"Mark Baker's *Centered-Set Church* is concept. With each story, he draws us in the world. We leave judgmentalism Hiebert's concept comes alive. A must-read for us who are called to lead churches to engage this world with the good news of Jesus Christ."
David Fitch, Northern Seminary, author of *Faithful Presence*

"When Jesus prayed for his future followers, he had only one thing on his mind—our miraculous, attractive, authentic, and authenticating unity. Mark Baker's book *Centered-Set Church* is helping this generation of believers become the answer to Jesus' prayer for his body and his bride."
Bruxy Cavey, teaching pastor at the Meeting House and author of *The End of Religion*

"When it comes to discerning what it looks like to live a Jesus-centered faith in a Jesus-centered community, it isn't an overstatement to say that Mark Baker's teaching and modeling of 'centered-set' Christianity completely revolutionized my vision of Christian formation within the local church. For years I'd hoped he'd put words on a page that could guide congregations—beyond the reach of his seminary class-rooms—and finally . . . it is here! *Centered-Set Church* is a must-read for any church desiring to authentically follow Jesus without the trappings of religiosity or rela-tivism. While many churches in North America have a track record for focusing on rule-based boundaries, this book paints a vision of a church transformed by a simple yet costly idea: What if Jesus were truly the center of a church's values, programs, community life, and discipleship? Without a doubt, that church's witness would be absolutely transformed. Church leaders and Christian readers, put this book at the top of your stack!"
Kurt Willems, pastor and author of *Echoing Hope: How the Humanity of Jesus Redeems Our Pain*

"*Centered-Set Church* is an immensely practical book brimming with eloquent the-ology and a lively hope in the loving spirit of Christ active in the world. It's not often that you find the practical and the lyrically beautiful so entwined. Baker embodies the traits he suggests the church needs to embrace to maintain a centered approach. Though clear about his vision, he presents his case with humility and vulnerability—something you don't often find in church manuals. I wish I'd had this book when I planted a church years ago. I highly recommend it to anyone involved in Christian community—church planters, lay leaders, and anyone who longs to glimpse the gracious love at the center of Christian faith."
Debbie Blue, pastor of House of Mercy in St. Paul, Minnesota, and author of *Sensual Orthodoxy*

"How can we hold beliefs and values without falling into gracelessness, self-righteousness, and conditional acceptance of others? In this excellent resource for churches, Mark Baker offers a practical alternative to help your community of faith keep firm convictions without drawing lines that promote polarization and judgmental attitudes. Highly recommended!"

César García, general secretary, Mennonite World Conference

"I can still vividly recall the moment of gracious encounter with the loving God who provides a covering from shame. That moment was unexpectedly in the middle of one of Mark Baker's lectures in his Discipleship and Ethics course. Dr. Baker provides helpful examples, reflective questions, and stirring testimonies from ministry leaders engaging in the work of moving from bounded or fuzzy toward restorative and centered systems. To say that the insights from the course and this book are transformative is to only begin to tell the story of beauty, love, and truth in this material. I highly recommend this book for those seeking to lead and be led in the way of Jesus, toward Jesus, and with one another."

Noemi Vega Quiñones, coauthor of *Hermanas: Growing Our Identity and Increasing Our Influence*

"Few concepts have had as much impact on my own work as a minister and theology lecturer as Mark Baker's explanation of the church in terms of bounded, fuzzy, and centered sets. I've been benefiting from Mark's work on this topic for years. Now with *Centered-Set Church*, we have Mark's full treatment of a paradigm that will surely shift the conversation and the church into a space of renewal and Christ-centered recalibration. Baker's advocacy for gospel communities that are defined not by theological fences or doctrinal fuzziness but by Jesus Christ the center will resonate with both new seminarians and seasoned ministry practitioners. *Centered-Set Church* will spark fresh, imaginative gospel hope in the hearts of the recently deconstructed, and it will provide a healing balm for the heavy-handed and the heavy-laden alike."

John Frederick, lecturer in New Testament and Greek at Trinity College, Queensland, Australia, and author of *Worship in the Way of the Cross*

CENTERED-SET

CHURCH

DISCIPLESHIP

AND COMMUNITY

WITHOUT

JUDGMENTALISM

MARK D. BAKER

Academic

An imprint of InterVarsity Press

Downers Grove, Illinois

InterVarsity Press
P.O. Box 1400, Downers Grove, IL 60515-1426
ivpress.com
email@ivpress.com

InterVarsity Press® is the book-publishing division of InterVarsity Christian Fellowship/USA®, a movement of students and faculty active on campus at hundreds of universities, colleges, and schools of nursing in the United States of America, and a member movement of the International Fellowship of Evangelical Students. For information about local and regional activities, visit intervarsity.org.

While any stories in this book are true, some names and identifying information may have been changed to protect the privacy of individuals.

Figure 6.1 is an adaptation of "Discipleship Cycle" graphic. Used by permission of The Meeting House, Oakville, Ontario.

The publisher cannot verify the accuracy or functionality of website URLs used in this book beyond the date of publication.

Cover design and image composite: David Fassett
Interior design: Jeanna Wiggins
Image: rainbow-colored orb: © Michel Leynaud / PhotoAlto Agency / Getty Images

ISBN 978-1-5140-0094-6 (print)
ISBN 978-1-5140-0095-3 (digital)

Printed in the United States of America ♾

InterVarsity Press is committed to ecological stewardship and to the conservation of natural resources in all our operations. This book was printed using sustainably sourced paper.

Library of Congress Cataloging-in-Publication Data

Names: Baker, Mark D. (Mark David), 1957- author.
Title: Centered-set church : discipleship and community without
judgmentalism / Mark D. Baker.
Description: Downers Grove, IL : InterVarsity Press, [2021] | Includes
bibliographical references and index.
Identifiers: LCCN 2021034695 (print) | LCCN 2021034696 (ebook) | ISBN
9781514000946 (print) | ISBN 9781514000953 (digital)
Subjects: LCSH: Church. | Judgment—Religious aspects—Christianity. |
Thought and thinking—Religious aspects—Christianity. | Prejudices.
Classification: LCC BV600.3 .B335 2021 (print) | LCC BV600.3 (ebook) |
DDC 262.001/7--dc23
LC record available at https://lccn.loc.gov/2021034695
LC ebook record available at https://lccn.loc.gov/2021034696
A catalog record for this book is available from the Library of Congress.

P	25	24	23	22	21	20	19	18	17	16	15	14	13	12	11	10	9	8	7	6	5	4	3	2	1
Y	37	36	35	34	33	32	31	30	29	28	27	26	25	24	23	22	21								

IN HONOR OF

Paul Hiebert (1932–2007) who had the creativity and insight to borrow set theory from mathematics and apply it to churches. Without his work this book would not exist. I am honored and privileged to have, since 1999, taught at the seminary that Hiebert graduated from in 1957.

DEDICATED TO

my students at Mennonite Brethren Biblical Seminary, now Fresno Pacific Biblical Seminary. Also, without you this book would not exist. Your challenging questions pressed me to refine and clarify my explanations of bounded, fuzzy, and centered sets. Your pertinent questions on application motivated me to produce a book to answer them. Things I learned from your efforts at doing centered ministry provided many of the examples and insights in the book. It has been a privilege to teach you, learn with you, and learn from you. May the conversation continue.

CONTENTS

1

DRAWING LINES
AND ERASING LINES

DRAWING LINES

While riding home from church when I was six years old, I looked disdain-fully at people who were mowing their lawns because I had learned that Christians did not work on Sunday. Though I don't recall anyone at church actually telling me that people who mowed their lawns on Sundays were reprobates, I viewed them that way. Not only did they perform forbidden tasks on the Lord's day, they obviously had not gone to church. This provided me a clear way of labeling some people as non-Christians.

By observing those who mowed lawns on Sunday, I could distinguish those who belonged to my religion from those who did not. At the age of six I had already absorbed and applied a line-drawing approach to Christi-anity, and I had the security of knowing that I was on the right side of the line. I was "in." As I grew older I continued to derive security from the lines I drew. As a teenager I felt morally superior because, in contrast to those around me, I did not cheat on tests, steal on the job, drink, dance, swear, smoke, or do drugs.

After I left home to go to a Christian college, two different encounters led me to rethink using rules to draw lines. First, I happened to visit a church that had a longer list of rules than mine. Sitting in a pew in the back, I became increasingly uncomfortable as the church filled up. All the males had on white shirts and ties. I did not. My hair was 1970s stylishly long; theirs was 1950s short. I felt shame for standing out and not complying with their rules. I was on the wrong side of their line. I imagined them looking at me and thinking just what I thought of people on the wrong side of lines I had drawn. Had I made others feel like this? I did not like it.

And, around the same time, I met some Christians who had a shorter list of rules than I did. They drank occasionally and enjoyed dancing. I faced a dilemma. My definition of Christianity told me that these people could not be Christians. In other ways, though, I recognized their faith to be more mature than my own. I either had to change my definition of a Christian or refuse to accept these friends as Christians. I concluded that legalism was the problem. I began to step away from my focus on rules, and I fully embraced my friends as Christians. I also began to see "legalists" as the ones who were not "good Christians."

Over the next seven years I continued changing and embraced new expressions of Christian discipleship: a simple lifestyle, total commitment to Jesus, openness to gifts of the Spirit, and commitment to social justice. I thought I had come a long way from my high school legalism until I sat in a Bible study and watched the teacher draw two diagrams on the board.

He drew a line that angled uphill and said: "Many evangelical students see their life as a progression from the legalism of their youth to a more mature Christianity, which stresses issues of lifestyle and justice and explores authentic Christianity. It appears they have moved forward." I thought, *Yes, that's me.* Then he drew a circle and at different points wrote *legalism, simple lifestyle, freedom to drink,* and *issues of justice.* He pointed to the circle. "They move along, but they are not going anywhere. They just change one means of judging themselves as superior for another."[1] I felt stunned. Perhaps I had not progressed as far as I had thought.

Stunned, yes, but I did not feel attacked because it was a gracious revelation—gracious in the spirit in which he did it and full of grace because it was a first step in my becoming more gracious toward myself and others. His observations led me to look at my life with new eyes. I saw that I had used the "broadening" of my faith perspective in the same way I had used

---

[1]John Linton, Bible study, "The Oregon Extension," Ashland, OR, January 1984.

the legalism of my youth: to draw lines between myself and others. Just as I had looked down on those who mowed their lawns on Sunday, I now looked down on those who did not share my new perspectives. Though I was self-righteously judging others, I also often felt judged by some people for things I did or believed. For instance, although my stance on US foreign policy in Central America caused some Christians to see me as a "good Christian," other Christians critiqued me. One church I attended maintained that, regarding social issues, opposing abortion should be *the* priority for all Christians. I agreed it was an important issue, but because I put more time and energy into other causes, I felt like I did not measure up to their standard. I was on the wrong side of their line.

Often when I read a book or heard a speaker, I would add something else to my list of what "true" Christians should support with their time and money. I tried to balance and carry this increasing load, but eventually it became impossible. Even I could not stay on the right side of the lines that I had drawn. So I would come up with a rationalization and then adjust the lines so that I could still see myself as a "good" Christian.

Such line drawing is a community activity, defining who belongs and who does not. It gives security, but it also stifles authenticity. During my first four years as a missionary in Honduras, I attended a charismatic church, but I never shared that fact with people from my home church in New York. I told them about my Honduran church but never identified it as charismatic. I told myself that no one had asked, but I knew that I had purposefully withheld that information because attending a charismatic church had not been a casual decision. I had spent hours exploring biblical texts about the Holy Spirit, reading books about the gifts of the Spirit, and discussing it all with others in Honduras. Eventually I had decided to step away from my home church's teaching that the gifts of the Spirit were for another age. I knew that this decision placed me on the wrong side of a line. Fearing shaming critique and rejection, I masked the truth and sealed off a significant aspect of my life from others. Though I remained in relationship with my New York church community, the shame that flowed from the lines we had drawn kept us from sharing our lives in a fully authentic way.

While lines provide clear guidance, they can also hinder us from hearing the Spirit's call. After four years in Honduras, I became a campus minister with InterVarsity Christian Fellowship and moved to Syracuse, New York. Others involved with InterVarsity recommended that I look for an apartment near the university, but I had just spent four years drawing a thick line between missionaries who lived with the poor and those who isolated themselves in nice houses surrounded by large walls in wealthy neighborhoods. Living with the poor was not only part of my definition of being a good missionary, but it had become a badge of honor. If I lived on the "wrong side of town," I would feel "in" with the circle of missionaries I most respected. There are certainly good reasons for living with the poor—in both Honduras and the United States—and the Holy Spirit has led me to do so at different points in my life. However, even more fundamentally, I think there are very good reasons to live in the context of one's ministry. Ironically, I had distorted an incarnational calling from one context into doing the opposite somewhere else. Rather than living within walking distance of the university and having students as neighbors, I thought I should live on the other side of the city, unconnected to any people or ministry, just so I could grasp the status of being on the "right" side of the line I had drawn. Thankfully, before I signed a lease, I was honest enough with myself to recognize the distortion, and I rented an apartment a few blocks from Syracuse University. I wish I could tell you I did it free from shame, but I was not yet that far in my journey.

I tell these stories not only to portray some of the problems that flow from line-drawing judgmentalism, but more importantly to display a common error. In college I recognized my legalistic self-righteousness, but I mistakenly thought that the legalistic rules were the problem. I viewed the solution as discarding the rules. I had not dug deeply enough. Although my perspectives about what it meant to be a good Christian had changed over the years, my drive to be right and my line drawing had remained constant. I had torn down one house and built another that looked completely different without realizing that both houses had been built on the same flawed foundation. My foundation of judgmental line drawing had prevented me from fully experiencing authentic Christian community in either house. This flawed foundation had also hindered me from experiencing the unconditional love of God.[2]

---

[2]Some material in this section is adapted from Mark D. Baker, *Religious No More* (Eugene, OR: Wipf & Stock, 2005), 34-36. Used by permission.

Because both houses were built on the foundation of line drawing, they had similar characteristics: gracelessness, conditional acceptance, fear, lack of transparency, lack of empathy, self-righteousness, and shallow ethical change. My intent had been to invite others to embrace the beliefs and practices that mattered to me, yet in the process I unintentionally fostered these negative characteristics. I am not writing this book to convince readers to let go of their beliefs and values, but to describe how we can affirm our beliefs and live out our values without producing the negative characteristics listed above. God worked in and through me during my early years of ministry, and I grew and changed in many positive ways. Yet until my foundation was rebuilt, I could not experience the full measure of new creation life in Christ.

I started drawing lines as a boy and kept drawing them for years. Others have different stories. Rather than drawing lines, some people try to erase lines and throw away all line-drawing markers. The following story displays the fruits of this approach.[3]

ERASING LINES

Dustin Maddox's parents grew up in restrictive, line-drawing churches. As adults they fled the church and did not return, but Dustin occasionally went to church with his grandmother. Once, when he was eight, an older woman told a group of children, "Jesus loves you so much that he died for you so that God will not send you to hell." Dustin thought, *That doesn't make sense.* He raised his hand and asked, "If God loves us, then why does God want to send us to hell?" The woman responded, "People who ask questions like that end up going to hell." At that moment, Dustin, like his parents, decided he was done with church. He did not want to end up like that woman. The stories he had heard from his parents and his experience with judgmental Christians in high school reinforced this conviction. His rejection of confident judgmentalism led him to align with those who took the opposite stance—a pluralistic approach to any truth claims.

However, Dustin did have some nonjudgmental Christian friends who did not turn him off, and he sporadically went to their church youth group. Through their encouragement, he made a last-minute decision to accompany

---

[3]Dustin Maddox, interview by author, Fresno, CA, March 6, 2018.

the youth group on a spring break mission trip to Mexico. The week was intense, both disturbing and exciting. He started the week by asking, "What is VBS?" only to find himself helping to run a Vacation Bible School program. The poverty he witnessed in Mexico disturbed and saddened him. Three brothers who walked a mile to come to the program caught his attention, especially the three-year-old, who made the trek barefoot. During a group prayer time, Dustin blurted out, "I don't know how this works, but God, if you are there, if you could get this kid shoes, that would be really cool." The next day the boy arrived wearing brand new shoes. Dustin recognized that any number of things might explain how that happened, but the startling answer to his prayer moved him deeply.

That prayer came in the context of a week of studies on the Sermon on the Mount, and Dustin was finding Jesus to be completely and utterly compelling, unlike anyone he had ever heard or experienced. During the final study, the day the boy arrived with new shoes, a youth pastor from another church did something that had never happened in Dustin's youth group. He gave an altar call, and Dustin went forward. In that moment of repentance and the Communion service that followed, Dustin encountered Jesus and sensed a call to something greater. He also recognized his short-comings and brokenness in a way that he never had before. Yet it was a guilt-freeing, shame-depleting experience that was radically different from what he had felt as an eight-year-old. God's love overwhelmed him.

Back home he became actively involved in the church and youth group. Rather than drawing clearly defined lines to distinguish Christians from non-Christians, his leaders worked to erase lines because they too had experienced the negative fruit of line drawing. Because they held onto enough of Jesus, Dustin made connections with what he had experienced in Mexico. It felt like a Christian space to him, but in many ways the spirit and practices of the youth group matched the world that Dustin had inhabited before the mission trip. The fundamental philosophy was "whatever works for you." Jesus seemed to be an optional add-on, a sort of a life coach mixed with relativism, even pluralism. In fact, things were so fuzzy and the imperatives so soft that Dustin felt no need to change his life in any significant way. He continued to party just as he had before. Later, when he began working at the church, his supervisor said, "Now that you are a leader, it is probably best if you do these things in a less public way." The softness of this suggestion displayed the degree of discomfort that the church felt with anything that might appear to be line-drawing exclusion.

Though Dustin did not experience any of the judgmentalism that drove his parents and his eight-year-old self from church, he began to recognize that the fuzzy, line-erasing approach also produced negative fruit. The flight from judgmentalism in the church led to a milder form of the "whateverism" Dustin had lived before becoming a Christian. The church often attracted Christians who were seeking an alternative to the line-drawing judgmentalism of their churches, and Dustin observed that as people got fuzzier and fuzzier, they eventually just left the church. As individuals wandered off, he sensed the church getting fuzzier too. Vague Christianity is not interesting or compelling, life-giving or transformative, and as the emphasis on genuine Christian orthodoxy decreased, the number of people leaving increased.

Just as I had sincere and positive motivations for drawing lines, Dustin (and others like him) had positive and sincere motivations for erasing them. Yet Dustin began to recognize deficiencies in the pluralistic, non-judgmental soil into which he and his friends had sunk their roots. The center of gravity was the autonomous "authentic self," and he saw his friends, both Christians and non-Christians, pursue many unhealthy actions that they easily justified by claiming that they were just trying to discover their true selves. They legitimized a whole variety of behaviors with little genuine reflection about how it might hurt themselves or others. In the end, what was determinative was subjective, "I can do whatever I want, however I want, whenever I want, and no one can tell me differently." There was no call or challenge to transformation, no imperative to work on deep-seated issues in one's being or character. Rather, the corporate culture was one of permissiveness because, "Who am I to tell you anything differently?" Common guidance was to "listen to yourself," which was offered without reins or constraints, without sharing a word of caution that our desires might mislead us because our feelings are fickle. More and more, Dustin realized that although the people in his church desired community, the soil in which the church was planted was not providing the conditions needed for true community.

Looking back now, Dustin sees how ineffective he was pastorally—not just because he never offered words of warning that were desperately needed, but because of the blandness of it all. Who wants to have a conversation with a pastor who is just super nice? As in, "Hey man, I am here to support you in whatever you choose." There is a role for people like that in our lives, but they don't draw us toward transformation. They don't challenge us by saying, "I know who you are and all that you could be; here are some things that do not reflect who God created you to be." If we are going to grow, we need people around us who can help us picture the kingdom of God by saying, "The path you are walking is not the way to life, but you can step into this kingdom life, because this is the life for which God made you."

The reality of Dustin's encounter with Jesus remained alive in his being, and themes from the Sermon on the Mount remained part of his experience. But as the years passed, he recognized that he had not been summoned to greater obedience to Jesus. He felt a strong push to try to fix the world but also an absence of any summons to sort out how to be a disciple of Jesus. He came to understand that many people in the church saw themselves as Christian authorities on the external world, but they did not recognize the need to obey anything beyond themselves in their individual lives. Despite his growing awareness about the negative aspects of the current he was in, he floated along because he didn't want to be associated with line-drawing rigidness.

In response to the self-righteous judgmentalism of a line-drawing church, it is understandable that Dustin—and others like him—pulled out their erasers and wiped out the lines. In response to the relativism and blandness of fuzzy churches, it is also understandable that other Christians have pulled out their markers to draw clearer and bolder lines. The intentions of both are positive, but the fruit is negative. Is there another option? A third way? I began to see the possibilities of a third way when I studied Galatians with Iglesia Amor Fe y Vida (Love, Faith, and Life Church) in Tegucigalpa, Honduras, in 1992 and 1993.[4]

---

[4]*Amor Fe y Vida* changed their name a few years ago to *Viviendo en Amor y Fe* (Living in Love and Faith). I am using the name they were using at the time, which is the name I used in Mark D. Baker, *Religious No More: Building Communities of Grace & Freedom* (Downers Grove, IL: InterVarsity Press, 1999).

NEW CREATION COMMUNITY:
PAUL'S VISION OF A UNIFIED TABLE

After working for three years as a campus minister with InterVarsity in New York and then attending seminary, my wife, Lynn, and I returned to Honduras as missionaries. A few years after we returned, I walked down a dusty street and into a simple house in Flor del Campo, a squatter neighborhood in Tegucigalpa, where six leaders from Iglesia Amor Fe y Vida were waiting for me. They talked earnestly as the late-afternoon sun beat down on the tin roof above us. By attending seminars and reading books, these leaders had come to embrace a holistic gospel, but other members of their church were not supportive of their desire to become more active in confronting injustices and addressing physical needs in their community. The leaders had invited me to teach seminars on holistic mission, hoping that I would help convince the rest of the church to support a more holistic approach. The opportunity to become involved with this group excited me, but as an outsider I felt reluctant to tell the rest of the church how to think. Also, I knew about the legalism of many Honduran churches, and so I was concerned that working for justice for the impoverished would become a new obligation for the church, a dividing line that would separate "true" Christians from others.

I proposed offering two four-hour workshops to give them tools they could use to study the Bible and together see a more holistic gospel in the Bible. As I prepared to lead these workshops, I made sure to include biblical texts that I thought would address the rampant legalism in the area.

After going over some basics in biblical interpretation in the first session, we continued the next week. At one point I read Galatians 5:2, "If you let yourselves be circumcised, Christ will be of no value to you at all," and started making the point that we need to move beyond a simple, literal interpretation of Scripture if it is going to impact our lives. I was getting ready to talk about the principle that was behind this verse when a woman raised her hand and said, "My friend tells me that now that I have cut my hair, I am not saved. Is that true?" I felt both compassion and bewilderment— compassion for the woman, who was afraid that she had lost her salvation, and bewilderment about the severity of her friend's line-drawing legalism. Attempting to keep the session on track, I suggested that she read the book of Galatians to discover the answer to her question. But as I attempted to continue with the teaching I had prepared, other hands shot up, and four people asked similar questions. Finally, I said, "Let's come back next week and study Galatians together." By reading Galatians together, I knew we would encounter texts that specifically challenged legalism and affirmed that salvation is by grace, not works.

Unlike my first season in Honduras, I now recognized the more foundational problem of line drawing, and so I was concerned that the church might draw new lines. But I did not have a coherent third-way alternative. In response to their line drawing, I emphasized God's grace, which was good, but as I look back on those years, I realize that I was providing pain relief medicine rather than addressing the underlying cause of the pain. I could see that part of the church's problem was their line drawing, but the solution I offered, talking about God's grace, had not actually worked in my own life. In my line-drawing years, I had preached salvation by grace, and yet I had lived out works righteousness. Thankfully, through the moving of the Spirit, more happened in the Galatians study with Iglesia Amor Fe y Vida than I anticipated.

In the midst of my preparations for our study on Galatians, I read an essay that Richard Hays had given at the Context and Hermeneutics in the Americas Conference.[5] Through that essay I saw that Paul's concerns go beyond the Galatian church's confusion about faith and works. Paul writes with passionate concern about the unity of the church community and how the principalities and powers were sowing division and enslaving people through judgmental line drawing. The following are some of the insights that emerged as the Amor Fe y Vida community studied Galatians together and began to see an alternative way, one that neither drew lines nor erased them.[6]

In Galatians 2:11-16, Paul recalls a beautiful scene of Jewish and Gentile Christians eating together in Antioch, where those whom culture and religion has separated are united in Christ. The table fellowship they share

---

[5]The conference was sponsored by the Theological Students Fellowship and Latin American Theological Fraternity (*La Fraternidad Teológica Latinoamericana*) and was held in Tlayacapan, Mexico, on November 24–29, 1983. Hays's paper as well as other papers from the conference are contained in Mark Lau Branson and C. René Padilla, eds., *Conflict and Context: Hermeneutics in the Americas* (Grand Rapids, MI: Eerdmans, 1986).

[6]I have condensed the narrative. I spent many weeks studying Galatians with this church. Then, the following year, after studying Galatians with Richard Hays as part of my doctoral work, the church and I worked through Galatians again, engaging the new insights that I had gained.

offers a concrete example of new-creation reality through the cross of Jesus Christ (Gal 5:15-16). To appreciate the radical nature of this table fellowship more fully, we must recognize the role of the table in the first-century biblical context.

In most cultures, whom you eat with matters. If someone invites you to share a meal, he or she is communicating something by that act. In some cultures, including the biblical world of the first century, the signifi-cance was much greater. To invite someone to share a meal communicated acceptance and honor. It was not done casually. In the world of Jesus, Peter, and Paul, Jews used the dinner table, along with circumcision and Sabbath observance, to separate themselves from non-Jews. By excluding non-Jews from the table, Jews could maintain their distinctive religious and cultural identity.

However, God uses a dream about food to lead Peter to begin the work of breaking down this barrier and to preach the gospel to Gentiles (Acts 10:10-44). Therefore, it should not surprise us that when Peter visits the church in Antioch, he comfortably takes his place at the table to share the meal with the other followers of Jesus—both Gentiles and Jews (see Acts 11:2-18; Gal 2:12).

Yet, tragically, the beautiful image of one united table of fellowship does not last. Some Jewish Christians arrive from Jerusalem, the mother church. Unable to overcome years of tradition and line drawing, they cannot eat with Gentiles; they sit at a separate table. Whether through explicit statements or the nonverbal implication of dining at a separate table, these emissaries from the Jerusalem church draw a line that communicates to the Gentile Chris-tians that they may join the Jews at their table only if they become circum-cised and follow other traditional Jewish laws.

Imagine the shame and abandonment that the Gentile Christians must have felt when the local Jewish Christians, who had previously eaten with them, left the table of union to join the newly arrived visitors at the Jewish-only table in the corner. They not only stopped eating with the Gentile Christians, but they also ceased celebrating the Lord's Supper together.[7]

---

[7]Most likely the "Lord's supper" in the early church was not a separate cultic event, but "an entire ordinary meal" that a Christian community may have eaten each time they came together. Quoted in Robert Banks, *Paul's Idea of Community*, rev. ed. (Peabody, MA: Hendrickson, 1994),

Paul tells us that Peter is afraid of those who are pressuring the Gentile Christians to become circumcised (Gal 2:12). Afraid of what? Before we imagine the scene, I invite you to remember a time when you felt that others were looking at you as if you were on the wrong side of a religious line. Now imagine what Peter thinks and feels as he sits at the table with the Gentiles, and the disbelieving stares of the emissaries from Jerusalem penetrate his being. He might imagine them going back to the church in Jerusalem, saying, "You will not believe what Peter is doing in Antioch. . . ." Under the scrutiny of their shaming gaze, Peter moves to the other table. Now imagine that you are another Jewish Christian who is still sitting at the table with Gentiles. You are not renowned like Peter; perhaps you are a new follower of Jesus. And then you see Peter, one of the twelve disciples of Jesus, leave. If he no longer thinks it is appropriate to eat at a table with Gentiles, how can you stay? Sadly, almost all the Jewish Christians leave the unified table—even Barnabas (Gal 2:13). Only one Jewish Christian—Paul—remains at the unified table with the Gentile Christians.

In response, Paul writes a passionate letter to the churches of Galatia to confront this practice of a group of agitators who are distorting the gospel and threatening the unity of the churches. They have drawn a line to communicate that the Gentile converts must live like Jews in order to be true Christians. The agitators seek to change the behavior of the Gentile Christians by shaming them and threatening to exclude them. Paul fears that the tragedy of the divided tables in Antioch will occur in Galatia as well.

In Antioch, Paul confronts Peter and reminds him that the Gentiles have a place at the table of God's people—not by fulfilling certain actions that Jews used to distinguish themselves from others, but by trusting in Jesus' faithful actions of obedience to God, even to the point of death on the cross (Gal 2:14-16).

Paul understands that the rules are not the problem. Rather, the problem is with line-drawing religiosity. Paul does not argue with Peter about the content of the line but confronts him for drawing the line in the first place. Similarly, he does not confront the agitators in Galatia for having the wrong set of rules. For example, he does not say, "Circumcision is not what

---

81; see also Philip Esler, *The First Christians in Their Social Worlds: Social Scientific Approaches to New Testament Interpretation* (London: Routledge, 1994), 52-53.

defines followers of Jesus; tithing distinguishes true believers from others. If you tithe, you have a place at the table!" Returning to the analogy I used at the end of my story about drawing lines, we could say that Paul does not argue about how to remodel the house. He digs deeper, proclaiming the need to rebuild on a new foundation.

Paul recognizes that someone with a line-drawing mentality might hear his critique of circumcision as an argument to draw a new line. That, however, would produce an anti-circumcision group that will be just as self-righteous and exclusive as the circumcision group. He makes it absolutely clear that he is not interested in drawing further lines of distinction. After arguing against the necessity of circumcision throughout the letter, he makes a stunning statement: "May I never boast except in the cross of our Lord Jesus Christ, through which the world has been crucified to me, and I to the world. Neither circumcision nor uncircumcision means anything; what counts is the new creation" (Gal 6:14-15). By centering on Jesus Christ, he points to a totally different way than either drawing lines or erasing them.

Although Paul does erase some lines that the Jewish Christians are drawing to separate themselves from the Gentiles, Paul does not take the fuzzy approach we observed in Dustin's story. Paul does not write, "Erase the lines—everyone is in!" In Antioch, he confronts Peter. Later in Galatians, he warns against a kind of "whateverism" (Gal 5:13), and he lists appropriate and inappropriate behavior (Gal 5:13-26), encourages loving confrontation when someone sins (Gal 6:1), and identifies some people as outsiders who are no longer part of the community of faith (Gal 4:30; 5:4, 9). Paul recognizes that the solution to disunity, judgmentalism, and confusion about works righteousness in Galatia is neither to draw new lines nor to erase all lines.

The members of Iglesia Amor Fe y Vida decided to leave behind their line-drawing paradigm as a way of defining their identity so that they could follow Paul in a radically different approach that would be centered on Jesus Christ and his saving work. I will share some of their adventure in this book.

My time with Iglesia Amor Fe y Vida was exciting. Though the changes were not easy, the new life we found together was profound and beautiful. Compare the question I heard from the fearful woman who had cut her hair with the comment that my wife, Lynn, overheard a few years ago from

Maria, a newcomer, who came to Amor Fe y Vida after experiencing line-drawing judgmentalism in other churches: "Now I have been changing, not because of rules and threats, but because I am loved."

We will also return to parts of Paul's letter to the Galatians later in this book. (For a more in-depth look at the points made in the previous paragraphs, see my forthcoming book, *Freedom from Religiosity: Studies in Paul's Letter to the Galatians*, in the Luminaire Studies series.) This brief glimpse reveals how line-drawing judgmentalism distorts the gospel and produces shame and division. Paul responds to this situation with deep concern and passion. Let us do the same.

MOVING FORWARD

Similar to my experience after reading Galatians, Dustin reached a turning point and began to move toward a third option after reading Leslie Newbigin's *Foolishness to the Greeks*. Newbigin argues that for too long we have viewed the Bible through the lens of Western culture, but now we need to look at Western culture through the lens of the Bible because Jesus has something to say to our particular cultural moment. This new stance led Dustin to an even more critical evaluation of the soil in which he had taken root, as well as the approach of his church. Although our experiences with line drawing and fuzziness are radically different, Dustin and I share something in our journey. Through the work of missiologist Paul Hiebert, both of us came to a deeper understanding of our past experiences and a clearer vision of the alternative that Paul models. The next two chapters will describe Hiebert's bounded-set, fuzzy-set, and centered-set models. The purpose of this book is not merely to explain these categories, but to help churches become communities that are centered on Jesus so that they can lovingly walk with each other on a journey of transformation. After describing Hiebert's categories, the rest of the book will focus on application—that is, how to live out a centered approach in the church.

I wrote this book for practitioners—pastors, small group leaders, para-church workers, youth group leaders, and Sunday school teachers. Much of the content of the book also comes from practitioners. Before I began writing, I intentionally sought out leaders who were seeking to apply the centered approach in their churches or ministries. I interviewed or met in focus groups with more than forty practitioners. Many of the examples and stories in this book are the fruit of those interviews. My interactions with these leaders did not merely serve to provide illustrations for concepts and strategies in the book. Rather, as I listened to these thoughtful leaders, I began to identify the common key elements for living out a centered approach. I wrote the outline for the book *after* the interviews. Thus this book is a collaborative project written both *for* practitioners and *by* practitioners.

I was compelled to write this book because I have seen and experienced the shame and alienation produced by bounded churches, the blandness of fuzzy churches, and the liberating transformation through Jesus Christ of centered churches. The categories themselves are not the gospel, but they provide a powerful instructional tool to help us live the way of Jesus in our time. After hearing about these three approaches, someone recently said to me, "I have not heard anything like this for a long time. This will radically reshape my faith. This is huge." May the same be true for you.

PART ONE

DEFINING THE PARADIGMS

TWENTY YEARS AGO, after a church service, my friend Larry Dunn approached me and said, "Mark, I read your book *Religious No More*. Have you read Paul Hiebert's work on bounded and centered sets?" When I replied that I had not, Larry countered, "You should." He knew he did not need to say more. Larry knew that, once I read Hiebert's article, I would see connections to my own work. Indeed, Hiebert's diagrams and definitions captured me immediately, clearly communicating something for which I had been seeking language. I wish I had read Hiebert before I had published that book, as it would have been better. Since reading Hiebert, I have become like Larry, looking for opportunities to introduce people to Hiebert's definitions of bounded, fuzzy, and centered sets.

As a professor, I work to come up with diagrams and drawings that I can use in class to illustrate concepts, as it is helpful to be able to visualize something. For the three stories I told in the first chapter—mine, Dustin's, and Paul's—Hiebert's concepts and diagrams clearly and concisely communicate the core dynamic of each. Some diagrams, however, not only illustrate an idea, but also generate new ideas, exciting the imagination with possibilities and propelling people to act. Hiebert's diagrams of bounded, fuzzy, and centered sets have done that for me and many others.

In chapter two, I will define these three paradigms and introduce Hiebert's diagrams for each. Then I will begin to describe what it means to be a bounded, fuzzy, or centered church. In chapter three, I will respond to the most common questions about how centered churches differ from bounded and fuzzy churches.

2

BOUNDED, FUZZY, AND CENTERED CHURCHES

WELDON NISLY'S ENCOUNTER WITH A NEW PARADIGM

Weldon Nisly grew up in rural Iowa. As a boy, he loved spending time with his grandfather, who was a bishop in the Conservative Mennonite Church. Throughout Weldon's childhood, the only church he knew had been influenced by his grandfather, whose leadership approach was similar to Paul's in Galatians. When Weldon was fourteen, his beloved grandfather died, and a marked change took place in the church as the new bishop started drawing lines to distinguish who was "in" and who was "out." Though Weldon did not have the language or categories to describe the difference, he felt it. As his insatiable desire to learn grew, he asked more and more questions, but the new bishop responded by saying, in effect, "These are the rules, these are our beliefs." Throughout Weldon's late teens, he kept asking deeper questions and searching for new answers until the bishop excommunicated him, and so Weldon parted ways not only with the bishop and that denomination, but with church in general. He stayed away for almost five years until he realized that his struggle was not with God, faith, or even the church, but a particular approach to church and belief. After joining the Mennonite church, he sensed a call to ministry and went to seminary in the mid-1970s.

As a new seminary student, Weldon Nisly heard Paul Hiebert give a presentation. He recalls, "I was blown away. It illuminated a profound insight for me and gave me tools for understanding what I had experienced in church." He now had words and categories to explain the difference between his grandfather's approach to church and the bishop who followed him. "What Hiebert presented challenged and excited me. It has been part of everything I have done in ministry for the past forty years."[1] What did Hiebert talk about that had such an impact on Nisly?

Thankfully, Hiebert later published the content of that presentation,[2] and many who have read his work on bounded, fuzzy, and centered sets have responded similarly to Weldon. When I first encountered Hiebert, I recognized that he was describing the paradigm in Galatians that the people of Iglesia Amor Fe y Vida in Honduras and I had glimpsed together, but Hiebert portrayed this paradigm with a clarity that I had lacked. For over twenty years now, I have used Hiebert's diagrams in my teaching—from seminary classrooms to indigenous churches in the Peruvian Andes.

Hiebert begins by asking, When is someone considered a Christian? Though the answer may differ from one church tradition to another, many people would have a clear response, just as Hiebert did. But then he became a missionary in India, where his clear means of answering that question did not function. To engage this question, Hiebert uses an example from India of a man named Papayya. Should he be considered a Christian after he hears a story about Jesus and salvation through the cross and says a prayer expressing his desire to worship Jesus with other Christians? What if Papayya refers to Jesus as God, or the Son of God, but uses a word for "God" significantly different in meaning than the English, Hebrew, or Greek terms for God? What if Papayya offers incense to a picture of Jesus on the shelf in his home, but does not take the other gods off the shelf? What if he starts attending church, but still participates in Hindu celebrations? When should Papayya be considered a Christian?

---

[1] Weldon Nisly, interview by author, Seattle, WA, February 15, 2018.
[2] Paul G. Hiebert, "Conversion, Culture and Cognitive Categories," *Gospel in Context* 1, no. 4 (October 1978): 24-29; revised and expanded in Paul G. Hiebert, *Anthropological Reflections on Missiological Issues* (Grand Rapids, MI: Baker Academic, 1994), 107-36.

In exploring this question, Hiebert argues that the way people conceptualize church and the category of Christian will shape how they answer the question about Papayya. Hiebert, a cultural anthropologist, borrows from mathematical set theory to describe three different ways to categorize people. He applied the theory to the issue of distinguishing between Christians and non-Christians. In this book I will apply it to the question of how a church discerns who is appropriately considered part of their church. To ask, "who belongs?" or "who is part of our group?" can include the question of whether someone is a Christian or not, but also more than that. In the first chapter we observed that I used line drawing to distinguish between Christians and non-Christians as well as to make distinctions between Christians.

BOUNDED, FUZZY, AND CENTERED SETS

Bounded sets. Hiebert explains that bounded sets have a clear, static boundary line that allows for a uniform definition of those who are within the group. In general terms, a bounded group creates a list of essential characteristics that determine whether a person belongs to that group. For example, a league soccer team is a bounded group. Such a team has a limited number of players. There are tryouts. Ability matters. A team also has other requirements, such as having a uniform, attending practices, paying dues to the league, and so on. Coaches draw a clear line to determine which players have the ability and meet the requirements to be on the team. As figure 2.1 illustrates, everyone who is not part of the team is on the other side of the line.

Fuzzy sets. A fuzzy set is similar to a bounded set, but the boundary line is removed—or at least less clear. The grounds for distinction are rather vague, and so the group is fuzzy. In the soccer example, imagine a city park where people gather on Sunday afternoons to play pickup games. The same people might participate week after week, but someone could miss several weeks and still show up and play. If others think that you are a lousy player, you might have a hard time getting on a pickup team, but how that would happen is not clear. Some people might play soccer each time they go to the park, while others might sometimes play ultimate frisbee. One week you might show up and find volleyball nets taking up the whole field. As figure 2.2 illustrates, group membership cannot be clearly established.

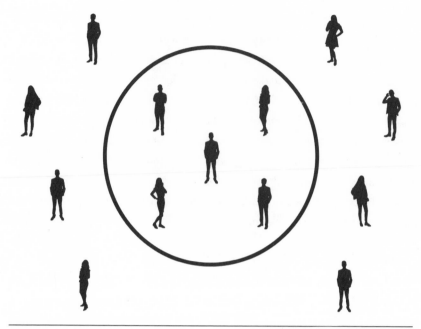

Figure 2.1. Bounded set

Figure 2.2. Fuzzy set

Though bounded and fuzzy groups differ radically, they share the same paradigm about how to define who belongs to a group, though they are positioned at opposite ends of a continuum. At one end, the boundary line is clear; near the other end the line gets increasingly vague and then totally disappears.

Centered sets. A centered set reflects a completely different paradigm. This third-way option is not on the bounded-fuzzy continuum. Rather than drawing a line to identify people based on their common characteristics, a centered set uses a directional and relational basis of evaluation. The group is created by defining a center and observing people's relationship with the center. As figure 2.3 illustrates, the set is made up of all who are oriented toward the center.[3]

Figure 2.3. Centered set

---

[3]Hiebert notes that relational sets are not limited to centered sets. They can also be defined by relationships to others in a common field. He limits his discussion to centered relational sets because of the correlation with Christianity and the church (Hiebert, *Anthropological Reflections*, 123).

Hiebert says that even though some people may be far from the center, they are part of the centered group if they are heading toward the center. On the other hand, some people may have been close to the center, but now are no longer part of the centered group because they have turned around and are moving away from it. Though the people within a centered group may not be uniform in their characteristics, they will all be heading the same direction.

In the soccer example, a centered approach would be when someone invites anyone who wants to play soccer to gather at a local public park on Saturday afternoon at three o'clock. In the diagram, those who show up are represented by the people whose arrows are heading toward the defined center, which is soccer. Those who do not show up to play are represented by the people whose arrows are turned away from the center. Some of those who show up may not be very good, but their lack of ability will not exclude them, because the invitation is open to all who want to play. If too many people show up, the organizers will start another game. The group will not define who can play and who cannot play based on ability or who can afford the fees.

After describing these three approaches to group membership, Hiebert applies the model to churches.

BOUNDED, FUZZY, AND CENTERED CHURCHES

Bounded churches. Bounded churches draw a line that distinguishes insiders from outsiders, Christians from non-Christians, or true Christians from mediocre Christians. The line generally consists of a list of correct beliefs and certain visible behaviors. In Galatians, the agitators display a bounded group approach by asking questions such as "Have you been circumcised? Are you believing the right thing and eating with the right people?"

All bounded sets have a sense of exclusion of those who do not meet the requirements. Often that leads to the insiders having a sense of superiority and increased status, but not always. Although those who make a sports team often exude a sense of superiority, there is generally no corresponding dynamic among those in bounded sets like Costco members or people with annual passes to national parks. In theory a church could be a bounded set and avoid the negative attitudes displayed in my line drawing in the previous chapter, but I have not seen that neutrality in reality.[4] For a variety of reasons, the lines drawn by bounded churches foment judgmentalism and communicate a sense of conditional love.[5] Therefore, in this book the definition of a bounded church includes the technical definition of a bounded set described in the previous section as well as the additional element that the boundary lines produce a sense of inferiority in the excluded and self-righteousness in the included.

The definition of a bounded set leads us to think of a church with a clear list of criteria used to explicitly state whether someone belongs. That does occur in bounded churches, for instance, if one does not affirm a list of beliefs one is told you cannot belong and your outsider status is made clear. Yet in bounded churches one's status in relation to a boundary line is communicated in a variety of ways. For instance, a teenager reported that after asking a question and suggesting an alternative to one of the church's beliefs, her grandmother said, "We do not believe that." The words themselves might simply be informational, and the grandmother did not state, "that belief disqualifies one from membership." Yet with an emphasis on "we" and the tone of voice communicated, the message was clear that if you want to be part of the "we," our church, you should not be thinking such things. One's status in relation to a line can also be communicated through silence and shunning. Similarly, people in bounded churches learn that many lines exist beyond those officially stated. They pick this up from what they hear people say about others, from facial expressions, and how people are treated—as insider or outsider. Unstated lines are no less real.

What churches come to mind when you read the previous paragraphs? Many of us might think of legalistic churches. And while the legalism of my youth provides a clear example of a bounded approach to church, my line drawing continued after I turned away from legalism. As my own

---

[4]To say that in theory a bounded church could be a "neutral" bounded group is not to imply there would be no negatives. Even if the judgmentalism of superiority was absent, some of the other negative dynamics explored in this chapter and the following would still exist.

[5]Some of the elements that pull bounded churches to stronger expression of the negative characteristics of bounded sets will be explored in other chapters, especially four and five, such as distorted concepts of God, human religious tendencies, and thirst for status.

story demonstrates, a church can practice bounded-group line drawing in a variety of ways. Boundedness is not limited to legalism. In fact, I have participated in churches that were self-righteously not legalistic, where we looked with disdain on legalistic Christians in the same way that they might have looked with contempt on those who fell short of their standards. Though we had radically different lines, we all drew lines in a bounded-set way. Bounded churches can use a variety of things to draw lines that define insiders from outsiders, including rituals, spiritual experiences, political commitments, activism, attendance, beliefs, and behaviors.

In critiquing a bounded approach to church, I am not critiquing anything that qualifies as a legitimate boundary. The problem is not with having a line that differentiates between things that are acceptable and unacceptable, but rather with how bounded churches use those lines to separate and categorize people in a judgmental way.

Fuzzy churches. Some churches recognize the problematic fruit of line drawing within bounded churches, and so they opt for what appears to be the obvious solution: they erase the line. This fuzzy approach to church comes naturally in many places today. As we observed in Dustin's story, the relativism and pluralism he brought from his cultural setting easily found a home in his fuzzy church. In a society that holds tolerance as the supreme virtue, a bounded church is problematic, whereas a fuzzy church is not. Yet as Dustin observed, fuzzy churches solve one set of problems while creating others.

Centered churches. Unlike fuzzy churches, centered churches can distinguish those who belong to the group from those who do not. In a centered church, God is the center focus. Therefore, the critical question is, To whom do we offer our worship and allegiance? In Galatians, we might imagine Paul asking centered questions such as "Are you living according to the new creation reality created by God's action through Jesus Christ? Are you trusting God for your security or placing your security in certain rituals and beliefs? In which direction are you heading?"

Two types of change happen in a centered church. The first is directional. Is someone facing the center or oriented in the other direction? From this perspective, conversion happens when someone turns toward the center. The second change relates to movement toward the center. Such movement varies because members do not move at the same pace. The group is unified by the first change because they are all oriented toward Jesus Christ. However, they are not uniform because the characteristics of the various members will differ due to their varying distances from the center.

In figure 2.4, we can distinguish those who belong to the group from those who do not by looking at the direction of their arrows. All those within the drawn line are part of the group. Though a centered church makes a distinction between Christians and non-Christians, as Hiebert observes, the emphasis is "on exhorting people to follow Christ, rather than on excluding others to preserve the purity of the set."[6]

Figure 2.4. Centered church: those who belong to the group

---

[6]Hiebert, *Anthropological Reflections*, 125.

Note how this approach differs from a bounded church, where the line defines the group. On the centered diagram, I can draw a line, but I draw the line by looking at the arrows. The line does not define the person's relationship with the group. Rather, the line emerges by observing a person's relationship with the center. If we erase the line, we still have the group. Both centered and bounded churches put energy and emphasis on what defines them. For a bounded group, it is the line of exclusion. For a centered group, the emphasis is on defining the center and maintaining a relationship with the center.

Distinguishing between approaches. Bounded churches, by nature, make those outside the group feel excluded. Both bounded and centered churches have a high sense of expectation for those in the group, whereas a centered church has a greater sense of welcome and inclusion because its identity does not depend on excluding others. A fuzzy group is also strong on inclusivity, but because it neither has a boundary line nor a center, it cannot communicate expectations to its members. Figure 2.5 highlights important differences between these three approaches to group identity.

The centered paradigm facilitates sincere and deep relationship because unity does not come from uniformity, but from a common orientation toward the center. There is space to struggle and fail because everyone recognizes that they are in process—moving closer to the center. Since centered unity does not come from uniformity there is also space for differences not possible in a bounded church. Commenting on Paul's response to a conflict over appropriate diet choices (Rom 14), Rachel Tulloch observes, "Unity is found not in agreement of all particulars, but in the direction of our actions and convictions. To whom do we eat or not eat? To whom do we celebrate or not celebrate? More crucially, to whom do we live or die? To whom do we belong?"[7]

A bounded church focuses on defining and maintaining the boundary, whereas a centered church focuses on defining the center and maintaining clarity about the church's center, which is, first and foremost, Jesus Christ—not only in terms of our beliefs about Jesus, but more importantly

---

[7]Rachel Tulloch, sermon preached at Wine Before Breakfast, University of Toronto, February 27, 2007, quoted in Sylvia C. Keesmaat and Brian J. Walsh, *Romans Disarmed* (Grand Rapids, MI: Brazos, 2019), 136.

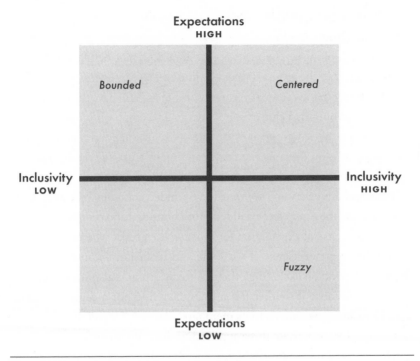

Figure 2.5. Comparing bounded, fuzzy, and centered groups

who Jesus is, how Jesus reveals God, and how the Spirit of Jesus remains alive and present today. The center is further defined by the Bible, the gospel, models of discipleship, and theological traditions that have shaped the community.

What so grabbed Weldon Nisly's attention and mine when we first encountered Hiebert's categories was the way they revealed how the foundation influenced the whole house built upon it. Yes, legalistic rules and a closed-minded rejection of questions were problematic, but now we saw how the seemingly disparate threads of our experience were part of one weaving created by a bounded-church approach. Hiebert's centered approach excited us because rather than compelling us to make minor adjustments to our line-drawing experiences, it pointed us toward a radical alternative. To explore the imperative of stepping away from the bounded-fuzzy continuum and to begin practicing a centered approach, I will return to my story, Dustin's story, and Paul's letter to the Galatians, as well as the experiences of other practitioners.

THE SHRIVELED FRUIT OF A BOUNDED CHURCH

Lines that shame. In Galatians 2, shame courses through the scene of the divided tables in Antioch. Peter feels it in the penetrating, disbelieving stares of the emissaries from Jerusalem. So he seeks to avoid further shame by leaving the united table and joining the Jews. But the Gentile Christians cannot go to that table because they are on the wrong side of the line and feel shamed. Shame was a major theme in my story as well. My fear of shame motivated me to stay on the right side of the lines.

A friend recently shared with me that a close friend who has been divorced for a few years practices linguistic gymnastics to avoid using the word *divorced* in relation to herself. Yet she can't always evade shame; for instance, it strangles her whenever she has to check the "divorced" box on a form. After suffering through many difficult years that culminated in her husband leaving and his affair coming to light, she experienced feelings of pain, anger, doubt, and guilt. Though most of these feelings had diminished with time, the weight of her shame had not. She had previously lived up to her church's expectations about appropriate behavior by remaining on the right side of the line, which had made her feel secure as a "good" Christian. But she knew how people in her church looked down on those whose behavior fell on the wrong side of the line because she used to judge others herself! Stuck in shame on the wrong side of the line, she could not erase the demerit and earn back her place on the right side.

Although not all bounded groups practice shaming, it is common in bounded churches. Drawing a line allows those on the inside to gain status and feel superior to those who do not meet the standards. In the previous story, no one actually said anything to shame the divorced woman, but she felt shame when she imagined what people were thinking.

Because I will mention shame frequently in this book, I will take a moment to clarify how I define it. Whereas guilt comes from an internal sense of moral failure, shame comes from falling short of the expectations of others. Guilt tells us, "I did something bad," and we feel it even if no one else knows about the transgression. Shame tells us, "I am bad," because we feel unworthy in relation to other people. Shame is related to feelings of humiliation, rejection, disapproval, loss of status, and abandonment.

Guilt is resolved through punishment, restitution, pardon, and forgiveness. Since shame is relational, release from shame must be relational by removing disgrace, receiving a new identity, restoring honor, and overcoming exclusion through reincorporation. Liberation from guilt comes through a restoration of right relationship with the standard; liberation from shame comes through the restoration of right relationships with the people around you.[8]

Lines that exclude. Line drawing not only shames, it also excludes. Sometimes the exclusion happens formally, and other times people on the inside subtly drift away from and exclude the offender. In some cases, the exclusion can be self-imposed.

For example, when I was in Tegucigalpa, Honduras, visiting the people of Iglesia Amor Fe y Vida, I asked a taxi driver if he went to church. He said, "I used to, but I went dancing." I asked if the church had disciplined him for dancing. He replied, "No, after I went dancing I never returned to the church." He knew which side of the line he was on now, and so he excluded himself.

Someone recently told me a story about how she had left her church because a relative who was part of the same church had divorced her husband. Though this relative had suffered years of abuse and unfaithfulness and her extended family had participated in the same church for years, everyone in the clan self-excluded. They stopped going to the church—parents, grandparents, siblings—because they "did not want to deal with the talk." As the example in the previous section suggests, though some may remain in their churches when they feel shamed, they tend to feel as if they are second-class Christians because they are standing on the wrong side of the line.

One can feel ashamed and excluded for both large and small infractions. Furthermore, line drawing can be found in both conservative churches and liberal churches, traditional churches and progressive churches. Just last

---

[8]I am not here making an argument for this being *the* definition of shame. Rather my purpose is to let readers know how I am defining shame in this book. Literature on shame has greatly expanded in recent years, and with it also various definitions of shame. There is much overlap, but also significant differences in concepts of shame—especially between those writing from a psychological perspective and those writing from a cultural-anthropological perspective. I am an expert in neither and have learned from and borrowed from both. For a short exploration of shame, including how the experience of shame is different in Western cultures than in honor-shame cultures, see Andy Crouch, "The Return of Shame," *Christianity Today*, March 2015, 32-41. For an in-depth explanation of honor-shame cultures and honor and shame in the Bible, see Jayson Georges & Mark D. Baker, *Ministering in Honor-Shame Cultures: Biblical Foundations and Practical Essentials* (Downers Grove, IL: IVP Academic, 2016).

week, I felt a familiar sense of shame for falling short of expectations. I felt "out" rather than "in." Have you felt the same? As one within the lines, have you ever felt the pressure to maintain certain standards or believe certain things? Have you thought, *What will they think of me if I don't . . . ?* Or, as one on the outside of religious lines, have you ever felt a shaming gaze of contempt from those on the inside?

Bounded from loving deeply. While many people appreciate the clarity of a bounded church and the security it offers, the boundary lines injure both those who are excluded and those who do the excluding. Outsiders experience the pain of not fitting in, and insiders sacrifice their distinct and complex individualities in order to belong. Such boundary lines hinder transparency because members find it difficult to express their struggles honestly when they are afraid of losing their standing in the church. While some bounded churches exclude people and some people choose to self-exclude, many people in bounded churches exclude a part of themselves. While they do not leave the group, they hide the part of themselves that does not fit. Metaphorically, we might say that they leave a part of themselves outside when they go to church.

I self-excluded a part of myself during my first years in Honduras. Although I shared some of my new perspectives and practices with my church in New York, including preaching a sermon that called them to live more simply so that they could give more to the poor, I never spoke of my new thoughts on the gifts of the Spirit nor the fact that I went to a charismatic church. I muzzled that part of me because I knew it would put me on the wrong side of their line. Boundaries may bind members together, but they can also leave people feeling bound and gagged, unable to share the depths of their beings. When people begin to categorize others according to lines, they are not free to love fully—or to *be* loved fully.

While a bounded church may appear to have unity because of the uniformity of its members, it is superficial. Bounded churches are characterized by gracelessness, conditional acceptance, shame, fear, lack of transparency, self-righteousness, and superficial ethical change.[9] I do not stand on the

---

[9] I describe concrete examples that display the characteristics listed in these sentences in the first chapter of Mark D. Baker, *Religious No More: Building Communities of Grace & Freedom* (Downers Grove, IL: InterVarsity Press, 1999), 17-33.

sidelines as an innocent bystander pointing out these negative things done by others—"the bad bounded-church people." In my own story, I can see how I lived out these characteristics even though it was never a conscious goal. This highlights two important observations. First, not only a guilty few produce the bad fruit of a bounded church. Second, most people in bounded churches are not seeking to produce the bad fruit that this book critiques. The people are not the fundamental problem. I do not look back harshly at my bounded-church self, nor at those in bounded churches today. My critique is not aimed at the people in bounded churches, but rather the paradigm. Sadly, practicing a bounded approach to church can even distort and undermine a church's clear belief in and proclamation of God's grace.

Preaching salvation by grace but living works righteousness. Who needs to hear that salvation is by grace? Obviously, those who think salvation is by works. Yet the theme of grace is a central element of Paul's letter to the Galatian Christians—people who had already experienced salvation by grace! The Jewish Christians visiting the church in Antioch and those emphasizing the necessity of Jewish practices in Galatia were all followers of Jesus. If you had asked them, "Are you saved by God's grace or your human effort?" they would have responded, "We are saved by God's gracious action through Jesus Christ." Yet Paul confronts them for sowing works righteousness. How could that be? What I observed in Honduras and my own life helped me answer that question.[10]

When I visited several bounded churches in Honduras, I heard clear proclamations of salvation by grace, and yet the people seemed to live out works righteousness—as if salvation was earned by human effort. This reality became even clearer when I talked with nonbelievers who lived in the neighborhood of these bounded churches. What was the message of salvation that the neighbors had absorbed from these bounded churches? Their line drawing had communicated more loudly than their statements about God's grace.

For example, after a Honduran woman told me that she had visited a church the night before, she said, "I almost accepted Jesus Christ last night."

---

[10]For a more in-depth explanation, see Baker, *Religious No More*, 84-87, and Mark D. Baker, *Freedom from Religiosity: Studies in Paul's Letter to the Galatians*, Luminaire Studies (Winnipeg: Kindred Productions, forthcoming).

When I asked her why she had not, she explained that she could not accept Jesus because she was a sinner. Rather than seeking God's forgiveness because she was a sinner, this woman had learned from her observations of churches and Christians that in order to accept Jesus, she had to first comply with the rules of the church. Because this woman could not marry her common-law husband for a variety of reasons, she could not cross to the right side of the line. Although she wanted to, the lines drawn led her to think she could not become a Christian.

My experience in Honduras led me to see the same dynamic in my life as well. At every point in the story that I recount in the first chapter, I would have said that God's grace, not my effort, enabled me to have a relationship with God. Yet I often lived as if my acceptance by God and others depended on staying on the right side of the line. A bounded church can easily lead people to view God's love and acceptance as conditional. This approach pulls people into contractual living, where if you do certain things, you're in, but if you break the contract you are out. Bounded churches may preach salvation by grace, but the paradigm itself pulls people to focus on human effort. If Paul were writing to my bounded self, he would proclaim the primacy of God's saving action over my efforts, just as he did to the Galatians—not to correct a mistaken doctrinal belief on my part, but to establish a foundation that would confront my bounded ways.

Sadly, line drawing not only distorts the content of the gospel, but it also undercuts the relational dynamic that is central to evangelism. As one ministry worker observed, "The bounded dynamic created within me a fear of being associated with or being influenced by those who are outside the group. It created a greater relational barrier that inhibited the very thing we were encouraged to do—build friendships with and evangelize non-Christians."[11]

Recalling the negative characteristics of bounded churches identified above, I do not mean to imply that these churches only produce negative fruit. There is good fruit as well. The point is not that everything about a bounded church is wrong and problematic, but that we can do better. We *must* do better. Many outsiders do not want to become Christians because of the negative fruit of judgmentalism and self-righteous superiority that

---

[11]Scott Carolan, email to author, December 17, 2019.

grows out of line-drawing churches. Philip Yancey describes in *What's So Amazing About Grace?* an instance where someone asks a prostituted woman trapped in addiction if she has thought of going to a church for help. "Why would I ever go there?" she cries. "I was already feeling terrible about myself. They'd just make me feel worse."[12]

THE MEAGER FRUIT OF A FUZZY CHURCH

Tolerance and partial love. As we observed in Dustin's story, a fuzzy approach produces churches that are less defined, less cohesive, and more relativistic. Rather than passionately dialoguing to clarify the truth, fuzzy churches focus on tolerance. This concern for tolerance leads people to qualify statements by saying, "This is just my opinion" and "You may think differently." Yet, as Will Willimon observes, "Jesus has a considerably higher view of friendship than that practiced in most churches, which amounts to: I promise never to hold you accountable if you'll do the same for me. Church as a gentile conspiracy of niceness, as a civil compatibility club rather than a community of truth."[13] I have observed such "whateverism" in fuzzy churches not only when people refrain from confronting others about sinful actions, but also when they are hesitant to describe certain actions or beliefs as inappropriate. In a fuzzy church, people are reluctant to talk about the need for personal transformation, let alone conversion, because it feels "intolerant" to call someone to repent, and the boundary lines are so fuzzy that there is no basis for repentance. For many in society who feel that the ultimate "sin" is to make someone else feel bad, this approach may not sound problematic, but some things hurt other individuals, ourselves, the church, and society. Because fuzzy churches do little to curb these destructive expressions of our shadow impulses,[14] they impede profound and life-changing love.

Individualism—alone together. The societal commitment to tolerance as the supreme virtue fuels fuzzy churches, it is often blended with individualism and relativism. These three forces work together to propel people

---

[12]Philip Yancey, *What's So Amazing About Grace?* (Grand Rapids, MI: Zondervan, 1997), 11.
[13]Will Willimon, *Accidental Preacher: A Memoir* (Grand Rapids, MI: Eerdmans, 2019), Kindle loc. 2672.
[14]Michael A. King, *Trackless Wastes and Stars to Steer By: Christian Identity in a Homeless Age* (Scottdale, PA: Herald Press, 1990), 128.

toward fuzzy churches and to see fuzziness as the only conceivable option. If individual freedom is seen as the ultimate good, then a bounded approach must be rejected. Individualism chafes at submitting to anything beyond the self. As Weldon Nisly said, "What Hiebert called 'fuzzy,' I have referred to as a kind of anarchist relativism lacking any structure or frame of reference beyond oneself."[15] How can we become disciples of Jesus Christ as Lord if we are part of fuzzy churches that are fueled by tolerance, individualism, and relativism?

Fuzzy churches are fueled by individualism, and they increase it. Social identity theory suggests that when a group's boundaries are more permeable, individuals in the group will engage in what social psychologists call individual mobility strategies.[16] Because both an individual's standing within a fuzzy church and the identity of the church itself are unclear, people will feel a greater need to act elsewhere to improve their personal lot, which will diminish their involvement in the church. In contrast, people in a bounded or centered church are more likely to commit their energies to improving the standing of the group. The individualism of a fuzzy church has a compounding affect. As individualism increases, attendance becomes more sporadic. Being alone together is less compelling than being part of a group identity, and this reality further undermines an individual's commitment to the church.

Relativism: a torpor of death. In *Exclusion and Embrace*, Miroslav Volf critiques the fuzzy approach, observing that if you consider all distinctions and differences as an inappropriate basis for exclusion, "You will have aimless drifting instead of clear-sighted agency, haphazard activity instead of moral engagement and accountability and, in the long run, a torpor of death instead of a dance of freedom."[17] Though "torpor of death" is strong language, Weldon Nisly observed the following from his experience pastoring a church in Seattle for twenty years (a cultural setting that lends

---

[15]Nisly, interview by author, February 15, 2018.

[16]H. Tajfel and J. C. Turner, "An Integrative Theory of Intergroup Conflict," in *The Social Psychology of Intergroup Relations,* ed. W. G. Austin and S. Worchel (Monterey, CA: Brooks/Cole, 1979), 33–47.

[17]Miroslav Volf, *Exclusion and Embrace: A Theological Exploration of Identity, Otherness, and Reconciliation* (Nashville: Abingdon, 1996), 65. Volf does not use the language of bounded, fuzzy, and centered sets in the text of his book, but I saw numerous connections, which he apparently sees as well, since he describes Hiebert's three categories in a footnote (71n3).

itself to a fuzzy approach): "I have pastored many people who had given up on the church because of their experiences in bounded churches. Yet they found it very difficult to live in a fuzzy place. You can't leave a bounded-set world and live in nothing. Bounded is deadly, fuzzy is also deadly. To live without any structure is equally deadly. It is not satisfying. It does not nurture. It is not fulfilling. You can't live just about what you are against."[18]

Wounded by fuzziness. If I hear someone say, "My church wounded me," I think bounded not fuzzy. The bounded approach takes an active stance—imposing and shaming. It feels aggressive; it is easy to imagine it wounding. In contrast, the negatives of the fuzzy approach, as described in the above paragraphs, flow more from inaction. I do not relate blandness and wounding. The image that comes to mind is not bruised fruit, but a fruit tree with a meager yield. So it caught my attention when in a class response paper, a student wrote: "I myself, have been wounded by a fuzzy set in a college ministry." Wounded? I asked her to tell me more of her story. Teresa Leonard shared with me, "At a point when I most needed direction and discipleship, I instead experienced a community of people lost and wandering. Metaphorically, many of us jumped off bridges while the rest watched. There were times I found myself on the rocks below, feeling fundamentally unseen and uncared for, wondering why my brothers and sisters in Christ were acting as observers." As the years have passed, others from the group have confessed that at various times they had felt they should intervene, but they never acted on the loving pull they felt. Why did they not act? Why did they not reach out to the brother or sister in Christ about to jump off the bridge? Leonard observes, "There seemed to be a pervading fear of being judgmental; the cultural atmosphere guided us more than the gospel. The high regard for individualism led many of us to believe that our actions did not affect others or that others' choices did not affect us. Thus, even in a Christian fellowship, we did not keep each other accountable in a real sense. Real love cannot exist without truth."[19] Fuzzy churches wound in a quite different way than bounded ones, but they do leave wounds.

---

[18]Nisly, interview by author, February 15, 2018.
[19]Teresa Leonard, written assignment ("Discipleship and Ethics" course, Fresno Pacific Biblical Seminary, Fresno, CA, February 3, 2021); email to author, February 5, 2021.

Fuzzy and bounded. While a bounded church focuses on drawing a line, a fuzzy church focuses on erasing all lines. As April Alkema observes, "Sometimes the group's only purpose becomes the work of not being bounded."[20] So even though a fuzzy church may know what it is not, does it know what it is? Can it provide people with a strong sense of belonging and group identity? Ironically, some fuzzy churches may end up having bounded elements. Simon Biasell, a student who strongly critiqued bounded churches in my ethics class, realized later in the semester, "I fooled myself to believe that because I'm a gay-affirming feminist who drinks fair trade coffee, I am accepting. However, I'm only accepting to those who agree with me. When I was conservative, I was just as accepting as I am now."[21] Was he fuzzy or bounded?

This question points to two important observations. First, some churches may don a veneer of tolerance and acceptance. They may appear fuzzy on the surface, but in reality they are judgmental of those who differ. In fact, some church leaders think that because of the instability in a fuzzy group, there is a tendency to slide toward boundedness. Second, varying degrees of boundedness and fuzziness can exist in the same church. This book describes them as pure and distinct categories, but the reality is more mixed.

Given the problems of bounded churches, a fuzzy approach seeks to erase the lines. Given the problems of fuzzy churches, a bounded approach seeks to draw thicker and clearer lines. Yet neither approach is radical enough. In order to produce rich and abundant fruit, churches must step away from the bounded-fuzzy continuum toward a totally different paradigm.

THE DEEP WELL OF A CENTERED CHURCH

By discerning group membership through people's trajectories and their relationship to the center, a centered church remedies the problems that motivate a fuzzy church to blur boundaries while also avoiding the negative fruit that grows out of a fuzzy approach. The centered paradigm provides the possibility of conversion and repentance, articulates what is appropriate

---

[20]April Alkema, written assignment ("Discipleship and Ethics" course, Fresno Pacific Biblical Seminary, Fresno, CA, fall 2017).

[21]Simon Biasell, reflection paper ("Discipleship and Ethics" course, Fresno Pacific Biblical Seminary, Fresno, CA, spring 2015).

and inappropriate, establishes a standard (the center), and calls people to a different way of living.

In Antioch Paul responds to the practices of a bounded church by taking a centered (rather than fuzzy) approach. He observes that "they were not acting in line with the truth of the gospel," and so he confronts Peter (Gal 2:14). The Greek word *orthopodeō* is translated as "acting in line," but a more literal translation would be "walking straight." This translation highlights the centered nature of Paul's confrontation. He even uses directional language: "They were not *walking straight toward* the truth of the gospel." Furthermore, rather than focusing on human action and the characteristics of the boundary line, Paul talks about the center and God's action—justification by Jesus Christ's faithfulness (Gal 2:16). When Peter separated himself from the Gentile Christians, he communicated through his actions that they had to meet certain requirements in order to be part of the family of God. By drawing this boundary line, Peter was not living as part of a centered church. Paul points him back toward the center.

Paul confronts Peter's boundedness in Antioch and that of the agitators in Galatia not only to counter its negative fruit, but also because he doesn't want it to inhibit the new creation possibilities of the centered approach (Gal 6:15). In a new-creation church, "There is neither Jew nor Gentile, neither slave nor free, nor is there male and female, for you are all one in Christ Jesus" (Gal 3:28). Such a church lovingly lives by the Spirit and bears the fruit of the Spirit, which Paul describes in Galatians 5. Similarly, this book advocates a centered approach not only to avoid the negative fruit of bounded and fuzzy churches, but also to encourage the new creation possibilities of centered churches.

In the dry Australian outback, it is too expensive for ranchers to build and maintain fences that will contain cattle on their huge properties. So rather than building fences, they dig wells. Though their cattle will roam, they will not roam far, because they must keep returning to the well to drink water.[22] The circumcision-advocating agitators showed up in Galatia with fence-building tools, but Paul dug wells. He wrote to the Galatians to exhort them to stay near the well of Jesus so they could keep drinking his life-giving water.

---

[22]Michael Frost and Alan Hirsch, *The Shaping of Things to Come: Innovation and Mission for the 21st-Century Church*, rev. ed. (Grand Rapids, MI: Baker, 2013), 68.

The cool, clean water that flows from the well of a centered church will attract thirsty people who long to be transformed through Jesus. I close this chapter with three examples of the fruit that grows when we turn from a focus on building fences to digging a well.

The fruit of a centered church. After Dustin began to pastor in a centered way, he experienced the promise and possibility of both loving acceptance and loving confrontation. A man in his church had spent decades listening to others without ever challenging them. Likewise, Dustin had listened to this man without challenging him. Then Dustin began to draw near the well of Jesus with this man and challenge him to take the biblical call to obey more seriously. In a recent conversation with Dustin, this man said, "Something new is happening. The way you listen to me and challenge me has been transformative."[23] Let us all join Dustin in a centered approach and thus love more fully.

Student leaders in a campus ministry wanted to tear down fences between people on their campus, and so they advocated for a fuzzy approach, thinking that if they used a less explicitly Christian liturgy each week, outsiders would feel more welcome. Near the end of the term, they invited a local pastor to lead a Communion service for the group. Before the celebration of the Lord's Supper, she explained the meaning of Communion in the Christian tradition, explicitly emphasizing the well as Jesus. She invited students to Jesus' table, using the same liturgy that she used regularly in her church. Afterwards, the student leaders expressed deep appreciation, saying, "We were fed by this service. It reminded us who we are and what this ministry is." They acknowledged that they now realized what had been missing in the services throughout the semester. May we all seek ways to blow away the fog of fuzziness and let the clarity of Jesus Christ shine forth.

Whenever I give seminars on Galatians, people come up to me at breaks and tell me about their painful experiences of being on the wrong side of a bounded church's fence. In the Dominican Republic, one man sadly told me how his teenage daughter, who loved to sing, had been growing in her relationship with Jesus, but she had been told that she could not be part of the worship group at her church because she had not been baptized.

---

[23]Maddox, interview by author, March 6, 2018.

Discouraged, she stopped going to church. After that same seminar, however, Pastor Robert Guerrero told me about two women in his church who were in the process of following Jesus but had not yet taken the step of baptism. Both had grown up in difficult family circumstances, and their current situations were pretty rough. When Robert invited them to sing in the choir, several leaders in the church became upset and pressed him to insist that they could not sing in the choir until they were baptized. Yet Robert felt confident that both women had turned their arrows toward Jesus, the center. He knew that singing in the choir might help these women walk toward Jesus, and so he did not give in to building fences but continued with a well-digging approach. As he passionately told me, "It was a wonderful thing. The women grew closer to Jesus, and the agnostic mother of one and the worldly father (a hired hit man) of the other both came to church to see their daughters sing. They thanked me profusely, with tears in their eyes, for what the church was doing for their daughters." Referring to the leaders with the bounded perspective, Robert sounded a lot like Paul in his letter to the Galatians: "What they want the church to be is not the gospel!"

In our churches, let us dig a deep well that is fed by the life-giving water of Jesus rather than focus our attention on building fences. May the fresh, cool water from this well, which will never fail, attract all who are thirsty.

3

RESPONDING
TO QUESTIONS ABOUT
A CENTERED CHURCH

WHEN TEACHING SEMINARY CLASSES or giving presentations to groups of church leaders from Buenos Aires, Argentina, to Winnipeg, Manitoba, or when sharing these ideas with friends at my dining room table, I always stop at this point and ask if anyone has questions. While I cannot pause and invite your questions here, I can respond to some of the most commonly asked questions in order to clarify what a centered church is—and what it is not.

NOT CHRISTIANITY LITE

A common question is "How about ethics and the demands of discipleship? A centered approach looks like Christianity lite." Yet a centered approach is not Christianity lite, because facing and heading toward Jesus, our center, will have significant implications for how we live out our life. A group of Christians in a centered church will look radically different from others in society. Still, you may be thinking, *Granted, but the reality is the bounded church takes Christian behavior more seriously and has a more robust Christian ethics than a centered approach.* Although there is an air of strictness and seriousness about behavior and ethics in a bounded church, a centered approach actually has greater potential for facilitating profound transformation. We can observe this difference in the changes reflected in people's lives from the following examples from bounded and centered churches.

Superficial life change in a bounded church. While doing research for an earlier book, I interviewed many people from churches in the Honduran neighborhood where I had studied Galatians with Iglesia Amor Fe y Vida.[1] One of the questions I asked was, "What does someone need to do to be an official member of your church?" One woman answered the question as most others had: the two key elements were being baptized and being legally married (unless you were single). Sitting in front of her humble home, this woman proudly told me that she was a member in good standing and taught a Sunday school class. After completing my questions I asked, "Could I interview your husband as well?" She replied, "He does not live here." I did not press for more information, but she continued, "We can't afford our own house. I will not live with his family, and he refuses to live here with mine. So I am here with our children, and he is with his mother on the other side of the city. But, actually, it is no good when we are together. We fight like cats." She looked down with sorrow and said, "There is much lacking on both sides." This woman was part of a bounded church. In one sense her church took marriage very seriously, insisting that people get married rather than living together. Yet in other ways they gave little importance to marriage. Hers was hurting, and her church did not intervene to help. She was a member in good standing—on the right side of the line, which is what mattered. This was not an isolated case. A woman from a different church said to me, "The leaders in my church are more concerned with what I wear than what I am like as a wife."

In bounded churches, those who successfully keep the rules receive affirmation and status, but there is not much emotional space to fail. Because of this, bounded churches tend to emphasize the clearly defined rules that are achievable, rather than talking about character qualities, such as patience, love, and unselfishness, which are harder to achieve or measure. Church planter Jim Tune made this point in a way that surprised his congregation

---

[1]The results of this research are presented in Mark D. Baker, *Religious No More: Building Communities of Grace & Freedom* (Downers Grove, IL: InterVarsity Press, 1999).

at Discovery Christian Church in Toronto. In the middle of the sermon, he pulled out a pack of cigarettes, and said,

> This is a marker. In evangelical churches, in conservative Christian circles, perhaps in our circle, this is a marker—a pack of smokes. You see, I could be an arrogant man, I could be an angry man, I could be a greedy man, and I could still probably be your preacher. But let me finish my sermon, step out to the parking lot and light up one of these—ask yourself—how much longer will I be your preacher? At the very least there's going to be a meeting![2]

A bounded church is strict about certain things, yet even in those things, does it prevent moral failure any more than a centered approach? In reality, it often does the opposite! Think, for instance, of sexual immorality in bounded churches. As long as people do not "cross the line," they are okay, but the deeper issues that lead someone to cross the line are typically not addressed. Furthermore, if someone is struggling with anything close to crossing the line, shame and fear often prevent that person from reaching out for help.

Profound life change in a centered church. The following stories reveal how centered churches are relationally rich communities that practice robust discipleship and prioritize transformation through the Spirit of Jesus. Beautiful things happen when commitments such as baptism and marriage are relationally motivated rather than behaviors that qualify some people to take their place on the right side of a line and relegate others to the wrong side.

Iglesia Amor Fe y Vida had similar rules as other bounded churches in the area, including the one about marriage. They had drawn a line and said that no one in a common-law relationship could be baptized, partake in the Lord's Supper, lead singing, teach, or collect the offering. Amor Fe y Vida did not openly refer to these people as fornicators as other churches did, but the line itself shamed them and forced them into the role of spectators in the church. After we studied Galatians together, the church sought to become less bounded and more centered. The process was not easy, because even though they earnestly desired to stop drawing lines

---

[2]Jim Tune preached this sermon in 2012. He is now president of Impact Ministry Group, an international church-planting ministry.

that caused shame and division, they also saw positive things about the marriage rule.[3]

The church decided to evaluate each individual situation before imposing any discipline on someone who was not legally married. Leaders who had been designated by the congregation visited Carmen.[4] They had a long conversation with her and spoke with her non-Christian common-law husband as well. They found that even though Carmen wanted to get married, her partner had repeatedly refused. The two had been together for seventeen years, and she had remained faithful to him. What most impressed the elders was the quality of the couple's relationship and parenting. As the leaders left their home and began walking up the dirt road toward their homes, one of them said, "I am legally married, but that couple has a much better relationship than my wife and I do."

In response to that visit, the church decided to invite Carmen to participate fully in the life of the church. The visit also provoked discussions about the health of marriages in the church. Rather than pronouncing new rules, the church asked a couple that had a strong marriage to lead weekly discussions about how to improve marriage relationships and parenting. This was a hard and painful step because a few of the church leaders themselves had serious struggles in their marriages. It would have been easier for everyone in the church to continue simply feeling content with the fact that they were obeying the rules about being legally married and remaining faithful to their spouse. Developing a relationship that kept Jesus at the center called for much more.

---

[3]In the Honduran context, advocating for legal marriage is a socially constructive action. Non-Christian women's organizations also work to encourage people who have common-law relationships to marry. Marriage gives legal protection to women and forces men to be more responsible. When combined with the church's emphasis on sexual fidelity, this rule makes a significant step toward stabilizing families in Honduras. Applied in a bounded way, however, the rule does not acknowledge the complexity of many people's situations. For instance, if a man married someone when he was young, left her without getting a divorce, later started living with someone else with whom he had children, and then became a believer, many churches would demand that he leave his present family and return to his original wife—even if he had been living with his current spouse for twenty years and his previous wife was living with someone else. If the man refused because he wanted to remain faithful to his common-law wife and support their children, he could never be baptized or become a member of the church. Although this situation may appear to be extreme, it is not rare. During my research, one man reported that he knew three people who had left their churches for this reason.

[4]In a number of stories in this book, like this one, I have changed the person's name. When I use the person's first and last name it is their actual name.

With time, as the congregation became more centered and less bounded, the level of vulnerability and honesty in the church increased. Jorge told me that he used to feel perfect when he was obeying all the rules, but it was superficial because his goal was to maintain the appearance of religious perfection. He shared that he did things so that others would be impressed and never talked to others in the church about his weaknesses and struggles— only his victories. Yet he and his wife were having difficulty with a son, and his first instinct was to hide this from everyone in the church. He did not want to ruin the image that he had a good Christian family. But instead of living according to his old pattern, he and his wife talked with church leaders about their son, and the leaders offered helpful ideas. Which church, bounded or centered, takes marriage more seriously? Which leads to more profound transformation?

We see this same dynamic in Jesus' teaching in the Sermon on the Mount. Jesus looks beyond the line to focus on deeper transformation. We could reword Jesus' statement as follows: "The bounded group tells you not to commit adultery, but I tell you that anyone who looks at a woman lustfully has already committed adultery with her in his heart" (Mt 5:27-28). Of course, to a fuzzy-church person, this comment might sound scary, but such a perspective interprets both parts of Jesus' statement through the lens of a bounded church. Simply to categorize something as inappropriate does not mean that we are living out of a bounded perspective.

A pastor who is working to move a fuzzy church to become centered recently said to me, "A centered church is not Christianity lite, and that is a good thing." As we observed in Dustin's story, contemporary Western society has embraced autonomous individualism and the freedom to do whatever we want as the path to a good life, which is often understood as a life full of pleasure. Yet this path does not produce a life of meaning because it inhibits the authentic community that all people crave. Meaning comes from sacrificial giving, serving, and committing to something bigger than ourselves. Community requires a high level of commitment to others and limits our options, so that we can't just do whatever we want whenever we want. Fuzziness is not the path to a thriving life.[5] Unlike bounded and fuzzy churches,

---

[5]These sentences are based on comments from a podcast by John Mark Comer and Mark Sayers, "True Individuality Is Found in Dying to Self (and Other Things You Don't Hear on the

a centered church guides us toward a path of transformation and more abundant life.

NOT UNIVERSAL INCLUSION

In contrast to the spirit of rejection and exclusion that emanates from a bounded church, a centered church has an invitational character. Unlike a fuzzy church, a centered church is not universally inclusive. Rather, it has a center, and one's relationship to the center matters. Returning to our example of centered soccer playing helps clarify this point. After the invitation goes out, a number of people demonstrate their interest in playing soccer by showing up on Sunday afternoon at three o'clock. These people's arrows are turned toward the center. If one person keeps picking up the ball and running with it, others will say, "You can't do that. This is not rugby." If the person continues to grab the ball, the others will say that she cannot participate until she is willing to play by the rules of soccer. That player was not centered on soccer. Similarly, a centered church invites all, but it does not include all. Those who want to be part of a centered church must be interested in building a relationship with Jesus Christ, the center.

Those who play soccer together would all agree on the rule of not using your hands. Similarly, those who are part of a centered church would all agree on certain important aspects of following Jesus. For example, Mennonites and other Anabaptist Christians would agree that a central element of following Jesus is a commitment to nonviolence. Imagine how a bounded Mennonite church might respond to someone who is not a pacifist? How might a fuzzy Mennonite church respond? Or a centered Mennonite church? I asked Weldon Nisly the latter question, as he has pastored Mennonite churches from a centered perspective for the past forty years. He told me about a man who had visited the church who was not a Mennonite, but was searching. In conversation the man told Weldon, "I don't know if I can ever be a pacifist." Weldon responded by saying, "What we invite you to, what Jesus invites you to, is to come and worship and be here. Do it for two or three or months, and let's keep talking. What you will find here is all

Street)," November 20, 2018, in *This Cultural Moment*, podcast, season 3, no. 3, 27:30, https://thisculturalmoment.podbean.com/e/true-individuality-is-found-in-dying-to-self-and-other-things-you-dont-hear-on-the-street/.

grounded in a Jesus of nonviolent love. That is what you will find. But we will not say, 'Unless you believe like us you can't be here.' In fact, I will walk with you along that journey. If you find that you genuinely cannot accept Jesus as we understand him, I will help you find a different church."

I asked Weldon if he had ever helped a non-pacifist find a different church. He said that he had and added, "We are always invitational and formational. You do not guard it by rules and boundaries. You call people into it. What we can't have is people trying to undermine our position. When we have experienced that, we have dealt with it through pastoral care, gentle reminders. We can't set aside what is central to us."[6] In the same way, soccer players would say, "If you use your hands, we will not be playing soccer. We can't just set that rule aside."

In Galatians, Paul criticizes line-drawing exclusion and writes beautiful words of inclusion: "There is neither Jew nor Gentile, neither slave nor free, nor is there male and female, for you are all one in Christ Jesus" (Gal 3:28). But Paul is not talking about universal inclusion. As Michael Gorman writes in *Reading Paul*:

> Some try to turn Paul's conversion and resulting inclusive gospel into a gospel that is so inclusive as to exclude no one. . . . The inclusion that Paul experiences, preaches, and practices is not an inclusion lacking teeth or limits. His gospel does not say, "All are welcome just as they are," but rather, "All are welcome just as they are to be apprehended by, and fully converted to Jesus Christ the Lord."[7]

Some may react against Gorman's placing limits on inclusion (and perhaps against this whole section). A pastor in a region with a high percentage of secular people has observed this resistance. He described a survey he sent to church members that invited them to rate their interest in a variety of topics and activities. One item referred to "resources to help you share the gospel with secular people," and a church member sent the pastor a text message telling him that she did not appreciate the language of "secular people" because it creates an us–them feeling. Although her fuzzy approach might shy away from making any distinctions, is it truly inappropriate to do so? As

---

[6]Nisly, interview by author, February 15, 2018.
[7]Michael J. Gorman, *Reading Paul*, Cascade Companions (Eugene, OR: Cascade Books, 2008), 19.

the pastor and I processed this response, we agreed that we must avoid using the phrase "secular people" in a judgmental and finger-pointing way. But as followers of Jesus, we quite appropriately must recognize that some people are not centering their lives on Jesus. We need language to describe those who are not part of our Jesus-centered communities—those we want to invite to come and join us as we drink from the life-giving water of Jesus.

DISCERNMENT RATHER THAN JUDGMENTALISM

A bounded group creates insiders by having outsiders. It builds its identity by differentiating itself from others and putting them down. Judgmentalism is a fundamentally selfish action because it accrues worth for oneself at the cost of others.[8] As Greg Boyd, a pastor and author, observes, "Judgments only serve the people who make them. They never help the person judged."[9] The lines of division in bounded churches do not make space for nuance or complexity in a person's life. The one standing in judgment observes an action or notes a statement of belief and makes a judgment without exploring the person's story. In this sense, judgmentalism focuses on actions or beliefs, but the especially damaging characteristic of judgmentalism is that the person, not just the action, is judged to be unacceptable. Bounded-church judgmentalism disdainfully categorizes others as outsiders, non-Christians, second-class Christians, worldly, heretics, some as too liberal, some as too conservative, and so on.

To avoid judgmentalism, fuzzy churches say, "We do not judge," and back up that statement with biblical teaching. For example, Jesus says, "Do not judge, or you too will be judged" (Mt 7:1), and Paul writes, "Let us stop passing judgment on one another" (Rom 14:13). Yet when people in a fuzzy church say, "We do not judge," they often mean, "We do not say anything about another person's actions or beliefs." Metaphorically, they would not tell someone who is using their hands while playing soccer to stop.

In contrast to these two approaches, the centered group evaluates, discerning the direction that someone is heading—not merely to determine

---

[8]Based on a dictionary definition judging is at times an appropriate action, but since many people associate negative meanings with this verb, I will use the word *judgmentalism* to refer to negative, inappropriate judging.

[9]Gregory A. Boyd, *Repenting of Religion: Turning from Judgment to the Love of God* (Grand Rapids, MI: Baker Books, 2004), 182.

whether someone belongs, but more to encourage the flourishing of the people who are part of the centered-church community. Others aid our thriving as the people God has created us to be by encouraging positive behaviors and helping us to turn away from negative behaviors, a process that requires both discernment and evaluation. Yet a centered church facilitates discernment without judgmentalism.

A centered church does not need to judge and exclude others in order to strengthen its identity. Because of the directional character of a centered paradigm, it facilitates the evaluation of an action or belief without categorizing the person. The focus of a centered church is on helping people move closer to the center rather than trying to make sure they are not crossing any lines. This process invites people to explore one another's stories, which creates space for nuance and complexity. Loving discernment in a centered church asks relational questions such as, "What in this person's life has led to this behavior?" A centered church's discernment includes concern for how one person's actions or beliefs may impact others, as we saw above in Weldon Nisly's comments. Furthermore, his response reveals how his discernment is motivated and guided by love for the person who seems to be moving away from the center. Thus discernment in a centered church is not selfish, because it is not about seeking status.

BOUNDARIES RATHER THAN BOUNDED

To live in the love and freedom of Christ, we must leave behind the judgmentalism of bounded churches. Jesus and Paul both call us to refrain from judgmentalism. Yet when we establish boundaries, it does not necessarily mean that we are living out of a bounded approach. I seek to have boundaries to keep my work as a professor from overwhelming the rest of my life. Pastors and counselors also use the term *boundaries* in a variety of positive and important ways, such as having appropriate boundaries in a relationship. Thus my critique of bounded churches is not a critique of all boundaries; it is good to have boundaries between appropriate and inappropriate behavior or beliefs. Psychologists tell us that without limits or boundaries, children will not flourish, and this is true for adults as well.[10]

---

[10]For example, see Margaret G. Alter, "The Necessity of the Law," chap. 2 in *Resurrection Psychology: An Understanding of Human Personality Based on the Life and Teachings of Jesus* (Chicago: Loyola

While boundaries can be good things, a bounded church twists and misuses them.

Of course, not all churches that have boundaries are bounded, because a bounded church is one *whose identity is defined* by the boundary line and who uses the boundary line to self-righteously divide the included (those who are superior) from the excluded (those who are inferior). Explicitly or implicitly, a bounded church's boundaries will communicate a sense of conditional love for those in the congregation.

People frequently say something like, "I love the centered approach, but there are times when we must use boundaries. We have bounded groups within our centered church." Then I ask, "Do the boundaries communicate a sense of conditional love, exclusion, and self-righteous superiority, or do they communicate responsibility, freedom, safety, and value?" If it is the latter, then it is not a bounded group as described in this book. For clarity of communication, however, in the rest of this book I will use the word *boundary* only in relation to bounded churches.

TO REJECT A BOUNDED APPROACH DOES NOT MEAN TO REJECT ALL GUIDELINES

Bounded churches also twist biblical laws and commands and use them to shame and exclude others. If we do not recognize this distortion, we will see the command or law itself as the problem. Yet stepping away from all guidelines that distinguish between appropriate and inappropriate belief and behavior sacrifices the important and beneficial aspects of the many ethical exhortations in the Bible, thereby creating new problems.

This leads to a question about the difference between a bounded and centered church's use of a biblical command. We will examine this difference in more depth in chapter six, but the following are some general observations. In a bounded church, standards and guidelines serve to divide those who are in from those who are out. But in a centered church, standards and guidelines help those who are moving toward the center become more

---

University Press, 1994), 19-32. In line with what I have written about bounded churches taking a good thing and misusing it, this chapter affirms the value of law and limitations, and yet, as Alter writes, "Law held as an ultimate value and demanding absolute loyalty destroys community and inhibits justice" (27).

Christlike. In a bounded church, the group (and individual) establishes its identity through its standards. But in a centered group, the group (and individual) establishes its identity through its relationship to the center.

I am including this section about rules and standards in an early chapter because it is a common point of confusion—not because they are the main focus in a centered church.[11] Furthermore, rules and laws can be problematic because they can feed people's desire to break them or to press as close to the lines as possible. Thus all rules, laws, and commands should be used and interpreted with discernment. Furthermore, the words themselves are problematic because of their close association with the line drawing of bounded churches. Those who have experienced an abusive authority figure pronouncing commands may react negatively whenever these words are used. For this reason, I use the term *guidelines* because it coheres with a centered-church diagram. Guidelines help guide us as we journey toward the center. However, *guidelines* could be interpreted by some as if they are mere suggestions that we can choose to follow, or not. That is not how I am using the term, but this does highlight that any of these terms will require framing and explanation. What is important here is to reveal how bounded churches misuse standards and rules, which can lead to the mistaken assumption that the rule or guideline itself is the problem and therefore has no place in a centered church. More appropriately, a centered church uses guidelines in ways that focus us on our relationship with the center, which is Jesus.

POWER OF THE PARADIGMS

To understand the nature of bounded, fuzzy, and centered churches, it is important to recognize that these three paradigms are active forces shaping churches. They are powerful. Regardless of what a bounded church may preach about grace and love, its character will communicate that you need to be on the right side of the line in order to be included. Bounded churches may state that Christ is the center, but the paradigm itself acts like a magnet and pulls people to turn and focus on the boundary line that defines the group and provides their security. At the other end of the spectrum, a fuzzy

---

[11]For instance, a focus on character and virtues is as important as command-based ethics.

church might talk about the centrality of Jesus Christ, but it does not actually have a center. The focus is still on boundary lines, but in this case their identity is defined by not having any boundary lines. The paradigm itself will undercut clarity. In a centered church our security and identity reside in our relationship to the center. Therefore, the paradigm itself, like a magnet, pulls our focus to the center—Jesus Christ.

In chapter two, we explored a narrow question: How does a church categorize who belongs, and who does not? We can now see that how we go about answering this question has far-reaching implications. For instance, the contractual character of a bounded church communicates that God's love is conditional and pulls people toward an emphasis on human performance. In contrast, the relational character of a centered church coheres with God's covenantal approach in the Bible. The centered paradigm itself helps people experience the biblical message that God is faithful to covenant promises even when we humans fail. A bounded approach pulls people to focus on the line rather than each other, which often leaves people standing near the boundary fence in isolation. Yet a fuzzy approach has no pull at all, and so people often wander in isolation. In a centered approach, as people move toward the center, they simultaneously move closer to others.

In *Playing God: Redeeming the Gift of Power*, Andy Crouch writes, "Status—at root, 'where you stand'—is about your place in line. It is about the human drive to be ranked above another, to be counted more worthy than another. . . . Status is about counting, numbering, ranking and ultimately about excluding."[12] Once the germ of excluding others is in the organism, it will infect the whole. The bounded paradigm does not explicitly seek to number and rank people, but the germ of exclusion it contains will pull people in that direction. We feel it in the Pharisee who prays, "God, I thank you that I am not like other people—robbers, evildoers, adulterers—or even like this tax collector" (Lk 18:11). James and John were among the twelve disciples, but they sought status above the others (Mk 10:35-45; see also Mt 20:21-28). Jesus counters this directly by saying, "Not so with you. Instead, whoever wants to become great among you must be your servant, and whoever wants to be first must be slave of

---

[12] Andy Crouch, *Playing God: Redeeming the Gift of Power* (Downers Grove, IL: InterVarsity Press, 2013), 156.

all" (Mk 10:43-44). Status-seeking is in fundamental tension with the kingdom of God because, as Crouch observes, "Every move up in line requires that someone else move back in line, the quest for status pitches us against our fellow image bearers."[13] Again, a bounded church does not openly promote ranking and status-seeking and may even teach against it, but the paradigm itself contributes to status differentiation with outsiders and also those within the church.

Although my bounded-group status-seeking was not as blatant as James and John, it was present (and still has a pull on me). I recall the pride I felt for Sunday school perfect-attendance medals I wore on my blazer as a child or for successfully reciting the memory verse. Of course, actually gaining status requires not just doing or believing the right thing—others must know about it. I recall many ways that, over the years, I would subtly work into conversation things that would score points in whatever bounded group I belonged to at the time—from mentioning my daily devotions to letting others know I lived with the poor, from carrying a Bible (of the right translation for that group) to name-dropping authors esteemed by the group. Note that the actions I sought to draw attention to were themselves good things. The problem is not incarnationally living with the poor or doing devotions. Rather it is the pull of the paradigm that seizes on those things as ways that, as Crouch observes, lead to us raising ourselves up and putting others down. Just as today on both the right and left we observe virtue signaling—acts that are more about enhancing one's image than actual social change—so too bounded-group status-grasping occurs in all types of churches, conservative and liberal.

A bounded church may work at being invitational and welcoming, but the lines of exclusion between insiders and outsiders will act as barriers that undermine and limit their hospitable efforts. In contrast, a centered church is invitational by nature because its character has no barriers, thereby keeping a pathway that leads toward the center open to all. Each individual can decide whether to head toward the center because the model does not post gatekeepers to preserve the identity of the group. Rather, the identity of the group rests in the center. As Stuart Murray says in *Church After Christendom*:

---

[13]Crouch, *Playing God*, 157-58.

Churches with healthy centers are secure enough to welcome those who are exploring faith and searching for authenticity. They are relaxed, non-judgmental communities where questions, doubts, dissent, and fears can be expressed, and where ethical issues do not preclude acceptance. They are inclusive without compromising, communities with deep convictions that are nevertheless open to fresh insights, churches that allow and encourage critical engagement with beliefs and behavior but test everything by its congruence with their founding story.[14]

While this book critiques bounded and fuzzy paradigms within the church and advocates a centered approach, it does not reject the people who participate in bounded and fuzzy churches. I affirm the strong desire of people in bounded churches to promote right beliefs and actions, but the bounded paradigm twists these convictions into line-drawing judgmentalism. To those practicing a bounded approach, I say, "Yes, you have appropriate concerns, but there is a better way that calls for even more radical life change yet avoids judgmentalism." Similarly, I affirm the strong desire of people in fuzzy churches to rid their congregations of an air of judgmental exclusion. To those practicing a fuzzy approach, I say, "Yes, take the loving step of getting rid of the lines of exclusion, but do more than that. You don't need to settle for the partial love of the fuzzy paradigm." The centered paradigm offers a radical and powerful alternative, one that guides people onto a path of life transformation.

PAUL'S CENTERED APPROACH

In the first chapter I used Paul's letter to the Galatians to introduce the third-way alternative I have called a centered approach. I will also give Paul the final word as we conclude these chapters of description. I invite you as you read these verses from the end of his first letter to the Thessalonians to look for things that match up with descriptions and observations from these chapters. How is Paul's centered approach evident?

Now we ask you, brothers and sisters, to acknowledge those who work hard among you, who care for you in the Lord and who admonish you. Hold them in the highest regard in love because of their work. Live in peace with each

---

[14]Stuart Murray, *Church After Christendom* (Milton Keynes, UK: Paternoster, 2004), 30-31.

other. And we urge you, brothers and sisters, warn those who are idle and disruptive, encourage the disheartened, help the weak, be patient with everyone. Make sure that nobody pays back wrong for wrong, but always strive to do what is good for each other and for everyone else.

Rejoice always, pray continually, give thanks in all circumstances; for this is God's will for you in Christ Jesus.

Do not quench the Spirit. Do not treat prophecies with contempt but test them all; hold on to what is good, reject every kind of evil.

May God himself, the God of peace, sanctify you through and through. May your whole spirit, soul and body be kept blameless at the coming of our Lord Jesus Christ. The one who calls you is faithful, and he will do it. (1 Thess 5:12-24)

Paul's final words point to the first observation in the next section. Although the centered-set paradigm is helpful, it is the Lord of the center, Jesus Christ, that will "do it"—not the model itself.

FROM DESCRIBING THE PARADIGM TO LIVING IT

When Weldon Nisly first encountered Hiebert's categories in the mid-1970s, few others knew about them. In recent years they have become increasingly well-known and have been described in numerous sermons, blogs, books, and podcasts. Books and presentations about *how* to practice a centered model, however, are lacking. Describing Hiebert's categories is of great benefit, but we must move beyond description and address the important question: How do we live out a centered approach? The rest of the book seeks to answer that question. Before we begin, however, I share the following two observations.

Centered model is a tool. The centered model is a tool that can help us better understand the nature and practice of discipleship in the church as articulated in the New Testament. Though the two-dimensional diagram is helpful, it cannot capture the full reality of a new creation community that is being transformed by the gospel of Jesus Christ. For instance, although the diagram depicts how people in the church get closer together as they draw nearer to the center, it fails to display the important relationship between the arrows. In addition, although it communicates something very important about the nature of a new creation community, it does not reveal how the church is an alternative culture in tension with the society in which it lives. The diagram does very well at communicating the movement of individuals, but it does not capture how the community of faith moves as a whole as it participates in God's mission. We would do well to imagine the whole diagram held within a moving arrow. Finally, in the diagram the center does not move; the focus, rather, is on the turning and movement of humans. But, as we will observe in the next chapter, the God of the center is always moving toward us. I point out these limitations of the diagram not to set it aside (or attempt to draw a new more complex diagram), but to underscore that it is a tool. It is not itself the gospel. It aids in understanding and living out part of what we are called to as followers of Jesus. Our calling is not simply to become organizations that have a centered character. Our calling is to become disciples of Jesus, to be the body of Christ in the world today. May this tool aid us in that calling.

Defining the center. The water that is in the well will shape a centered church. The water is at the core of the church because it sustains the church and determines its direction. If the church moves away from the center, they move away from the life-giving water. Therefore, defining the center is of utmost importance for a centered church. For Christians, the center is the God revealed by Jesus Christ. The following chapter will explore the importance of having Jesus as the center. However, saying that Jesus is the center is not a complete definition. The center is also defined by a church's theological beliefs and how a church seeks to follow Jesus. Although Christians will hold many things in common, the content of the center will differ from church to church. For instance, Wesleyan, Reformed, and Orthodox churches will define their centers differently. Some churches will include the practice of infant baptism, while others will include the practice of adult baptism. Churches will have different stances on ethical issues and different perspectives about what behaviors should be identified at the center. Beyond placing the God as revealed by Jesus Christ at the center, this book will not define any additional core convictions of the center. That is up to individual churches. Rather, this book will focus on how to belong to one another and journey together toward the center as defined by your church or ministry organization.

Recognizing that churches will define what it means to have Christ as the center in different ways means that some of the examples in this book may not reflect what some readers would place at the center. For instance, in this chapter I use the example of pacifism within a Mennonite church. Nonviolence is part of the center of Mennonite churches, but it is not at the center of many others. Though your center may be different from Pastor Weldon Nisly's, you can still learn from the centered way he interacted with others, and you can apply that to your involvement with your organization or church.

While it is important to consider how a denomination can use a centered approach, or how churches from different denominations in the same city can interact in centered ways, my focus will be on how individual churches or ministries can apply this paradigm to their contexts.

CONCLUSION

I pray that the stories and examples in these first three chapters will motivate you to move away from fence building or fuzziness toward well digging. The potential of a centered approach is great, but putting it in practice is not easy. After Jose, a young Peruvian Pentecostal pastor, participated in a three-hour seminar I facilitated on Galatians, he rose from his seat in the last row and said, "I was not sure about all this at first, but you have convinced me. Yet this will mean more work for me. A bounded-church pastor can just make the rule and apply it, but a centered-church pastor needs to get involved in people's lives. I want my church to become more centered so I am willing to put in the extra effort." These chapters have placed you next to Jose in that seminar. How do you respond to his comment? What thoughts and feelings have you experienced as you have read these opening chapters?

PART TWO

FOUNDATION OF A CENTERED-SET CHURCH

AFTER I PRESENT THE CENTERED-SET MODEL as an alternative to bounded and fuzzy churches, and answer initial questions of clarification, people frequently respond with excitement—and more questions. Many find that the centered approach resonates deeply, and though they might not have realized it before, they suddenly realize how much they desire an alternative to their bounded or fuzzy experiences. Along with passionate hope come many questions. They ask, "What do you do when _____?" (many things fill that blank: disagreement with the church's doctrinal statement, a couple living together, poor attendance at worship team rehearsals, etc.). They ask, "What do you do about membership in a centered church?" or "Don't some things, like recovery ministry, have to be bounded?" or "How can you exhort people to action, to tithe, to love their enemies in a centered way?"

Those questions motivated me to write this book. I wanted to provide a resource to address these questions in concrete and practical ways—and chapters six through twelve will do so. Plunging immediately in the next chapter into "how-tos," however, would repeat the error of ignoring the foundation, as displayed in my story in the first chapter.

A foundation supports a building and enables it to stand. Similarly, a centered church needs the foundational elements described in the next two chapters to support the practices described in the later chapters. Rather than immediately seeking "how-to" tips, let us first ask, "What are the foundational elements we need in place for the methods in the rest of the book to function?" We must lay a centered-church foundation in order to build a centered church. I have dedicated chapter four to the single most important aspect of the foundation—the God of the center. In chapter five, I will present several other elements foundational to building a centered church.

4

THE GOD OF THE CENTER

IT IS NOT ENOUGH TO SAY simply that God is at the center of a church. We must describe who God is, because our conceptions about God will influence whether we do church in a bounded, fuzzy, or centered way, and the paradigm of our church will influence how we view God. Doug Frank recalls how his experience of growing up in a bounded church led him to conceive of God as the big, unkindly Eye.[1] Philip Yancey's bounded-church experience left him "feeling [he] must somehow earn God's approval."[2] He describes his journey in seeking to correct and heal from this view in *What's So Amazing About Grace?*[3] Of course, others from bounded churches have different images, which are not all as harsh as these. Perhaps most commonly, people blend together various images of God. For instance, one leader in a bounded church often spoke about God's love, yet one day in the middle of a Sunday school class discussion, she became teary and said, "I do not talk about it much, but in the depth of my being, I am afraid of God, afraid I will fall short, and he will punish me."

How might a fuzzy church influence its members' concepts of God? In *Almost Christian*, Kenda Creasy Dean reports that youth from churches who

---

[1]Doug Frank, *A Gentler God* (Eugene, OR: Wipf and Stock, 2020). Frank uses the unkindly Eye description in autobiographical reflections in "Naked but Unashamed," in *Proclaiming the Scandal of the Cross: Contemporary Images of the Atonement*, ed. Mark D. Baker (Grand Rapids, MI: Baker Academic, 2007), 122-34.

[2]Philip Yancey, *What's So Amazing About Grace?* (Grand Rapids: Zondervan, 1997), 33.

[3]Yancey, *What's So Amazing?* See also Philip Yancey, *Soul Survivor: How My Faith Survived the Church* (New York: Doubleday, 2001).

"are devotees of nonjudgmental openness, self-determination, and the authority of personal experience" often "view God as either a butler or a therapist, someone who meets their needs when summoned ('a cosmic life-guard,' as one youth minister put it) or who listens nonjudgmentally and helps youth feel good about themselves. . . . God watches over them without making demands of them. God, above all else, is 'nice.'"[4] She sees this per-spective developing in churches that have "lost track of Christianity's mis-sional imagination . . . [supplanting] the gospel with a religious outlook that functions primarily as a social lubricant."[5]

Though we can observe a correlation between church paradigms and peo-ple's concepts of God, such a correlation does not prove causality. Does the church model create the concept of God or the reverse? As I observe above, my sense is that our paradigms and concepts about God are intertwined and reinforce each other. In both bounded and fuzzy churches, other factors also shape our views of God. For instance, in the memoir *Memories of God*, Roberta Bondi connects her nightmares of God as a stern father figure to her experiences in her grandparents' church. Yet her childhood church was not the only factor, because her earthly father also influenced her view of God. She thought her heavenly Father was like her earthly father, only more so. She describes her father as a loving man, but one who "tolerated no imperfections or weakness in other people, no laziness, no disobedience from his children. . . . I loved my father so much, yet I knew I could never please him. . . . I could not possibly believe my human father loved me as I was. And if this was true of my earthly father, how much more must this be the case with my heavenly Father."[6] Similarly, Kenda Creasy Dean describes societal and personal factors that contribute to a fuzzy church's view of God, such as cultural pluralism and societal values of tolerance, autonomy, and individual freedom.[7]

I write the above paragraphs not only to reveal some of the negative fruits of bounded and fuzzy churches, but also as a cautionary word. What

---

[4]Kenda Creasy Dean, *Almost Christian: What the Faith of Our Teenagers Is Telling the American Church* (Oxford: Oxford University Press, 2010), 17, 28. Her research is based on the National (US) Survey of Youth and Religion, 2002–2003.

[5]Dean, *Almost Christian*, 37.

[6]Roberta C. Bondi, *Memories of God: Theological Reflections on a Life* (Nashville: Abingdon, 1995), 24-25.

[7]Dean, *Almost Christian*, 30-37.

Roberta Bondi describes is quite common—simply take the human characteristics we know, enlarge them, and call that God. We can observe this throughout time and cultures. For instance, Greek philosophy defined ideal human traits and then described God as the ultimate expression of them. Other Greeks were less abstract, the gods of their myths, such as Apollo, Athena, and Zeus, were depicted as humans writ large. A centered church is radically different from a bounded or fuzzy church in large part because the descriptions of the God at the center are radically different. If we trust in our human assumptions and speculations about God, our views of God will mirror the harsh or bland ones described above. Instead, let us follow the counsel of Martin Luther:

> You must not climb up to God but begin where he began—in his mother's womb he became man—and deny yourself the spirit of speculation . . . you should know no God at all apart from this man, and depend upon his humanity. . . . In this matter, of how one should treat God and act towards God, forget about speculation about his majesty. . . . We know of no God excepting only the incarnate and human God. . . . If you are concerned about your salvation, forget about all ideas of law, all philosophical doctrines, and hasten to the crib and to his mother's bosom and see him, an infant, a growing child, a dying man. Then you will escape all fear and errors. This vision will keep you on the right way.[8]

During a class discussion, one of my students, Christa Wiens, suggested a way to put Luther's counsel into practice. When you imagine God doing something, such as judging with an unkindly eye or passively being nice, see if you can picture Jesus doing it. If not, adjust your thinking to line up with Jesus.[9]

This chapter seeks to establish a strong foundation by exploring and describing the God of the center. Let us begin by committing to look at Jesus so that Jesus can shape our concept of God. Let us do so with humility and a healthy skepticism of our human concepts of God, which we have absorbed from other sources—including bounded and fuzzy approaches to church. Let us approach this chapter with the recognition that we are not simply

---

[8]Martin Luther, commentary on Galatians 1535 (Gal 1:3). This translation in Gerhard Ebeling, *Luther: An Introduction to His Thought* (Philadelphia: Fortress, 1970), 235.

[9]Christa Wiens, post to online forum (Fresno Pacific Biblical Seminary, December 3, 2019).

compiling important information to put in the center. The center is not a list of our beliefs about Jesus, but the person of Jesus. We will draw insights from Jesus about how to live out a centered approach. More significantly, placing the God who is revealed by Jesus at the center will help us begin to undo the negative concepts that we may have absorbed from bounded and fuzzy churches.

STATUS-SEEKING IN THE WORLD OF JESUS

During the time of Jesus, people sought to protect their honor, gain more honor, and improve their status. They constantly measured the status of others and knew that others were measuring their status as well. As Cicero commented, "Life was lived under the constant, withering gaze of opinion, everyone constantly reckoning up the honour of others."[10] Occasionally we see this scrutiny explicitly described in the New Testament. For instance, at a banquet in Luke, Jesus talks about how the seats at the table are ranked according to one's status, and he counsels his listeners about how to avoid shame and gain honor in that setting (Lk 14:7-11). If this dynamic was as prevalent as Cicero suggests, why isn't it mentioned more in the New Testament? In part, because those who listened to Jesus and received the original New Testament letters did not need to be told about this reckoning. Status-seeking was a given, and so it did not need to be mentioned. Furthermore, when it is mentioned, those of us from other cultural settings may not have eyes to see it. For instance, just a few verses after the previous passage in Luke, Jesus says,

> When you give a luncheon or dinner, do not invite your friends, your brothers or sisters, your relatives, or your rich neighbors; if you do, they may invite you back and so you will be repaid. But when you give a banquet, invite the poor, the crippled, the lame, the blind, and you will be blessed. Although they cannot repay you, you will be repaid at the resurrection of the righteous. (Lk 14:12-14)

The repayment is not just about getting a meal, but accruing status. A person gained honor when they received dinner invitations from people with status.

---

[10]Cicero, *Epistulae ad Quintum Fratrem* 1.1.38, quoted in J. E. Lendon, *Empire of Honour: The Art of Government in the Roman World* (Oxford: Clarendon, 1997), 36.

Inviting people with status to a meal was strategic and calculated. Those who accepted would be duty-bound to reciprocate, which would honor the host. But a host could not reach too high, for if he invited someone who refused the invitation, the host would suffer shame and lose honor. Jesus lived his life in a world that paid high attention to status—who was in and out, high and low.[11]

Think of who you have shared meals with recently. Who has invited you to a meal? Whom have you invited? And why? An invitation to a meal can communicate inclusion, a desire to establish a more intimate or deeper relationship with someone. This was even more true in Jesus' setting than in Western society today. Dennis Smith, who writes about social practices in the New Testament world, observes that at that time, "Whom one dines with defines one's placement in a larger set of social networks. Because of the clear boundary-defining symbolism of table fellowship in the ancient world, banquets became a significant feature of various identifiable social groups. The social code of the banquet represents a confirmation and ritualization of the boundaries that exist in a social situation. The act of dinning together is considered to create a bond between the diners."[12]

Thumb through the Gospels. Take note of how often Jesus is at a meal, hosting a meal, or talking about table fellowship.[13] The table clearly played a central role in Jesus' life and teaching—in part because of its power to communicate acceptance and inclusion. Jesus, however, was not the only one using table fellowship with intentionality. Table fellowship played a central role in the Pharisees' campaign to return holiness to Israel. They brought a heightened practice of purity to meals—what they ate and with

---

[11]For a description of the honor-shame dynamic in the New Testament world, see David deSilva, *Honor, Patronage, Kinship & Purity: Unlocking New Testament Culture* (Downers Grove, IL: InterVarsity Press, 2000). For a briefer description of honor and shame in the Old Testament and New Testament, see chapters four and five of Jayson Georges and Mark D. Baker, *Ministering in Honor-Shame Cultures: Biblical Foundations and Practical Essentials* (Downers Grove, IL: IVP Academic, 2016). Even better than a description, read a well-researched narrative that enables you to feel how honor accrual, shame avoidance, and status consciousness pervaded daily life, e.g., Bruce W. Longenecker, *The Lost Letters of Pergamum: A Story from the New Testament World* (Grand Rapids, MI: Baker Academic, 2003); James L. Papandrea, *A Week in the Life of Rome* (Downers Grove, IL: IVP Academic, 2019).

[12]Dennis E. Smith, *From Symposium to Eucharist: The Banquet in the Early Christian World* (Minneapolis: Fortress, 2003), 9-10.

[13]For example, see Mt 8:11; 22:1-4; 23:23-26; 25:1-13; Mk 7:1-23; 12:39; 14:3-9; Lk 7:36-50; 10:38-42; 11:37-52; 12:35-38; 14:1-24; 15; 17:7-10; 19:1-10; 22:14-38; Jn 12:1-11; 21:12.

whom they ate. The table provided them with an excellent tool to pressure others to follow the law just as they did. They rewarded the observant with status through table fellowship; they denied status and communicated disapproval of the non-compliant by refusing to invite them to meals. They made bounded-group lines clear through table fellowship. Jesus used meals to erase those lines.

JESUS' ALTERNATIVE TO BOUNDED RELIGIOSITY: LUKE 15

At the beginning of Luke 15, we read that tax collectors and sinners are "coming near" to Jesus because they want to listen to him (v. 1). Whereas others exclude and shame these "sinners," they are attracted to Jesus and feel free to go near him. The bounded-group religiosity of the Pharisees communicates to these sinners that they can't belong with those who are truly living as the people of God until they clean up their act, but Jesus apparently communicates the opposite, and this upsets the guardians of the boundary lines. What if other religious leaders start doing the same as Jesus? The lines will lose their power, and the scribes and Pharisees fear that wayward people will not repent and change their ways. From the Pharisees' perspective, the pressuring lines of their bounded group must stay in place if there is going to be holiness in Israel. While the Pharisees try to get people to change their lives by threatening to exclude them, Jesus does the opposite.

Jesus not only lets these sinners come close and listen to his teaching, but he invites them to share table fellowship. Based on what we learned in the previous section on table fellowship, this invitation would have communicated acceptance in a powerful way, and so it would have been particularly upsetting to the Pharisees. I imagine this scene as follows.

The outcasts in the community, such as prostitutes, tax collectors, those who do business with Gentiles, and those who do not go to the synagogue or comply with diet and Sabbath laws, wake up with amazement as they remember how great it felt to spend time with Jesus the day before. They recall with wonder how Jesus had invited them to dine together. Drawn to the unaccustomed feeling of acceptance and inclusion, and curious about the kingdom of God that Jesus described, they leave their homes and look for Jesus. When they find him, they draw closer. Jesus stops his teaching to welcome the new arrivals and greet them by name. They soak up his love and acceptance. Then a group of scribes and Pharisees pass by and start listening from the edges, not wanting to get too close to the sinners in the crowd. Some of the Pharisees begin to point out to one another the various disreputable people who are standing near Jesus. They talk loudly among themselves, grumbling and complaining so that everyone can hear. They try to shame both Jesus and the outcasts by saying, "This Jesus fellow welcomes sinners and eats with them!" Their words pierce the outcasts, deflating their feelings of acceptance and inclusion.

Jesus responds to the shaming comments of religious line drawing by telling the entire crowd, both the religious insiders and the outsiders, three parables: the lost sheep, the lost coin, and the lost sons.

Jesus need not explain the meaning or significance of ancient customs, but many of these details might be lost on Westerners, who are from a different time and culture.[14] To connect the parable of the lost sons with readers in our time, I will retell it from the perspective of a neighbor who lives in the village. The following expanded version of the story provides more explanation and highlights the scandalous shame and radically gracious honor of the original parable in Luke 15:11-32.

Amazing things have been happening in one family in our village! The younger son asked the father for his inheritance. Can you imagine? Have you ever heard of such a thing? What nerve! What disrespect! He might as well have said, "Father I wish you would die."

Of course, we all expected the father to scorn the younger son, perhaps disown or stone him, just like it says in Deuteronomy 21. Instead, he gave his younger son the inheritance! It also amazed us that his older son never intervened or at least protest that he didn't want to have anything to do with his younger brother's action and the disgrace he'd brought to the family.

As news spread around town, a lot of people were pretty upset, and I think the younger son started feeling uncomfortable. So what do you think

[14]I gleaned many of the insights on the cultural background for this parable from Kenneth E. Bailey, "The Pursuing Father," *Christianity Today*, October 26, 1998; Kenneth E. Bailey, *Poet and Peasant and Through Peasant Eyes: A Literary-Cultural Approach to the Parables in Luke*, combined ed. (Grand Rapids, MI: Eerdmans, 1983), 158-206; Kenneth E. Bailey, *The Cross & the Prodigal: Luke 15 Through the Eyes of Middle Eastern Peasants*, 2nd ed. (Downers Grove, IL: InterVarsity Press, 2005).

he did? We thought he would give the land back to his father, but he tried to sell it. Can you imagine, selling ancestral land, the very land that God gave our forefathers? What will his father have to live off when he grows older? And where will this son raise his family? What will his children inherit? Such disrespect! So inconsiderate!

Trying to sell the land only made things worse for the son. Each person he tried to sell it to got angry and insulted him. He finally found someone to buy it—a merchant newly arrived to town. The son couldn't have felt very welcome here after doing such shameful things, so he took the money and left town.

He went to a Gentile land, where he squandered all his money. Then a famine hit, and since he was a foreigner, no one felt obliged to help him. So there he was, living in a foreign land, hungry, and feeding pigs for a living. We heard he was so hungry that he wanted to eat the pig food! He'd obviously lost all his dignity—just think, a Jew, feeding pigs for a living! and eating their food!

The son was starving, but he knew that if he returned home, he would face the scorn of the village. After all, we had shamed him before he left—how much more would we shame him in his degraded condition? He had blown his complete inheritance in a Gentile land! He must have been worried about his father's anger, and he certainly knew about the *kezazah*, our custom of banishing anyone who lost or sold family inheritance among Gentiles. He would have known that when he returned, we'd break a large pot of roasted nuts and declare, "You are rejected from this community!"

Desperate, the son hoped that his father would give him a job as a worker so he could pay back the inheritance and escape the ban. But he didn't know if his father would even talk to him, and so he decided to apologize first, in the hope that his father would listen to his request. As he walked home he carefully crafted his speech.

"Father," he would say, "I have sinned against heaven and before you; I am no longer worthy to be called your son; treat me like one of your hired hands."

He must have wished there was a back way into town, but our homes are clustered all together, and our farmland spreads all around the village.

I was one of the first to see him, and he was a sight—dirty, thin, barefoot, wearing patched-up clothes that looked like rags. He walked with his head low, obviously hoping that we would not recognize him. I was glad to see how bad he looked. I didn't want my sons running off like he had! We all started yelling at him and insulting him, "You worthless pig!" "Leave our village, you foreigner!" As a crowd gathered, people began the *kezazah* ceremony to ban him from the village.

But all of a sudden, people began looking down the street. His father was running—yes, *running*—toward us! We were all shocked. In our culture, men do not run. Older men wait for others to approach them. Running is for children, not elders. How shameful—just imagine what he exposed, his robes flying up in the air!

Then the father hugged and kissed his filthy son. While the son stood there in shock, we all shut up. We could not insult or ban the son when his own father was welcoming him home. In fact, his father was humiliating himself to stop us from shaming his son.

Then the son said, "Father, I have sinned against heaven and before you; I am no longer worthy to be called your son." He didn't say anything about being a hired hand. I think the father's reaction changed the son's whole perspective. He must have been amazed by his father's love and acceptance and grateful for the way his father had saved him from our scorn. Maybe he realized he couldn't bring about a reconciliation on his own or try to buy back his relationship with his father. He had done more than waste money; he hurt his father, so all he could do was ask for mercy.

The father left no doubt he was accepting the son back. He responded by telling his servants to put sandals on his son's feet, a ring on his finger, and a fine robe on him. Without a word of rebuke, the father covered up his son's filth and restored him as a true son. He also told the servants to prepare a feast and kill the fatted calf—not even a lamb or a chicken! Then he told them to invite the whole village. I was glad to hear that! The father not only accepted him back, but he *honored* him and *celebrated* his return in the presence of the entire village. But that's only half the story.

As everybody began to arrive at the father's house for the celebration that evening, I got to the house just as the older son returned from his work in the fields. I paused to let him enter so he could take his place as a greeter at his father's party, according to our custom. But he stopped and asked a servant what was happening. The servant explained, "Your father is celebrating and welcoming back your brother." The older son turned away from the house, saying, "I'm not joining in this celebration. I deserve a party, not my brother." In our village, you never refuse an offer of food, but the older son refused his own father! He made a huge scene in front of the guests, which was as shameful to the father as the younger son's request for an inheritance.

Then I saw the father look out the door at all the commotion. I expected the father to be furious and to put his older son in place for insulting him, but the father came out and pleaded with his son to join the celebration. For the second time that day, the father sought to restore a dishonoring son.

But the older son continued to insult his father. He spoke with no respect, without using a title, as he yelled in his father's face, "Listen! For all these years I have been working like a slave for you, and I have never disobeyed your command; yet you have never given me even a young goat so that I might celebrate with my friends. But when this son of yours came back, who devoured your property with prostitutes, you killed the fatted calf for him!"

Once again, the father went out of his way to try to bring the older son into the family celebration, shaming himself for the sake of his son. He responded, "Son, you are always with me, and all that is mine is yours. But we had to celebrate and rejoice, because this brother of yours was dead and has come to life; he was lost and has been found."[15]

With those words, the parable ends. Jesus leaves the listeners wondering. Does the older son go in and join the celebratory meal, or does he leave in disgust? Is the family ultimately restored? To understand why Jesus stops the parable without a conclusion, we need to remember the two groups of people who are listening in Luke 15:1-2.

On the one hand, there are sinners and tax collectors, those who are outside of the acceptable boundaries of society. On the other hand, there are the Pharisees and scribes, those who are respected and admired in the society. To the tax collectors and sinners, Jesus' words communicate that God welcomes them and is willing to demonstrate his love—even at the expense of his own reputation.

By not finishing the story, Jesus tries to communicate to the Pharisees and teachers of the law that he wants them to finish it. Functionally, Jesus is saying, "I'm offering love and forgiveness to these people. Will you come in and join the welcome-home party?" Jesus ends the story mid-scene because the listeners' response to this invitation will become the conclusion to the parable.

---

[15]This story is adapted from Georges and Baker, *Ministering in Honor-Shame Cultures*, 102-5.

Jesus also wants to communicate something else to the Pharisees. Anyone in his culture would see that the older son, although keeping the letter of the law, has done shameful things that damaged his relationship with his father. Through the parable, Jesus tells the scribes and Pharisees, "You are sinners, too!" But like the father in the parable who comes out of the house to invite the older son to take part in the celebration, Jesus does not scorn or reject the Pharisees. He invites them to join him in welcoming the excluded people. Jesus expresses God's gracious welcome to everyone—the sinners as well as the Pharisees and scribes.

Although we commonly call this the parable of the prodigal son, the central figure is the father. The father reaches out in love to both sons—the one lost in a foreign land, the other lost at home. By inviting both sons to come together and eat at one table as a family, the father pursues restoration and harmony. The father willingly suffers shame to communicate love and forgiveness with each son personally and to restore their relationship as a family. As my former student Sherri Nozik observed after reading my paraphrase of this parable, "The father also communicates that it is his table, his celebration, his decision. The table is open to the prodigal younger son, bitter older son, judgmental onlookers, everyone, wherever they stood."[16]

The parable reveals the loving nature of God and also interprets the meaning and significance of Jesus' ministry among those who have been shamed. As God incarnate, Jesus lives out the parable of the lost sons and the pursuing father through his table fellowship. If Jesus had focused on saving his reputation and honor, he would have turned his back on the tax collectors and sinners when the Pharisees and scribes grumbled about the way he ate with sinners. To save face, he would have walked off with the religious leaders. But by making the interests and status of others a higher priority than his own, he stands in solidarity with the excluded and told the three parables in Luke 15. Like the father in the parable, Jesus steps out on their behalf, absorbs their shame, and restores their identity and dignity, a costly demonstration of unexpected love that he enacts even more profoundly at the cross.

---

[16]Sherri Nozik, email to author, November 6, 2019.

I invite you to take a few minutes and reflect on Luke 15 through the lens of bounded, fuzzy, and centered approaches. What does the above retelling lead you to see in the text? How does Luke 15 add to your understanding of bounded, fuzzy, and centered? I will list below a few of my responses to these questions.

BOUNDED, FUZZY, AND CENTERED APPROACHES IN LUKE 15

One could look at bounded, fuzzy, and centered approaches and evaluate them as options—each with pros and cons, but not as right or wrong. However, this is not Jesus' approach. Jesus confronts the bounded religiosity of the Pharisees as sin. Jesus' actions and words in this chapter boldly critique any practices that shame or exclude those on the fringes of society. As Miroslav Volf observes, "Since he who was innocent, sinless, and fully within God's camp transgressed social boundaries that excluded the outcasts," it exposed those "boundaries themselves [as] evil, sinful, and outside God's will." Jesus's hospitality stands in stark contrast to the Pharisees' bounded ways. "By embracing the 'outcast,' Jesus underscores the 'sinfulness' of the persons and systems that cast them out." I find especially powerful Volf's observation that to deem sinful this practice of exclusion "names as sin what often passes as virtue, especially in religious circles."[17]

The meaning and significance of this parable changed radically for me after I gleaned cultural insights from Kenneth Bailey and read the parable in the context of the first two verses of Luke 15. First, I saw that the older son was not as sinless as he thought—and I recognized myself as such an "older son." Both the Pharisees and the Mark Baker you met in the first chapter viewed their personal behavior as virtuous, and they also saw their seriousness about line-drawing exclusion as praiseworthy. Jesus confronts it as sin.

Once again, I want to underscore that it was not just the legalistic ways of my teenage self that Jesus would confront as sin, because my disdainful,

---

[17]Miroslav Volf, *Exclusion and Embrace: A Theological Exploration of Identity, Otherness, and Reconciliation* (Nashville: Abingdon, 1996), 72. Richard Beck discusses this same page from Volf in relation to the purity codes in Jesus' day in *Unclean: Meditations on Purity, Hospitality, and Mortality* (Eugene, OR: Cascade Books, 2011), 78.

twenty-something progressive attitude toward "legalists" was just as bounded. Today, Jesus would confront the bounded ways of both fundamentalists and progressives, and he would invite both groups to dine at the table with those whom they view with contempt.

As we discussed in the previous chapter, a bounded approach prioritizes rules and a fuzzy approach seeks to dispense with them, whereas a centered approach has rules, but uses them differently. In the parable, we see this in the way that the father prioritizes relationship over rules with both sons. As Volf observes,

> What is so profoundly different about the "new order" of the father is that it is not built around the alternatives as defined by the older brother: either strict adherence to the rules or disorder and disintegration; either you are "in" or you are "out," depending on whether you have or have not broken a rule. He rejected the alternative because his behavior was governed by the one fundamental "rule": relationship has priority over all rules. Before any rule can apply, he is father to his sons and his sons are brothers to one another.[18]

To say that Jesus prioritizes "relationship over rules" does not suggest that his radical inclusiveness is fuzzy. The Pharisees and the older son seek to draw lines because they see themselves as "in" and superior to those who are "out." Jesus does not say "whatever." Through the parable, he confronts the Pharisees for their superiority. The father in the parable, who represents God, is not fuzzy either. He does not let the older brother simply stay outside. He addresses what is broken and presents an opportunity to change. A centered approach presses for more than a fuzzy approach—for transformation in ways that are life-giving and enriching for all involved. The radical forgiveness of the father for the younger son could be misinterpreted as fuzziness, but note how the father describes his wayward younger son as "lost" and "dead" (Lk 15:32). These are not fuzzy terms. As Dustin Maddox observes, "The father did not say, 'Oh, he was just on a journey of self-discovery and realized that he was now in a more integrated and healthy place to come back to his family.'"[19] Jesus, and a church that is centered on his radically inclusive love, will always care if someone is lost or found, dead

---

[18]Volf, *Exclusion and Embrace,* 164.
[19]Dustin Maddox, focus group discussion of an early draft of *Centered-Set Church,* October 24, 2019.

or alive. Jesus and a centered church offer "direction from lostness, life out of death, restoration from brokenness."[20]

This parable also gives a narrative depiction of the centered-church diagram (see figure 2.3 above). The text says that "The tax collectors and sinners were coming near to listen to him" (Luke 15:1, NRSV). The arrows of these characters are headed toward Jesus. I can also imagine the scribes and Pharisees standing a bit removed, arms crossed and scowling. Their body language communicates the opposite directional stance—they are not headed toward Jesus. When the younger brother leaves his father and home, he is heading away, but then he turns around and heads back home, back toward his father. Note how there is no line for him to cross for him to be "in." His father embraces him before he gives his speech. To be "in" again, the son simply has to turn toward his father. When the older son refuses to go into the dinner party, he communicates that his arrow is heading away from his father. The parable communicates even more than the diagram captures, because both the father in the story and Jesus as he tells the story take initiative. The center reaches out to people rather than sitting passively.

Much of this book explores the character traits, practices, and insights that can help a church live out a centered approach. They are important. Let us learn from and imitate Jesus' actions in Luke 15. But the methods themselves are not enough. We must ensure that the God revealed by Jesus and the God represented by the father in the parable is at the center of our churches. Let us proclaim with clarity and boldness this God, who is radically different from our humanly conceived gods. Let us invite people to meet Jesus, to experience his unconditional loving embrace, and to receive his invitation to sit down and join others at his table—not because of who they are or what they have done, but because we all have a seat at the table through Jesus. The God of the center, the water in our well, is the most important element of a centered church. As we gather together at this table of Jesus, our churches will become more centered.

JESUS AS RADICALLY INCLUSIVE, NOT FUZZY

The parable reveals how Jesus not only avoids a bounded approach, but also actively confronts and critiques it. It also reveals how Jesus doesn't simply

---

[20]Maddox, focus group discussion, October 24, 2019.

erase all the boundary lines and live out a fuzzy approach. We can see him living out of a centered approach throughout the Gospels. Consider just a few examples.

Jesus calls people to repent and believe in the good news (Mk 1:15). That reflects a key element in a centered approach—turning away from something and reorienting to a new center. Jesus offers ethical teaching that clearly identifies some actions and attitudes as in alignment with the center, the kingdom of God, and others as inappropriate. In the repeated couplets in the Sermon on the Mount (such as "It was said to the people long ago, 'You shall not murder, and anyone who murders will be subject to judgment.' But I tell you that anyone who is angry with a brother or sister will be subject to judgment." [Mt 5:21-22]) Jesus does not make things fuzzy, but he expands the commands of the bounded approach so that they become even more challenging. He calls for life transformation rather simply trying to pull people across a line.

In Luke's narrative about the calling of Levi, a tax collector, Jesus begins by saying to Levi, "follow me" (Lk 5:27). In this first command Jesus focuses on relationship, not rules. His command is directional and implies not only orientation but also movement. To follow someone will require ongoing movement. The narrative says that Levi "got up, left everything and followed him" (Lk 5:28). Then Levi honors Jesus with a banquet (Lk 5:29). A Pharisee would never accept such an "honor" from a tax collector because the rules say they cannot eat with tax collectors and sinners. So, when Jesus accepts this honor, the Pharisees complain. Jesus' response is not rooted in the values of fuzziness. He does not lecture the Pharisees about the importance of tolerance, but he challenges their line-drawing exclusion, making it clear his alternative is not fuzzy "whateverism." Eugene Peterson's translation in *The Message* captures this dynamic well: "I'm here inviting outsiders, not insiders—an invitation to a changed life, changed inside and out" (Lk 5:32).

We see this repeatedly; here are just two other examples. In John 8, Jesus rescues the woman caught in adultery from the shaming threats of the line-drawing scribes and Pharisees by first offering words of healing restoration and then saying, "Go now and leave your life of sin" (Jn 8:11).[21] In the house

---

[21]As noted in the NIV, this pericope was not in the earliest manuscripts. Likely it was part of the oral tradition and added to John's gospel by later scribes.

of Simon, the Pharisee, Jesus offers acceptance and grace to a woman who has been shamed and excluded by Simon and his other guests (Lk 7:36-50). Jesus confronts Simon's line drawing when he defends and honors the woman at the risk of his own reputation. Again, his response does not convey fuzzy inclusiveness because forgiveness is central to the story. We only say, "You are forgiven," when there has been an offense. Therefore, "You are forgiven" is centered, not fuzzy, language; it is directional language (Lk 7:48). It communicates the way a person was headed was not the right path; what they were doing was not in line with the center.[22]

Whereas the Pharisees' bounded-group strategy is to work for transformed lives through shaming and threatening exclusion, Jesus frontloads not accusation and threats but *grace* as the foundation for transformation. He extends radical inclusivity, but not radical tolerance. As Volf observes,

> He was no prophet of "inclusion" for whom the chief virtue was acceptance and the cardinal vice intolerance. Instead, he was the bringer of "grace," who not only scandalously included "anyone" in the fellowship of "open commensality," but made the "intolerant" demand of repentance and the "condescending" offer of forgiveness (Mark 1:15; 2:1-17). The mission of Jesus consisted not simply in *re-naming* the behavior that was falsely labeled "sinful" but also in *re-making* the people who have actually sinned or suffered misfortune. The double strategy of re-naming and re-making, rooted in the commitment to both the outcast *and* the sinner, to the victim *and* the perpetrator, is the proper background against which an adequate notion of sin as exclusion can emerge.[23]

When Jesus confronts bounded religiosity as sinful, he does not embrace fuzzy-group tolerance. Rather, Jesus models a totally different option—a centered approach.

UPENDING PRIVILEGE AND STATUS

The previous pages focused on how the Pharisees use line drawing to promote holy living. Yet in their day, as in ours, the lines of division also provide security, permit the Pharisees to love selectively, and to establish

---

[22]I explore these and other elements in this passage in-depth in Marcos Baker, *Centrado en Jesús: Teología Contextual* (Buenos Aires: JuanUno1 Ediciones, 2017), 87-94.
[23]Volf, *Exclusion and Embrace*, 72-73 (emphasis in original).

status over others by constantly evaluating their position in relation to the lines. This is not to imply that the Pharisees practice bounded-group religiosity in a calculated way in order to accrue status over others. I do not picture them as a group gathered in a back room, strategizing about how they can use religious rules or beliefs as a way to gain superiority over others. Most people draw religious lines with sincere concerns and motivations. Yet in a society that is saturated with status-seeking, a bounded group easily absorbs that mentality, and their practices can become tools to grasp at superiority and status. In this way, status, superiority, and privilege can become unconsciously woven into the fabric of bounded churches.

In *Playing God*, Andy Crouch argues that Jesus does not give up power, but extensively uses power to teach, heal, forgive, calm storms, and so on. However, Jesus intentionally gives up and turns away from "the privilege that would so naturally be offered in the wake of these acts of power. . . . He simply never accumulates privilege."[24] After his miracles, after feeding the thousands, after crowds praise him shouting "Hosanna," he pulls away. As Crouch observes, "Those who are preoccupied with status must constantly expend their energy on sorting out the status of those around them. But Jesus, completely unconcerned with his own rank or place in the pecking order, shows a corresponding lack of interest in associating with the 'right sort' of people."[25]

Thus Jesus is concerned with privilege and status only so that he can upend it. In Jesus' day, a servant would wash people's feet, and if no servants were present, the person with the least power and status would get a towel and water and wash everyone else's feet. Yet Jesus, the most powerful person in the room, washes his disciples' feet. In this act, he not only ignores the status hierarchy, but overturns it. Through his example, he calls his followers to do the same. As Crouch observes,

> Jesus simply never had a thought except to restore, redeem and create a new community among whom power would be used always and only for flourishing. In such a community, privilege and status can only be disdained and

---

[24] Andy Crouch, *Playing God: Redeeming the Gift of Power* (Downers Grove, IL: InterVarsity Press, 2013), 165.
[25] Crouch, *Playing God,* 165.

discarded. They are distractions from the real calling of image bearers: to be fruitful and multiply, far as the curse is found.[26]

Therefore, churches must turn away from bounded methods of establishing group identity that encourage and facilitate privilege and status-seeking. It is one thing to reject an approach that would add fuel to the fire, but Jesus did more than that. He lived with indifference to status in a society fully aflame with status achievement. How was he able to do so? I think it was because his identity was secure. He did not need to enter the status contest because he was secure in his relationship of love with his Father. Regardless of what others thought of him or what status points he gained or lost, he knew his Father loved him. He was secure in his belovedness.

Just as a bounded church's methods contribute to enflaming status measurement and its pressures and shame, a centered church's methods help people turn away from privilege and status. They do not, however, cleanse it from our system nor protect us from the shaming power of society's status machine. As Debbie Blue acknowledged in a sermon, "There is something in me that lurches toward building my identity over against another." We create our identity in community based on a competitive framework. We know we are good people because we know who the bad people are. "It is almost like we do not how to feel good except by comparing our goodness, our beauty, our intelligence, our righteousness over against others." Simply drawing a centered-set diagram on a white board is not enough to free us from line drawing. It is not the method itself but experiencing belovedness from the God of the center that provides security and freedom from status-seeking. Blue concludes her sermon, "Jesus wants to free us to love and create community that doesn't involve the condemnation of others What does it look like to be set free and trust in the love of God? [It is] a radical coming alive, opening up, not feeling clinched by judgments, not feeling compelled to hide our vulnerability; [it is] the capacity for being more relaxed, less competitive."[27] The loving embrace of God is a key element of the foundation for a centered church.

---

[26]Crouch, *Playing God*, 166.

[27]Debbie Blue, "Sucking All the Power out of Death: John 11:17-44," House of Mercy, November 22, 2020, www.houseofmercy.org/sucking-all-the-power-out-of-death/. See also Debbie

It is easy to write words about God's love, but as we observed at the beginning of this chapter the concept of God proclaimed by Jesus does not come naturally to us. We must constantly return to Jesus to ensure that Jesus is our center rather than our human ideas about God. This is a key difference from a bounded church. A bounded church preaches the gospel to outsiders, and once people have responded by crossing over a line, they no longer need to keep hearing and responding to the gospel. From a bounded-church perspective, those who are "in" just need ongoing reminders about boundary-line standards. In contrast, returning to the well metaphor, we don't go to a well and draw water to drink only once. We must keep returning to the well and quenching our thirst again and again. In the same way, the gospel is not only "good news" for one moment in our lives. A centered church, therefore, will continually remind us of the gospel of Jesus Christ and will reorient us to the God of the center again and again.

For a centered church to flourish, its center and foundation must be the God who is revealed by Jesus. The following chapter will describe several other foundational elements.

Blue, "A Different Story: Mark 15:21-39," in *Proclaiming the Scandal of the Cross: Contemporary Images of the Atonement*, ed. Mark D. Baker (Grand Rapids, MI: Baker Academic, 2007), 62-72.

5

FOUNDATIONAL ELEMENTS

DOCTRINE

A pastor told me that his denomination has an official group named the "Doctrinal Fencepost Committee." For a bounded church, this is a great name because it conveys a sense of caring for the fenceposts, which likely includes clarifying any confusion about doctrines and making sure everyone stays on the right side of the fence. The doctrinal fencepost committee also deals with those who climb over the fence into doctrinally suspect territory. If this denomination shifted to a centered approach, what should they do with their "Doctrinal Fencepost Committee"? Perhaps disband it? Although much about the committee clashes with a centered approach, they concur on one point: beliefs matter.

In a centered approach, defining the center is of utmost importance. Returning to the sports metaphor, before we can play, we must agree on the center. Are we playing soccer or American football? Which sport's rules are at the center? Similarly, for a church to live out the centered approach, it must define the center. The previous chapter addresses a key question in defining the center: Who is the God of the center? A church's center will include many other things: the Bible, statements of belief, vision and mission commitments, and ethical direction.

If a church tears down its fences and opts to begin digging a well, it should not do away with its committee, but reformulate how it cares for the denomination's central doctrines. In the above scenario, the church might decide to establish two committees: a "Caring for the Well Committee" that does the ongoing work of defining the center and maintaining its clarity, and an "Alignment Committee" that helps people and the congregation stay in alignment with the center. Pulling down fences and moving toward a centered approach does more than merely change how a committee responds to someone out of line with the church's central beliefs. Shifting from fence building to digging a well also changes the *role* of beliefs within a church. When doctrines are treated as a fence, they function as a litmus test. In a bounded church, doctrine can degenerate to mostly a means of defining who is in and who is out. A centered church frees doctrine to be much more than right belief. Doctrine becomes life-giving well water by helping people in the church align with and journey toward the center. In *The Drama of Doctrine*, Kevin Vanhoozer says, "Doctrine . . . gives direction as to how individuals and the church can participate fittingly in the drama of redemption."[1] When understood in this way we recognize that our theological beliefs are not only part of the content of the center but also part of the foundation that enables centered discipleship.

ETHICS AS GIFT

Because rules about behavior play such a major role in many bounded churches, I will devote significant attention to ethics in this book. Later chapters will include many specific examples about how to address behavior in centered ways. Foundationally, how we frame ethics will greatly influence whether we live out our ethics in bounded or centered ways.

The Bible contains numerous commands and a significant amount of ethical instruction. What is the purpose of these commands and ethical instruction? How are they experienced in a bounded church? In my story, I used the biblical Sabbath command as an evaluative tool. Numerous people have told me that they imagine God doing the same—sitting in heaven with a list of rules, checking off whether we comply or not. I doubt I ever would have said that the reason God gave us laws and commands was to have a means of evaluating our standing, and yet the reality is I experienced them in that way. I used ethical norms as means of evaluating my

---

[1]Kevin J. Vanhoozer, *The Drama of Doctrine: A Canonical Linguistic Approach to Christian Doctrine* (Louisville: Westminster John Knox, 2005), 78.

standing and the standing of others. Are you doing well as a Christian, or not? Are you in or out?

I remember considering myself a good Christian when I faithfully had daily devotions. I wasn't only concerned with being in or out, good or mediocre. I was also thinking about how I could earn something. Rather than praying and reading the Bible for the richness it added to my life, at times it devolved into seeking a reward for the act itself. I remember leaving my college dorm room with the feeling that my day would not go well if I had skipped devotions that day. I had the sense of a reward being withheld. Those who view the "big eye in the sky" as more threatening may fear punishment for not complying. In either case, the purpose of biblical commands is seen as providing a means of evaluation. But this perspective does not cohere well with the God described in the previous chapter. How will having the God revealed by Jesus Christ in the center influence how we understand the ethical content in the center? God's earliest response to human sin in the Bible provides a metaphor that can help us answer this question.

In Genesis 3, God responds to Adam and Eve's disobedience by first seeking out Adam and Eve (Gen 3:8-13). Then God tells them of the consequences of their actions (Gen 3:14-19). Next God provides garments of skin for them. Finally, God expels them from the garden to prevent them from further disobedience in relation to the tree of life.

Why does God provide garments of skin for Adam and Eve? God is helping them deal with the consequences of their sin. Garments were not in God's original design. Adam and Eve brought the shame they felt upon themselves, but God does not abandon them. God gives them clothing so that they can cover themselves with something better than fig leaves. In concrete terms, the garments lessen their feelings of shame; the skins that God provides bring the humans closer to the way they had been before they sinned, when they were without shame. God does not reject humans, but responds to their rejection by choosing to continue to be with them and for them.

Biblical commands, imperatives, guidance, counsel, ethics, and wisdom are like the garments: gifts from God to help us deal with the consequences of our sin. Not all ethical instructions in the Bible, however, are a direct response to sin as the garments were. Therefore, it is better for us to focus on the purpose of the garments. Biblical ethics, like the garments, help us live closer to the way that God created us to live. It might be helpful to think analogously of loving parents. Appropriate limits, rules, and guidelines are gifts to children. Psychologists tell us that a lack of limits will hinder children from thriving.[2] God gives us ethical guidance not to test us, but to enable us to thrive. The commands and lists of appropriate and inappropriate behavior in the Bible are a gift from God that is not only given for our individual thriving. Rather, Christian ethics are rooted in God's gracious and loving action to heal the whole world. God offers ethical direction to Christian communities as part of God's mission to transform the world, to bring about a radical change in our direction.

Why did God give the Ten Commandments and the law to Israel? You will answer that very differently depending on how you conceive of ethics and God's relationship to humans through ethics. How might the law be viewed through the lens of the "ethics as gift" paradigm? Through this lens, we can see that the law provided Israel with guidance about how to live together by both limiting destructive behavior and also encouraging positive behavior. The law provided directives that would improve their relationships with God, other Hebrews and foreigners in their land, and the creation. The law was intended to help them in their role as coworkers and cocreators in God's mission so that they could be a blessing to others. The law warned them about the consequences of disobedience, but as Galatians 3:17-18 points out, the law was not given as a precondition for God's loving accompaniment. The law came after God's covenantal commitment to Israel. God gave the law to Israel just as God gave garments to Adam and Eve. God's love is not conditional. We do not need to obey God's law for God to express love to us.

I invite you to take a few minutes to think of some specific commands or laws in the Bible. Look at them first through the lens of ethics as a bounded-group standard. Then look at them through the lens of an ethics-as-gift paradigm. What differences do you notice in your feelings and thoughts?

---

[2]Margaret G. Alter, *Resurrection Psychology: An Understanding of Human Personality Based on the Life and Teachings of Jesus* (Chicago: Loyola University Press, 1994), esp. ch. 2, "The Necessity of Law."

A centered church embraces ethics as a gift not only to avoid the detri-mental impact of a bounded church's approach, but also to experience the positive impact that ethics can have on our life. A fuzzy church tends to lack clear ethical guidelines, which can lead to bland "whateverism" and painful stumbling in our daily life. Ethical exhortations in a centered church flow from love and contribute to the thriving of individuals and the community. Christian ethics is, as theologian Norman Wirzba observes, part of an apprenticeship in love: "Seeing Christianity as a school or laboratory that trains people in the ways of love is the best way to understand the work and mission of the church. . . . Christian faith is really one long apprenticeship in which we work to understand and then root out the many ways we devise for falsifying or simply denying love."[3] The reality is that we have many behaviors and values that impede love and therefore impede our ability to thrive. An ethic that enables love to thrive is a gift.

I begin the seminary ethics course I teach with the following question: Are biblical commands primarily an evaluative tool or a gift to help us thrive? Year after year the written responses to this class session both sober me and excite me. They sober me because so many students, whether from a bounded church or a fuzzy church, acknowledge they have seen the bib-lical commands as an evaluative tool. Their responses also excite me because I get to witness the impact that describing biblical ethics as God's gift has on them. It is as if the lecture flips a switch, and they begin to connect state-ments about God's love with God's commands. Their papers exude a sense of liberation, hope, and excitement for new possibilities. I encourage you to start a conversation like this with a few others sometime today or this week. Present someone with the ethics as a gift paradigm. I expect the fruits of these conversations will compel you to continue sharing it with others.

In a centered church, seeing God's ethical direction as a loving gift enables us to join the psalmist, David, as we sincerely recognize the life-giving value of God's commands.

The law of the LORD is perfect,
    refreshing the soul.

---

[3]Norman Wirzba, *Way of Love: Recovering the Heart of Christianity* (New York: HarperOne, 2016), 7-8.

The statutes of the LORD are trustworthy,
    making wise the simple.
The precepts of the LORD are right,
    giving joy to the heart.
The commands of the LORD are radiant,
    giving light to the eyes.
The fear of the LORD is pure,
    enduring forever.
The decrees of the LORD are firm,
    and all of them are righteous.

They are more precious than gold,
    than much pure gold;
they are sweeter than honey,
    than honey from the honeycomb.
By them your servant is warned;
    in keeping them there is great reward. (Ps 19:7-11)

NAMING

Naming is a central activity in Madeline L'Engle's novel *A Wind in the Door*, the sequel to *A Wrinkle in Time*. As the characters in the book explain it, naming helps someone become more the person that she or he was meant to be. As the story unfolds, readers observe that naming requires discernment, is rooted in love, and is a process that utilizes both words and actions. Naming both calls and aids people to live more fully as the people whom God created them to be, more in the image of Jesus Christ. One key element in the book is that someone cannot name himself or herself. Naming affirms individuality but stands against autonomous individualism.

Perhaps the most obvious type of naming is when someone says something affirmative about us that gets to the core of who we are and calls us to live that out. Coupled with this is the act of helping people peel off debilitating false labels that others have stuck on them. Naming also includes helping people identify and change behaviors that hinder them from thriving and living out their calling. Furthermore, naming helps people develop positive behaviors and character traits.

A foundational quality of a centered church is that it seeks to name people. Fuzzy tolerance will lead to incomplete naming. A centered church includes a focus on behavior because it is part of naming. Yet emphasizing ethics does not automatically name someone. The line-drawing shaming of a bounded church not only hinders naming, but actually un-names people.

Having naming as part of our foundation reinforces the directional character of a centered church. To name others is to help them move toward the center and live more as the person God has created them to be. Thinking of ourselves, individually and corporately, as namers will lead us to disciple, counsel, and provide pastoral care in more centered ways. To be a namer pulls us beyond simply being "nice." It also pulls us beyond simply keeping people on the right side of the line. Let us continually remind ourselves that we are namers. Keeping that in mind will help us stay on the centered way.

FREEDOM FROM THE POWERS

In the fall of 1983, a lecture at the one-semester Oregon Extension study program grabbed my attention, disturbing me deeply yet leaving me wanting more. After four years of ministry and teaching high school in Honduras, I had become a student again. On that memorable day, Doug Frank wove together insights from sociologists Peter Berger and Jacques Ellul in a lecture contrasting religion and Christian revelation.[4] He described religion as something humans construct as a security system that gives us the means to draw lines defining who is in and who is out. (Many years later, I would describe this as a bounded group.) Religion also provides us security by giving us the means to please and appease God or the gods. Frank said that the fundamental assumption of religion is that humans must take the initiative and attempt to move God to act through our actions.

None of this would have rattled me if Doug Frank had contrasted other religions with Christianity, but he gave many examples of Christian religiosity—including ones that mirrored my life, such as my thinking around daily devotions and the line-drawing tendencies I describe in the first chapter. If I had heard Frank's lecture a few years earlier, I imagine I would have reacted defensively or perhaps just dismissed it all. But after

---

[4]Doug Frank, lecture, The Oregon Extension, October 31, 1983.

four years of ministry in Honduras I was worn down from working to stay on the right side of the lines I and others had drawn and burdened by all the to-dos I had piled on myself. Doug Frank's words unsettled me but rang true.

Frank was not, however, anti-Christian. He did not dismiss the gospel of Jesus Christ. Rather, following Ellul, he said that Christians had a propensity to turn Christian revelation into a religion. Ellul says that religion is like an arrow that moves upward, perceiving human action as the fundamental determinant for how God acts toward humans. In contrast, the fundamental heart of Christian revelation is God's gracious action toward humans. The gospel is like an arrow that moves downward, following the impulse of God's loving initiative (see figure 5.1).[5]

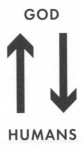

Figure 5.1. Human initiative/religion versus divine initiative

Frank's lecture, like Christian revelation itself, not only exposed and confronted religion, but also pointed to the possibility of liberation from religion. In one sense he called into question everything that I had dedicated my life to, and at the same time he excited me with unimagined possibilities for my life. I left the lecture shaken but convinced, and asking, "How about the church? How can we have a non-religious church?" This question consumed me. I had never been so engaged by a topic for an academic paper. I read Ellul and Berger and had numerous conversations with Doug Frank. One paper was not enough, of course, and I continue to explore this question.

Two points from that original paper serve as foundational elements for practicing a centered approach to church. First, Ellul maintains that all humans have a propensity toward religiosity. Second, Ellul includes religion within the principalities and powers. As a power, it seizes and transforms our human religious drive and our human religious systems into a force that is greater than the sum of those two things. Ellul argues that religion is a force that we cannot on our own resist or control.[6]

---

[5]Jacques Ellul, *Living Faith: Belief and Doubt in a Perilous World* (San Francisco: Harper & Row, 1983), 129.

[6]See Jacques Ellul, *Ethics of Freedom* (Grand Rapids, MI: Eerdmans, 1976), 152.

Therefore, living out a centered approach is not just a matter of using the right techniques. It is not a simple matter of saying "we are going to practice the centered methods in this book." First, because bounded ways are the default. They come naturally to humans. Furthermore, we are not simply wrestling with one set of methods versus another, but with spiritual forces. We will look again at Jesus and Paul to illuminate these two points.

Jesus and the Pharisees: purity battles. We risk missing valuable lessons for life if we simply view the Pharisees as the bad guys and think, *Of course those legalistic, salvation-by-works men were against Jesus.*[7] Let's take a charitable, or at least a more objective, look at why the Pharisees are so upset with Jesus. Why do they complain about him eating with tax collectors and sinners (Mt 9:11; Lk 15:2)? Why is Simon the Pharisee scandalized when Jesus lets a sinful woman touch him (Lk 7:39)?

First, the Pharisees did what comes naturally to humans. They divided everyone into us–them categories in bounded ways. We do not have to teach people how to be bounded! (As noted, fuzzy groups tend to drift back to boundedness even if their boundedness comes from their sense of superiority over those whom they view as judgmental and intolerant.) The psychologist Richard Beck tells us that in addition to this us–them tendency, humans have a hardwired revulsion to anything disgusting. One important point of clarification is that the revulsion itself—that is, the desire to separate from or eliminate the object of disgust—is hardwired, but what is categorized as disgusting is learned.[8] Think of something you find disgusting, such as a cockroach floating in a drink or coming across an animal that died days ago. Now, think of a human action you find disgusting—something that repulses you. In the time of Jesus, the people labeled as tax collectors and sinners were considered unclean—that is, disgusting. So when the Pharisees reacted against Jesus' table fellowship with sinners, they were not only disturbed at a rational level about

---

[7]To be clear, I am saying this as a caricature. See Mark D. Baker, *Religious No More: Building Communities of Grace & Freedom* (Downers Grove, IL: InterVarsity Press, 1999), 84-87, for a clarifying discussion of this caricature. Although the Pharisees most likely did not teach salvation by works explicitly, they did, in practice, live out works righteousness.

[8]Richard Beck, *Unclean: Meditations on Purity, Hospitality, and Mortality* (Eugene, OR: Cascade Books, 2011), 18.

doctrinal differences, but were repulsed, offended, and concerned about contamination spreading.

Many things that disgust us are actually contaminants, and we should stay away for good reasons. In relation to purity, however, Beck points out three key mistakes that the Pharisees made and Jesus challenged. First, they considered things to be contagious that were not. Second, they identified people themselves—not just their actions—as contagious and disgusting. Third, they operated with a negativity dominance that "places all the power on the side of the pollutant. . . . [From this perspective] Jesus doesn't purify the sinners. The sinners make Jesus unclean."[9] Jesus challenges these mistakes. He separates people from their actions and reverses negativity dominance. Contact with Jesus purifies. Jesus counters another mistake related to security when he invites the Pharisees—and others—to put their security not in lines that create an us–them dynamic, but in relationship with God—a center.

Though humans today do not use the same categories as the Pharisees to draw lines, avoid contamination, and garner security, we must recognize that the same human tendencies live within us. To practice the against-the-current, centered ways of Jesus, we do not need just a manual, we also need the transformative Spirit of Jesus to work in our lives. United with Christ, we can recognize what the Pharisees could not: those whom we might naturally view with contempt or as a threat to our church's purity can be cleansed by Jesus. We can risk inclusion because the purifying power of Jesus Christ is greater than the stains of sin.

As a final observation, we must recognize that Jesus' confrontation of bounded ways led to the cross. Resistance was strong. We, too, must expect resistance from the spiritual force that killed Jesus. Once again, we turn to Paul to understand this force more fully.

Paul: the same enslaving power at work in paganism, Judaism, and Christianity. Buried in the middle of Paul's letter to the Galatians, there are two sentences that are remarkable when brought together. In chapter one of this book, I described how the line-drawing judgmentalism of a bounded

---

[9]Beck, *Unclean*, 30. Beck uses the graphic example that if feces touch a cheeseburger, the cheeseburger gets ruined, not vice versa. He argues that the Pharisees operate from that negativity dominance when they interpret Jesus' actions.

approach tore apart the celebration of the Lord's Supper in Antioch. Paul writes to the Galatian churches out of his concern that they are heading down the same path.

In Galatians 4, first, referring to himself and other Jewish followers of Jesus, Paul writes:

> So also, when we were underage, we were in slavery under the elemental spiritual forces [*stoicheia*] of the world. But when the set time had fully come, God sent his Son, born of a woman, born under the law, to redeem those under the law, that we might receive adoption to sonship. (Gal 4:3-5)

Note that he describes his previous experience in Judaism as enslaving. A few verses later he writes about paganism in exactly the same way. Addressing the Gentile Christians he writes:

> Formerly, when you did not know God, you were slaves to those who by nature are not gods. But now that you know God—or rather are known by God—how is it that you are turning back to those weak and miserable forces [*stoicheia*]? Do you wish to be enslaved by them all over again? (Gal 4:8-9)

I imagine the recipients of the letter immediately wanting to protest and clarify, "No, Paul. You do not understand. We are not turning back to paganism. We are taking on practices of the people of God." But Paul is not confused. He knows that they used to practice pagan religiosity (Gal 4:8), and now as Christians they have begun to follow certain Jewish religious practices (Gal 4:10, 21; 5:2). Paul calls this turn toward following Jewish traditions a return to a previous state (Gal 4:9). How can this be? Judaism and paganism are not the same thing. Paul knows this. He does not actually say that they are returning to the same practices, but that they are returning to the same state of enslavement. Table 5.1 displays that although the religious traditions and practices were different, the enslaving forces, *stoicheia*, were the same.

The *stoicheia* (elemental spiritual forces) enslaved Paul as a Jew. The *stoicheia* enslaved Galatian Gentiles as pagans. Now, as followers of Jesus, the Galatians are at risk of being enslaved again by the *stoicheia*. Paul is not saying that paganism, Judaism, or a line-drawing version of Christianity are the same thing. Rather, he is saying that they can all be used by *stoicheia* as tools of enslavement.

Paul	formerly practiced Judaism	enslaved by *stoicheia* (spiritual forces)
Galatian Gentile Christians	formerly practiced paganism	enslaved by *stoicheia* (spiritual forces)
Galatian Gentile Christians	as Christians adding Jewish boundary-line practices	threat of enslavement again by *stoicheia* (spiritual forces)

Table 5.1. Enslavement by spiritual forces in Galatians 4

What exactly are *stoicheia*? I will not delve into all the details of the translation here,[10] but I view *stoicheia* as a word to be included in Paul's list of principalities and powers. Therefore, I affirm the NIV's translation ("elemental spiritual forces"), which captures the sense that *stoicheia* are spiritual (meaning they are more than human principles or powers), and they are forces (meaning they are more than just individual demons).

Colossians can help us further understand how Paul uses the term. In Colossians 2:8 he warns against captivity to the *stoicheia*. In Colossians 2:15 he proclaims that Jesus Christ has triumphed over the principalities and powers through the cross. He follows this by stating:

> Therefore do not let anyone judge you by what you eat or drink, or with regard to a religious festival, a New Moon celebration or a Sabbath day. . . .
>
> Since you died with Christ to the elemental spiritual forces of this world [*stoicheia*], why, as though you still belonged to the world, do you submit to its rules: "Do not handle! Do not taste! Do not touch!"? These rules, which have to do with things that are all destined to perish with use, are based on merely human commands and teachings. Such regulations indeed have an appearance of wisdom, with their self-imposed worship, their false humility and their harsh treatment of the body, but they lack any value in restraining sensual indulgence. (Col 2:16, 20-23)

From Galatians and Colossians, we can observe that *stoicheia* enslave. While Paul connects them to religious rules and practices, he does not connect them to one specific religion. Paul does not divide good religions from bad religions. He does not equate elemental spiritual forces solely with paganism. In the terms of this book, we might say that the *stoicheia* take up

---

[10]For a more detailed discussion, see; Marcos Baker, *Gálatas*, Comentario Biblico Iberoamericano (Buenos Aires: Ediciones Kairos, 2014), 166-83; and Baker, *Religious No More*, 87-90.

the rules and rituals of paganism and turn them into bounded-group religion. The *stoicheia* also take up the Law, given by God, and turn it into bounded-group religion. And in Antioch, we can observe how the *stoicheia* also take up the rules and practices of the followers of Jesus and turn them into bounded-group religion. As we observed in previous chapters, the problem is not first and foremost the rules, but the elemental spiritual forces that turn rules into ways of seeking status with God and humans and judging and excluding others.

An ongoing struggle. Paul pronounces strong words of warning both to the Galatians and the Colossians, but he combines his warning with a proclamation of the gospel: the possibility of being freed from these elemental spiritual forces (Gal 1:4; 4:4-7; 5:1; 6:14-15; Col 2:15). The good news is that through union with Jesus Christ we can live in freedom from the bounded-group religiosity of the *stoicheia*. Note, however, that this is not a "one-and-done" step of freedom. The Colossians, Peter in Antioch, the Jewish-Christian agitators in Galatia, and the Gentile Christians in Galatia had experienced the saving work of Jesus through God's grace. Yet Paul confronts them all with words of warning about the enslaving power of religion in the hands of elemental spiritual forces. Therefore, rather than resting confidently in a "correct" understanding of salvation by grace, for instance, and assuming that Paul's words in Galatians do not apply to us, we would all do well to regularly imagine Paul saying to us, "How is it that you are turning back to those weak and miserable forces [*stoicheia*]? Do you wish to be enslaved by them all over again?" (Gal 4:9).

Though these warnings from Paul are vitally important, let us also remember Paul's positive promises. Through Christ there is new creation, liberation from the normal ways of the present evil age (Gal 1:4; 6:15). At the heart of the church is not a diagram or a list of new methods about how to be centered, but incarnation, God in the flesh, cross, resurrection, and the indwelling of the Holy Spirit. This center enables us to become something radical, new, not natural so that we can live out a centered approach to discipleship and the church.

Recall that Doug Frank's lecture both unsettled and excited me. The liberation through Christ that Paul proclaimed was the exciting part. Although Frank's lecture and my reading of Ellul called into question many of my actions and attitudes, I also sensed the possibility of being liberated from the tyranny of line-drawing Christianity. During those weeks in the fall of 1983, I experienced the grace of Jesus Christ in new and profound ways and began to experience freedom from religion the power. Colossians 2:15 was becoming true in my life as religion the power was exposed and disarmed by the life, death, and resurrection of Jesus Christ. I saw the lines of bounded-group religiosity for what they were—not divine but human constructs. They began to lose their power over me.

What do we take from this look at bounded-group religiosity through the lens of Jesus and Paul? What does this mean for us as we seek to practice a centered approach to church? First, there will be resistance. Second, we must not only present information about a centered approach, but also proclaim freedom through Christ from the enslaving distortions of the spiritual power of bounded-group religiosity. Third, we must recognize that we are in an ongoing struggle with religion as an enslaving spiritual power. Therefore, ongoing discernment and proclamation are necessary. Finally, we must go deeper than I have in this brief section. I recommend the following books that contrast the enslaving religion of the *stoicheia* with the way of freedom in Christ: Jacques Ellul, *Subversion of Christianity* and *Living Faith*; Bruxy Cavey, *The End of Religion: Encountering the Subversive Spirituality of Jesus*; and Mark Baker, *Freedom from Religiosity: Studies in Paul's Letter to the Galatians*.

LOVE

Jesus and Paul both sum up all of God's law as love (Mk 12:28-31; Jn 13:34-35; Rom 13:10; Gal 5:14). Rather than reducing love to a mere section within these two chapters on the foundational elements of a centered church, the reality is that love permeates the whole foundation. Ethics are a gift that have been given to us by God in love. True naming is an act of love, and without love, it will be an act of un-naming. The God of the center, whom we explored in chapter four, is a God of love. Our doctrines describe that loving God. In chapter six, we will discuss some methods of exhortation that can be used in a centered church, but without love, the approach will not be centered. In chapter seven, we will discuss some of the character traits of a centered church, but love is not only one quality in a list, but the fundamental characteristic.

A bounded church can function without love and impedes loving fully. The line of separation is not a line of love. A fuzzy church can also exist without love, and it falls short of full caring and thus true love. For a centered church to flourish and to be experienced by its members as centered, there must be love. Love must permeate everything that a centered church does.

The God of the center, doctrine, ethics as gift, naming, freedom from the power of religiosity, and love provide a foundation. Let us now explore how we can build a centered approach on this foundation.

PART THREE

DISCIPLESHIP IN COMMUNITY

WHAT HAVE BEEN KEY MOMENTS of change or significant seasons of transformation in your life? What provoked reorientation or moved you closer to the center—Jesus and Christlikeness? I invite you to take a few moments and respond to these questions.

Instruments of transformation. As I look at the responses to those questions that I jotted down in a few minutes, I observe four categories of instruments that God has used to bring about change and growth in my life. This is not a complete list; if I gave more time to this exercise, additional categories would likely emerge. Even so, the following four categories are instructive.

Words of challenge and calling. As I recounted in chapter one, my early twenties were years of radical change, a continual redefinition of what it meant to be a "good Christian," and an attitude of self-righteous superiority. In my midtwenties, Doug Frank, a professor at a study program I participated in, listened to one of my rants about the mistaken ways of other Christians. He agreed with my critiques, but at one point he said, "Mark, you are sounding pretty pharisaical." It was a moment of reorientation. His words stopped me in my tracks and marked my first step toward the centered way that I describe in this book.

Four years out of college, I sat in the living room of Howard Newsom, who had been a beloved college professor and mentor. He urged me to go to seminary or graduate school, and I responded, "No, not interested." Then I listed all my critiques of higher education. He listened, looked me straight in the eyes and said, "I think you are afraid to go. Why are you afraid?" That conversation began a reorientation toward further study, and it began a long journey of Jesus' liberating me from the shame and fear that were buried in my being.

Doug and Howard both spoke strong, direct words of challenge that penetrated to the core of my being, exposing things so hidden that I was unaware of them. While their words stung a bit, I did not feel attacked or put down, but cared for and loved. Why didn't I experience their confrontation in a bounded way? We will explore that question in this part of the book.

Books. I also thought of several books that God has used as instruments of reorientation in my life. I recalled reading several books that left me feeling unsettled as one paradigm crumbled while also being energized by a sense of possibility emerging from a new way of thinking and living. I happened upon some of these transforming books myself, but most often other followers of Jesus urged me to read them. For instance, part of the reason Doug Frank's confrontational words led to such life-giving transformation was that he and other professors in the study program had assigned *Brother to a Dragonfly* by Will Campbell. They had also urged me to read Karl Barth. Those authors communicated that we are sinners, but God graciously loves us. I had heard and read the word *grace* many times before, yet through their writing, I experienced God's grace in a new and profound way.

Life experiences. My life experiences have also shaken my assumptions and challenged my paradigms and contributed to reorientation. For instance, as described in chapter one, during college I forged friendships with others who clearly had a more intimate and profound relationship with God than I did, and yet they were on the "wrong" side of lines I used to define "good Christians." Or, a few years later, when I stepped off the plane in Tegucigalpa, Honduras, extreme poverty confronted me every day—not just the beggars on the streets or the shacks visible on the hills around the city, but neighbors with whom I interacted daily. My immersion into this reality provoked me to ask questions I had never considered before. I began to read the Bible with new eyes, and the changes God worked in my life through that experience continue to influence how I live today.

Mentorship and learning by doing. The final category that came to mind was serving as a camp counselor at Northern Frontier Camp in the Adirondack Mountains of New York from when I was sixteen through my college years. My father, who was the director, viewed discipleship and leadership development as a central purpose of the camp. I began as a junior counselor, observing and being mentored by someone with more experience. Yet right from the beginning, I had opportunities to learn by doing. Within a few years, I began to mentor others and took on more leadership and teaching responsibilities—and I also continued to be mentored by others. This experience changed me and reoriented me in so many ways, providing skills, character formation, confidence, and biblical knowledge.

On the surface, this final category, which transpired over many years in a nondramatic fashion, appears quite different from the previous three. Yet the difference is less than it appears. Howard's question to me was birthed out of a mentoring relationship, and Doug's question began one. I presented the encounter with extreme poverty itself as provoking transformation, and there is truth to that, but the reality is that others walked with me in that experience. Some, like Blake Ortman, mentored me through his questions, comments, and modeling. Others, like Santos Carcamo and Jacobo Sanchez, wrestled together with me about how we were called to respond as Jesus followers. Others thrust books into my hands. The categories all blend together. Discipling others includes modeling, providing experiences, confronting, asking questions, providing resources and more. In this book I will often use the word *intervention* as an umbrella term to capture the sense of taking initiative to intervene in a variety of ways that orient others toward the center.

SIGNIFICANCE OF THESE CATEGORIES

I did not do the above exercise in order to write the introduction to this part of the book. Rather, another book led me to ask these questions. After I took the time to respond, I saw several connections to this book. The activity underscored for me why this third part of the book on discipleship in community is the largest.

Discipleship that orients and reorients, challenges and calls people, is imperative in a centered church. If we are not aiding each other in moving toward the center, we are not a centered church. Could the interventions I describe above happen in a bounded church? Yes, but they would come draped with a sense of obligation and lend themselves to self-righteousness. Could these interventions happen in a fuzzy church? Yes, although some of them would be framed in a much less direct way. They would be fuzzier in order to avoid the negativity of the bounded approach. So although the process of discipleship can take place in bounded and fuzzy churches, it is qualitatively different in a centered church.

Although the discipleship interventions I describe in chapters six through ten are imperative in a centered church, the number of chapters here is not meant to imply that discipleship is more important than other aspects of ministry, such as worship, teaching, or service. I am giving these interventions more space in this book because these are areas where we can most easily slip into bounded or fuzzy ways.

The chapters that follow include significant attention to loving confrontation like I received from Doug Frank and Howard Newsom. However, the centered approach is not just, to give one example, about Paul confronting Peter and telling him he is off-track. Rather, in Paul's letters, we observe positive exhortation and words of calling, and we also can easily imagine the mentoring he did of those who ministered with him. To emphasize this broader sense of intervention and journeying together, I am using "discipleship" as the overall title for the section—discipleship done in and by community. Discipleship is a formational process of becoming more Christlike. Someone who disciples others walks with them toward Jesus, intentionally sharing life with them, modeling, naming them, guiding them, exhorting them, and learning from the Bible and the Spirit together. The discipler points disciples to resources for learning, mentors them in practices, values, and character, and gives them opportunities to learn by doing—training them so they can train others.

MOVING TOWARD APPLICATION

The chapters that follow do not describe one "right" centered way of responding to a situation. Rather, they describe one *possible* way to respond in a centered manner, but it is not the *only* possibility. Because there can be a variety of centered responses to similar situations, the invitation is not to try to repeat the exact words and actions as they are described here, but rather to observe the qualities and characteristics that make certain responses more centered than others. In chapter six, we begin this section on centered discipleship by addressing the issue of language that we use in centered exhortation.

6

CENTERED EXHORTATION

UNDERMINING LINE-DRAWING RELIGIOSITY

Clearly, a centered church must include exhortations—calls for people to align their lives with the center. Just as clearly, a centered church must avoid using exhortations with a bounded character, such as, "You should do X to demonstrate to God and others that you are a good Christian." Yet merely stripping away the language of line-drawing religiosity from our exhortations is not enough. People who have been shaped by bounded religiosity will tend to drape any command with a cloak of conditionality. Even without threatening words, they will fear that they will be shamed if they do not comply.

For instance, recall my experience deciding where to live when I moved to Syracuse. The obvious thing to do was to rent an apartment near Syracuse University, my place of ministry. Yet I had heard many times, and given, the exhortation: "Live with the poor." We might call this a naked imperative, one that is stripped of any explicit conditional, bounded language. I, however, wrapped that naked command in robes of bounded religiosity and a God of conditional love. I imagined the badge of honor I would wear if I was found to be on the right side of the line drawn by myself and others. I also imagined the shame I would feel if I fell short of that line. In the end, I opted to live a few blocks from the university, but not without some shame. Even though just months earlier I had heard Doug Frank's lecture, read Jacques Ellul, confessed my religious ways, and experienced

God's grace in new and profound ways, there was still a lot of bounded-church religion in my being. Those were the clothes I most naturally draped onto naked imperatives I heard.

Those naked imperatives became toxic when I cloaked them with a religious concept of God and a bounded-group approach to Christianity. Through Ellul, I had discovered that I had toxins in my system, but I later realized that it is one thing to discover the toxins and another thing to flush them out completely. I decided to pour into my being sermons that countered a religious concept of God and repeatedly emphasized God's loving initiative. I read and reread books of sermons by Karl Barth and listened to sermons by Earl Palmer and Robert Hill.[1] (Today, I would add to the list sermons by Debbie Blue and Grace Spencer.[2]) I kept at it, absorbing these messages of God's unconditional love for a few years until I sensed that the level of toxins had diminished significantly. Over time, my default way of hearing naked exhortations began to change because my concept of God had changed.

Pouring in the good news of the God revealed by Jesus Christ will aid in diluting our internal religious tendencies. Think of it as a general shower. Yet there will remain parts within us that are especially entrenched in a view of God as judgmental or God's love as conditional. When I felt fear rising in my being from the threat of being found on the wrong side of a line, I would invite those shamed parts to rest in Jesus' embrace. Rather than a general shower of religious undermining statements, bringing these parts into Jesus' presence was more like spot cleaning. The love of Jesus is a powerful cleanser! This is ongoing work, of course. I continually need to hear the good news of God's loving initiative in both general and particular ways.

If the first step to exhort in a centered way is to strip away bounded language from our imperatives, the second step is to surround those exhortations with statements about God's unconditional love. As Robert Hill

---

[1] Karl Barth, *Deliverance to the Captives* (reprint, Eugene, OR: Wipf and Stock, 2010); *Call for God: New Sermons from Basel Prison*, rev. ed. (Norwich, UK: Hymns Ancient & Modern, 2012); Earl Palmer Ministries, www.earlpalmer.org/teaching-and-preaching; Marsh Chapel Sermon Archive, https://blogs.bu.edu/sermons/.

[2] Debbie Blue's sermons are available at the website of House of Mercy Music Hall & Church, www.houseofmercy.org/category/sermons/ and in a published collection, Debbie Blue, *Sensual Orthodoxy* (Saint Paul, MN: Cathedral Hill Press, 2003); Grace Spencer's sermons are available at www.graceospencer.com/sermons.

observes, "Paul was ever answering the question of what we should do by saying something first about what God has done."[3] In more technical terms, Paul's imperatives flow from his indicatives. To speak or write in the indicative mode is to indicate or point, to give information and state realities. Therefore, let us respond to people's natural tendency to think we must do things to earn the acceptance of God and others by showering them with indicative statements about the primacy of God's loving action.

In this, quantity matters. In Paul's letter to the Romans, he has eleven indicative chapters before turning to three-and-a-half chapters of ethical exhortations, and he ends the letter with indicative content. In the letter to the Galatians, Paul has four and a half indicative chapters before turning to the imperative mode in chapters five and six, and he concludes with indicatives that undermine bounded-church attitudes. Quantity matters because our natural tendency is to assume that acceptance is conditional, and one short statement about God's grace is not enough to overcome it. Paul spoke first about what God has done, and he spoke *more* about what God has done.[4]

Unfortunately, unlike Paul, many preachers commonly speak much more about what *we* ought to be doing.[5] Many of us have this model so engrained in our mind and being that it is difficult to do otherwise. We replicate what we have heard, and so we naturally focus on human action and "shoulds." I saw this in myself, and so I read and listened to preachers who would help change the tapes that were already playing in my mind, as mentioned above.

A particularly effective indicative that undermines religiosity is to proclaim God's graciousness. In any exhortation I seek to state explicitly that

---

[3]Robert A. Hill, "What a Friend We Have in Paul" (sermon delivered at Asbury First United Methodist Church, Rochester, NY, October 12, 1997).

[4]The vast majority of the Bible is indicative, providing information about God and humans. A common use of general indicatives in exhortation is to use God as an example. It is fine to do this—for instance, to point to Jesus as a model of loving enemies—but this type of indicative does not counter our natural bounded-group religiosity. People easily hear such an indicative exhortation as an "ought" with which they must comply in order to meet the standard. Therefore, our exhortations must always include indicatives about God's unconditional love along with any statements that use God as an example of the action the exhortation is focused on.

[5]The emphasis on the human is not limited to bounded-church sermons so often filled with oughts. This focus can flow from an over-emphasis on seeking to be relevant and contemporary or from the fuzzy approach of not wanting to offend with too much God-talk. Jill Trites, a pastor in Hamilton, Ontario, told me, "I seek to be intentional in my focus on Jesus. If I am preparing a sermon on vulnerability I want to have more Jesus than Brené Brown."

God's unconditional love means that God will forgive us even when we trip and fail in trying to do whatever I am exhorting people to do. This statement lessens the possibility of people interpreting what I am saying in a religious way. The first time I intentionally did this was at an InterVarsity Christian Fellowship conference in upstate New York. The organizers asked me to give a talk on the importance of daily devotions. I spoke about the value of daily prayer and Bible reading and gave ideas about different devotional practices. Then I ended by saying, "If you miss a day or even stop for a week, God will love you just as much. Start again the next day. God will welcome your prayers and speak to you again through the Bible." Saying that felt counter-intuitive, because I had spent twenty minutes emphasizing the value of devotions and the importance of discipline and developing this habit. In making this statement about God's grace, I felt I had lessened the pressure. The bounded-church Mark Baker would not have said those words of grace, but they are true. So I continue to proclaim the truth of God's graciousness in the midst of any words of exhortation.

Seasoning our speech with indicatives that undermine bounded-church religiosity by proclaiming God's unconditional love will help people experience commands in a more centered way, but the wording of the imperatives themselves is also important. In the sections that follow I will introduce means of transforming our exhortations so that they can have a more centered character.

INDICATIVES CHANGE THE CHARACTER OF IMPERATIVES

Imperatives linked to indicatives. There is no mistaking Paul for being fuzzy. He piles one imperative on top of another. In fact, he writes three-and-a-half chapters of commands near the end of his longest letter (Rom 12:1–15:13). He begins Romans 12 with a call to commit to and orient our lives around the God of the center: "Offer your bodies as a living sacrifice. . . . Do not conform to the pattern of this world, but be transformed by the renewing of your mind" (vv. 1-2). Note, however, that Romans 12:1 begins with "Therefore." Paul links this command to what has come before, making this verse a response to all that he has already said in his letter. While "therefore" sometimes only refers to the previous sentence, this verse is a hinge point in the letter. Paul has written about sin, humans turning from God, and God's initiative in providing a restoration of relationship and salvation. After eleven chapters of indicative material that is focused primarily on God's merciful action, Paul pivots to talk about our human response to God's loving action. He writes, "Therefore . . . in view of God's mercy . . . offer your bodies as a living sacrifice" (v. 1). The chapters of exhortation that follow this transitional verse are linked to the preceding indicative material.

Paul links indicatives and imperatives not just in relation to broad swaths of a letter as seen above, but also at the level of individual commands. For instance, indicative: "Since, then, you have been raised with Christ," imperative: "set your hearts on things above." Indicative: "For you died, and your life is now hidden with Christ in God." Imperative: "Put to death, therefore, whatever belongs to your earthly nature: sexual immorality, impurity, lust, evil desires and greed, which is idolatry" (Col 3:1, 3, 5). According to bounded-group religious thinking, if you do X, then God (or the church) will respond by giving you Y. But Paul turns religious thinking on its head and undermines bounded-group judgmentalism by linking his exhortation to an indicative about what God has already done.

Let us follow Paul by linking our imperatives to indicatives about God's action. The link can join large amounts of material, as in Romans 12:1, but it can also join an indicative statement with a command in a single phrase or sentence, such as:

- ▶ "Forgive as you have been forgiven";
- ▶ "Having been loved by God, love others"; or
- ▶ "Having been reconciled with God, let the ripples of that reconciliation extend to others."

Linking an exhortation to an indicative makes it clear that what we are called to do flows from what God has done. Imperatives are frequently linked to indicative statements about who we are because of God's action, thereby calling us to live out of who we are. We see this at work in the following line from an Earl Palmer sermon: "You are loved, love one another. Live out the grace that has happened to us." Linking imperatives to indicatives pours sand into the gears of a bounded church. Because Palmer's exhortation is surrounded by indicative statements about God's grace and loving inclusion, it is hard to hear it as something we must do to get on the right side of a line.

There are a variety of ways of stating indicatives and linking them to imperatives. Take for instance this example by Natalie Reinhart: "Can you imagine the possibilities that could emerge in your family, friendships, workplace, schools, if we responded to our enemies through our own experience of God's mercy and grace?"[6]

Empowering indicative. When we link imperatives with indicatives, we make it clear that God's action precedes our own. However, imperatives can still leave people feeling burdened by the difficulty of the challenge and slide them into a bounded mentality. We can counter the burdensome feeling with indicatives about how God empowers us. Such indicatives not only point to how God enables us to carry out a command, but they often add a sense of invitation, promise, and possibility. One of my favorite songs from Iglesia Amor Fe y Vida in Honduras includes the line, *"Porque tu Dios es amor tu puedes amar"* (Because your God is love you can love). God and Jesus not only show us what love is, but God's love also enables us to love (1 John 4:7-12).

Although listening to Earl Palmer or Debbie Blue can help change the soundtrack we are used to listening to in our minds, we do not have to be a master preacher like them to practice centered exhortations. In the ethics course I teach at Fresno Pacific Biblical Seminary, my students must write an exhortation with a clear call to action in a centered way. It is not an easy assignment. Their first drafts often are either too fuzzy or too bounded, but many have done excellent work. I share some of their lines with you not just to illustrate my points but also to stimulate your imagination. How might you use similar language as you are leading a small group, preaching a sermon, sending a text message, posting a blog, or engaging in conversation over coffee?

Consider the following examples of empowering indicatives:

God has reconciled with humanity; because of Christ, reconciliation with each other is possible. Our restored relationship with God and the power of

---

[6]Unless otherwise noted, examples in this section that are not my own are from the assignment in my Discipleship and Ethics course, which is described in the following section.

the Spirit allows us to do the impossible in the face of our enemies. God is making all things new! (Grace Spencer)

The transforming Spirit of God, living and active in our midst, empowers us to embrace, bless, show hospitality to, offer kindness to, those persons afflicted with the same malice that crucified our Lord . . . that would have us crucified. (Brad Isaak)

The following two examples combine an imperative linked with an indicative with an empowering indicative:

Take hold of His hand as He offers you a freedom that you have never before known. You have no need to live in the shame of deception but are free to speak openly and honestly. Therefore, I urge you to speak with the authority of the truth, because you can! Choosing to speak the truth will become less a decision and more an outpouring of Christ working from within you; so, let your honesty come from your feelings laid bare and know that in the love of Christ, you will blossom forth into the person that you have been made to be! (Bryan Taylor)

You are loved and forgiven. Be who the Spirit has empowered you to be. Be who you are. Love. (Heather Ediger)

As we consider how we can deliver centered exhortations, let us follow Paul's example by intentionally using empowering indicatives that undermine religiosity, linking indicatives with our imperatives, and using more indicatives than imperatives.[7]

AVOID "SHOULD" . . .

I try to avoid using the words *ought* or *should* when discussing Christian actions. People often experience these words as shaming darts thrown from a stance of superiority. Of course, that is not the case with every *should* or *ought*. Yet because the words flow so easily out of my mouth, a moratorium works better for me than trying to filter out any shaming darts from more appropriate uses. I have found that avoiding these words heightens my awareness of how I talk about action and behavior. *Should* and *ought* are lazy exhortations because they do not require any explanation. For example:

---

[7]For exemplary exhortations that use the various types of indicatives in this section, see the "Ethical Exhortations" portion of the Discipleship & Ethics website, www.discipleshipandethics.com/exhorting-ethically/.

You should read the Bible.

You shouldn't get drunk.

You should help the poor.

But consider how these exhortations change when you replace the *should* with *if*.

If you read the Bible . . .

If you get drunk . . .

If you help the poor . . .

This does not suggest that we must always say "if" instead of "should." For instance, I might say, "God calls us to help the poor because. . . ." The point is that when we pull *should* or *ought* out of a sentence, we must engage the exhortation more fully, and we often end up speaking in a way that carries a greater sense of invitation and possibility.

Of course, rather than pulling out *ought* and revising the sentence, one could just drop the exhortation. A fuzzy church avoids "should" and "ought" language, but it does not seek an alternative, and so it puts life-giving imperatives in the closet with the shame darts. A centered approach seeks alternatives.

. . . AND USE CENTERED ALTERNATIVES

Paint a vision: "imagine." Rather than imposing behavioral expectations with the finger-pointing word *should*, we can attract people to different behavior by painting a vision of the good life according to the kingdom of God. Vision-casting can be broad and general, but it can also be as specific as any "ought."

For example, Dylan Aebersold, a youth pastor, focuses on energizing a collective imagination for a life lived in the ways of Jesus. The youth group's formal times together follow a trajectory: "Cultural commentary and critique; statements of identity made in the indicative mood; exhortations made in the imperative mood; and then allocating and designing space to actually imagine together what this stuff looks like lived out in our days at school, work, extracurriculars, etc." At an end-of-the-school-year meeting, he asked students the following questions:

▶ Where have you seen God's presence in your life over the past school year? (What transformation did you experience?)

▶ When you think about the upcoming summer season, what kind of transformation do you imagine occurring in your life?

▶ What are some things (rhythms, disciplines, relationships, etc.) you can imagine that could help lead you to a place of allowing God to bring transformation?

Rather than ending a discussion about gratitude by saying, "You should be grateful," he encourages the youth to work together in small groups to imagine the following:

▶ What are the disciplines/practices that can help gratitude take root in our lives?

▶ How do you imagine your life and your rhythms as being marked by gratitude?[8]

Journey words: directional language. A bounded church demands people move across the line, but then it becomes fairly static—you are in, not out. A fuzzy church is fuzzy; it is difficult to call for movement or change. A centered church, however, invites people on a journey. It is not static because we have not yet arrived. Through the Holy Spirit's work, we continue to be transformed to become more Christlike. With Paul, we say that we have not arrived and so we continue to press on (Phil 3:12-14). The most effective centered-church leaders overflow with directional vocabulary.

Journey language does three important things. First, it communicates that there is always a next step. Second, it is gracious. While setting the bar high, it also roots the whole process in grace. We are not simply in or out by complying or not complying. Instead, we are all in process together. As church planter Keith Miller observes, "When we understand ethics as a trajectory toward fullness in Christ rather than a standard of being good enough, we are able to celebrate any movement on that trajectory instead of dwelling on the shortcomings of an incomplete attempt."[9] Third, every use

---

[8]Dylan Aebersold, emails to author, May 9-10, 2019.
[9]Keith Miller, "Ethics as Trajectory Rather Than Standard" (post to online discussion forum for the course "Following Jesus," Fresno Pacific Biblical Seminary, September 26, 2017).

of a directional term contributes to a centered culture and undermines a fuzzy or bounded approach. Let the examples that follow stimulate your imagination about how you might be able to use more directional language in your ministry context.

Youth pastor Jordan Hogue begins a series on dating by saying, "I want to talk about the practicalities." He identifies the practicalities as establishing boundaries to set ourselves up for success, how to avoid letting someone treat us in a degrading way, how to avoid lowering our standards. Then he makes it clear that all these practicalities are held "within the idea that everything in our life should point us to Jesus." As discussed in chapter two, establishing boundaries is not the same thing as having a bounded approach. A centered approach can utilize standards, but they are set in a different framework. Jordan's final sentence above roots the previous statements in a centered approach. He ends each session in the series with directional language, stating, "We can talk about boundaries, about things you can do to protect yourself. Those things have their place, but an even more important question is, 'Does this person point me closer to Christ?' If the answer is 'no,' then it is a problem—even if you are keeping the 'rules.'"[10]

The Meeting House in Oakville, Ontario developed what they call a "discipleship cycle" that communicates a directional rather than a bounded approach. Darrell Winger, executive pastor, states that the words Trust, Grow, Give, and Go in figure 6.1 are key, but just as important is the repeated directional question: What is your next step?

The circle form of the framework communicates that it is an ongoing process. As Winger explains, "We all have a next step. Whether a seeker or long-time disciple." The journey is corporate, and everyone works on these discipleship steps together. Just as there is not an end stage when someone finishes, there is not a single starting place. "People can enter at any point," Winger says and emphasizes that trust is not a one-time event. Not only are there new steps of trust, but there is an element of trust involved in growing, giving, and going as well.[11]

---

[10]Jordan Hogue, interview by author, April 2, 2018.

[11]Darrell Winger, focus group discussion, The Meeting House, Oakville, Ontario, January 22, 2018.

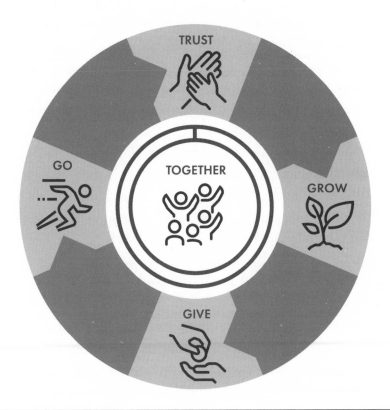

Figure 6.1. Discipleship cycle

The Meeting House uses this language in their preaching and teaching, and it also weaves it into their "huddles," groups of three or four that meet as part of the weekly home church gatherings. Huddles ask three fundamental questions:

- ▸ What do you sense God might be saying to you through this week's teaching?
- ▸ What is something you can do to respond?
- ▸ How can we help?

In addition, the huddles pick and choose from a list of questions including these, beginning each question with "Since the last time we talked. . . ."

- ▸ How have you encountered Jesus, and what has he been challenging or encouraging you about through Scripture, people, or other ways?

▶ What has been your greatest area of temptation, struggle, or sin—and how can we help you overcome that?

▶ When have you served others and loved well (or missed opportunities to do so), including serving your church, investing time in your family, helping your friends, showing kindness to strangers, and loving your enemies?

▶ Have you had a spiritual conversation with someone outside our church community—learning about their beliefs and sharing your own?

▶ Is there anyone you need to ask forgiveness from, or offer forgiveness to? What is holding you back from doing that?

▶ How have you actively sought to be a peacemaker (someone who is helping to create peace), in your own conflicts or disputes, or in those around you?

▶ How have you handled your finances (shopping, saving, giving, investing) and your possessions (using, sharing, loaning, giving away) in ways that reflect the priorities of the kingdom of Christ?

▶ Are there any distractions (media, hobbies, pursuits) that draw too much time and energy away from the loving life you are called to live?[12]

Jill Trites, a pastor at Eucharist Church in nearby Hamilton, Ontario, says that some of these questions might not work in her church, because many people have come from bounded churches and are deeply distrustful of bounded frames of reference. Therefore, they gravitate toward a fuzzy approach. In light of this reality, Eucharist Church sees it as important to ask directional next-step questions, though they do so in a softer way. In their small groups, they ask a similar basic question, "What is God saying to you, and what are you going to do about it?"[13]

While it is important to formalize directional language as The Meeting House has done, we must also develop the habit of seasoning our speech

---

[12]From The Meeting House document, "Home Church Huddles," September 2019. For the complete list of questions see www.themeetinghouse.com/static/pdfs/Policies-and-Statements /Huddle%20Questions_September%202019.pdf.

[13]Jill Trites, interview by author, February 12, 2018.

with it. Pastor Phil Schmidt often uses the word *journey* to reinforce the centered dynamic of his church, such as talking about the "faith journey" and "journeying together."[14] Youth pastor Ryan Cody repeatedly uses the phrase "arrows, not lines" when discussing biblical texts that contain commands. He tells the youth, "Standards are in the Bible, and often we fall short. Commands are given to draw people back to fullness, to *shalom*. Commands are arrows pointing to what God desires, calling us to move in that direction."[15]

REPENTANCE: TALKING ABOUT SIN

In a centered approach, the key move is to turn toward the center. When we turn toward Jesus, we also turn away from some things. We will explore the evangelistic use of conversion language in chapter twelve. A centered approach regularly uses the language of turning throughout the faith journey. Being *for* something is a key step toward recognizing that some paths are better than others because certain paths are destructive and our choices matter. To abandon using the word *should* because it is a shame dart does not mean that we become fuzzy. A centered church will use the language of turning and calls for repentance in ways that promote deep and profound transformation and go far beyond what the "should" lines of a bounded church demand.

In the Bible study that I lead in the Fresno County Jail, I regularly invite inmates to repent—to turn away from something and to turn toward the way of Jesus. I do this even after men have converted and made an initial turn toward Jesus. For instance, I call the men to repent from keeping up appearances of materialistic success at any cost and to turn toward putting security in our identity in Christ. In a circle of gang members, I invite the men to repent from a lifestyle of seeking revenge and to turn toward Jesus' way of forgiving. Of course, these invitations are embedded in Bible studies that paint a vision of the alternative. They are not single-lined, lazy "should" imperatives. Any call to repentance is a confrontational "no" to certain ways of being and living in the world. In a centered approach, there is also inherent "good news" of a better way. Although at times sobered by the challenge, the men also express a longing to live in the way of Jesus and to be freed from

---

[14]Phil Schmidt, interview by author, February 16, 2018.
[15]Ryan Cody, interview by author, April 23, 2018.

the many burdens they carry. Yet many people today (not just those in fuzzy churches) shy away from using the word *repent* or the word it is often linked with in the Bible, *sin*.[16]

I recently began a sermon on Mark 1:1-8 by asking, "When is last time you used the word *sin* in a conversation?" My assumption was that for many, myself included, it had been a while. Why? In a society where tolerance is the supreme virtue, it often seems inappropriate to talk about sins. But why is this word even avoided in some churches? Perhaps it is in response to the ways that sin has been perceived as a war on pleasure. Or it may be that the word *sin* is associated with bounded churches and self-righteous, finger-pointing people who shame others. Or, perhaps the word is linked with an image of a judgmental God—"the big eye in the sky"—and people have abandoned the word *sin* as they have run away from that concept of God.

All these reasons for moving away from the language of sin are understandable, but have we moved too far? Two authors would respond with a strong, "yes." The first, Mark McMinn, is a Christian counseling professor who describes how he did not talk about sin much because he considered himself to be a grace-oriented counselor. But then he began to wonder if we could fully understand or experience grace without a robust understanding of sin. He acknowledged that by not talking about sin "a true understanding of grace has also been lost, because it cannot exist without a language of sin."[17]

The second, David Brooks, writes about sin in *The Road to Character*. A New York Times columnist, Brooks did not yet identify himself as a Christian when he wrote this book, but, like McMinn, Brooks advocates for pulling the language of sin out of the dustbin. He writes,

> Sin is a necessary piece of our mental furniture because it reminds us that life is a moral affair. . . . No matter how hard we strive to replace sin with non-moral words, like "mistake" or "error" or "weakness," the most essential parts of life are matters of individual responsibility and moral choice: whether to be brave or cowardly, honest or deceitful, compassionate or callous, faithful

---

[16]For example, see 1 Kings 8:47; Is 59:20; Mk 1:4; Lk 5:32; Acts 2:38.
[17]Mark McMinn, *Sin and Grace in Christian Counseling: An Integrative Paradigm* (Downers Grove, IL: IVP Academic, 2008), 19, 22.

or disloyal. . . . To banish words like ["sin,"] "virtue," "character" . . . and "vice" . . . means we think and talk about these choices less clearly, and thus become increasingly blind to the moral stakes of everyday life.[18]

Later in the book, Brooks reflects on David Chappell's analysis of the civil rights movement in *A Stone of Hope*. One stream of the movement had an optimistic view of human nature and believed that through education and appeal to reason, people would gradually see that racism is wrong. The other stream, led by Martin Luther King Jr., emerged from the biblical prophetic tradition. King declared, "Instead of assured progress in wisdom and decency, man faces the ever present possibility of swift relapse not merely to animalism, but into such calculated cruelty as no other animal can practice."[19] King's more serious consideration of the human propensity toward sin led him—and those who worked with him—to be more realistic about others, more humble about themselves, more aggressive in their fight against racism, and better able to deal with pain, suffering, and setbacks.

Although bounded-group religiosity often talks about sin in harmful ways, the fuzzy-group alternative of banning the term also is also problematic. A centered approach requires us to talk of sin, for reasons that McMinn and Brooks indicate, and because a centered approach requires us to turn away from something—sin—in order to turn toward the center. Propelled by McMinn and Brooks, as I prepared for my sermon on Mark 1:1-8, I decided to preach on sin.

Knowing that I would be encouraging listeners to think and talk more about sin, I sought to practice what I was going to preach in the days before I delivered the sermon. I did not do very well. As I prayerfully reflected over my days, asking how I had sinned, not much came to mind. In part, I think this is because the "list" view of sins is so deeply embedded in my being. In my youth I would occasionally slip up and then confess my infraction, but in general, I steered clear of the sins on the list in my mind—things like lying, cheating, stealing, swearing, drinking, and so on. At a theoretical level, I agreed with McMinn and Brooks, and I was working on a sermon advocating the same thing, but personal application was not going well.

---

[18]David Brooks, *The Road to Character* (New York: Random House, 2015), 54.
[19]Brooks, *Road to Character*, 146.

Midway through my sermon prep, however, a shift happened. John the Baptist proclaims "a baptism of repentance for the forgiveness of sins" (Mk 1:4). The word *repentance* stood out to me. As I rode my bicycle home from the seminary that day, instead of asking, How have I sinned today?, I found myself asking repentance questions: How am I heading in the wrong direction? How have I gotten off-track today?

In response to these questions, the word *interruption* came to mind. I had interrupted others a couple of times during the seminary faculty meeting. Interrupting someone was not on my sin list, and it never would have come up as an answer to the question, How have I sinned today? Yet this was not a new revelation. I had been working on interrupting others less. But in the space of repentance and prayerful openness, something new happened. A question came to mind, perhaps by God's Spirit: "What are you communicating when you interrupt?" I responded, "I communicate that what I have to say is more important than what the other person is saying." I had an immediate and powerful response. "I do not want to be that kind of person. I repent. I want to change." What a different experience simply by changing the word in my reflection from *sin* to *repent*. This is a helpful change, yet we must do even more.

Although I believe there is value in using the word *sin* and related words *sins* and *sinners*, it is more important to use language that communicates the concept of sin. Whether because of having accepted the belief that tolerance is the supreme virtue, or having been beaten down by a bounded church, the words *sin* and *repent* lead many to assume that a centered church that uses this language is a shaming, excluding church. The language itself carries so much baggage we may need to use alternatives. For instance, I often say, "You are hurting yourself and others." We can use words such as *dehumanizing, alienation, broken, damaging, inappropriate, hurtful,* or phrases such as *resisting God's Spirit, sowing discord, hindering flourishing,* or *God is calling you to more.* Ted Steenburgh, who works with individuals who have experienced the rejection and judgmentalism of bounded-group religiosity in profound ways, finds any sin language to be a trigger, and so he has flipped the language. He gets at the concept of sin or inappropriate behavior by talking about positive ideals. He observes, "My mind might say, 'that is bad, that is sin,' but I frame a comment to suggest that [the path] may not be the ideal thing for that person. I seek to convey not a tone of judgment, rather a tone of opportunity."[20]

It makes a big difference if the voice talking about sin and repentance is the loving God revealed by Jesus, or a big, accusing, eye in the sky. A loving God, like a loving mother or father, still disciplines us and calls us toward repentance, but it feels significantly different from a shaming, scolding call to turn away from sin. Jesus calls for repentance and challenges us to turn from sin, but his call is draped in love. Let us not simply return to using the language of sin. Rather, when we use the language of repentance and sin, let us always bind it to Jesus and wrap it in the nurturing love of God.

IT IS POSSIBLE: MODELS TO IMITATE

The central question in this chapter has been how to exhort others without leaving them feeling that they have stepped into a bounded church. I have suggested the following as key elements to centered exhortations:

1. include indicatives that undermine line-drawing religiosity,

2. include words of grace,

3. use more indicative than imperative content,

4. link imperatives with indicatives about God's action,

5. include empowering indicatives,

6. avoid using the words *ought* or *should*

7. invite people to imagine an alternative,

8. use directional journey language,

9. use alternative language for *sin* and

10. connect *sin* and *repentance* with statements about a loving God.

Note that on this list I do not suggest that we soften the challenge or lower the standards. In fact, when I give students the assignment of writing an ethical exhortation, part of their grade is based on the strength of the challenge that is communicated through imperatives. It is possible to

---

[20]Ted Steenburgh, focus group discussion, The Meeting House, Toronto, Ontario, January 21, 2018.

incorporate the above suggestions and deliver strong, ethical challenges in a centered way.

I end this chapter with five examples of centered exhortations. Though the first four examples are from sermons, this does not imply that this chapter is only for preaching. The above list and the models that follow can be applied in many settings, including personal conversations, counseling sessions, Bible studies, presentations, and Sunday school classes. The final example is taken from a mission statement of a centered church.

In this first example, note how Jean Janzen says, "may we," instead of, "you should," and how she uses the word "imagine" along with a question to urge practical application in an invitational way. Note also how she uses the directional language of conversion and has a clear and strong emphasis on God as the fundamental actor.

> May we, this week, allow the Gracious Spirit to convert us from our limited and pinched generosity to an extravagant generosity to God and to others. Imagine the form that could take this week. May we be converted from a withholding of love for those who differ from us, whether it is religious, race, economic, or sexual orientation, recognizing our common humanity. Who might the Spirit move you to reach out to this week? And may we, this week, be converted from hiding under our own goodness and allow God's love to wash us and dress us once again. Thanks be to God for the wideness in his mercy.[21]

How might the form of Janzen's imperatives undermine the impulse to interpret her words in a bounded religious way? How might the form of her imperatives also contribute to more action and more profound change?

Robert Hill displays another alternative to "you should" by saying, "let us." Note how he repeatedly links his imperatives to indicative statements about what God has already done and who we are. How might this help his listeners hear his exhortation in a centered rather than bounded way?

> People of faith, let us live in newness of life! Let us set aside our resentment of things past. Let us set aside our desire to even the score. . . . Let us pardon one another even as God has pardoned us. Let us receive others favorably,

---

[21]Jean Janzen, "Conversion: The Prostitute, Luke 7:36-50" (sermon delivered at College Community Church, Mennonite Brethren, Clovis, CA, August 17, 2003).

even as God has accepted us. And let us in faith take what is offered to us—Jesus Christ. Let us in faith receive the gift of forgiveness, the treasure of life itself. And as forgiven people, let us forgive others.[22]

John Casey not only encourages people to take actions in response to all that God has done for them, but he also guides people to recall and actually feel again what God has done for them. Then he draws those indicatives together into the phrase, "as one loved," which he links with the imperative, "step forward." He offers various examples of actions, which feed people's imagination about what they might do while also reinforcing the exhortation to do something! He ends with a strong invitational sense of possibility, not just: "you ought to do this" but, "do a small thing and you may contribute to a great thing—God's kingdom work."

> I invite you to recall the simple ordinary ways that God stepped toward you, Almighty God came after you and drew you to Himself. Just to go back and recall those small ordinary things that happened that God used draw you to Himself and take in God's love for you all over again. And then to step forward as one loved, believing small ordinary things are powerful in his Kingdom and under his hand. To go bless a child, bless a grown daughter, bless a grandchild, to bless a clerk in a store where you regularly go, and to believe that somehow that could be the beginning of the Kingdom of God rolling towards that ordinary person. You could in that very small ordinary step be continuing the work of Jesus in bringing the Kingdom of God. God's great kingdom coming near in all of His ordinary people, stealing away to be with Him; doing the hard work of resolving differences, having dinner with people very different, blessing others with ordinary words, gifts and actions just as the Spirit of God leads us. Very simple small, invisible Spirit-led acts advancing God's rule.[23]

This next example is from the end of my own sermon on Mark 1:1-8, addressing sin and repentance. What methods that I have described in this chapter can you observe?

> Who do you imagine calling you to repent, God as police officer with a list of laws, or God like a parent, mentor, or pastor? With the sin list mentality the

---

[22]Robert Hill, "First Forgiveness" (sermon delivered at Asbury First United Methodist Church, Rochester, NY, March 4, 2001).

[23]John Casey, "This Kingdom's Small Beginnings—so Un-American, Matthew 13:31-35" (sermon delivered at Blanchard Alliance Church, Wheaton, IL, April 3, 2011).

objective is to not sin so God, the police officer, will leave me alone. In contrast, I invite the loving God into my life with hopeful expectation that the call to repent will contribute to a more abundant life.

I will end by suggesting a daily practice you might take up. Four steps:

▶ First, focus your mind on an image of God's nurturing love: perhaps Jesus' loving gaze, God giving you a maternal hug, a caring shepherd; use an image that works for you.

▶ Second, in the security of that love, ask God: What are you calling me to repent from today? Reflect, listen, think back over your day.

▶ Third, confess, repent—make a commitment to change direction.

▶ Fourth, rest in God's loving forgiveness.

What might happen if we take up this practice? What might God be lovingly calling you to repent from? What are ways God might be calling you to turn around, change direction?

God loves you, and because God loves you, God calls you to repent, calls you to leave behind attitudes, practices, habits, thoughts, and turn to new ways that will be better for you, for others, for creation.[24]

The words we use matter—not just in moments of exhortation and sermons, but in other contexts as well. Think, for instance, of the benefit of writing the mission and values of a church in a centered way. The process itself would be formational, and having a centered statement would set the church on a trajectory toward becoming more centered. Note the ways that Neighborhood Church in Visalia, California, makes clear their centered approach—one that is neither bounded nor fuzzy—in the following statement of their mission and values.

> Neighborhood Church exists to inspire people wherever they are to live like Jesus wherever they go through:
>
> *Authenticity.* We live in such a way that people see the real us. We share stories that are real, no matter how messy they are. We start conversations where no question is off limits.

---

[24]Mark D. Baker, "Repentance, Sin, Mark 1:1-8" (sermon delivered at College Community Church, Mennonite Brethren, Clovis, CA, December 10, 2017).

Inclusion. We won't let anything get in the way of relationship. We provide a place for people to belong even before they believe. We build bridges with all people regardless of labels.

Restoration. We partner with God to make the world better. We look for opportunities to join God at work in our city. We give generously of time and resources to benefit others.

Grace. We extend God's love to people no matter what. We refuse to dispense shame as a way to motivate people. We will always default to grace over religion.

Transformation. We submit to a process of radical change that orients our lives around Jesus. We teach the life of Jesus as the model for our lives. We design all of our environments to promote relationships that produce life change.[25]

This chapter has focused on words. I urge you to borrow from this chapter by using words such as these! Look for ways to practice centered approaches to exhortation. While words matter, however, we cannot live out a centered approach simply by changing our words of exhortation. We must also consider how the *character* of ministry leaders and the *characteristics* of a church or ministry influence our approach to church. We will explore that in the next chapter.

---

[25]"Who We Are," *Neighborhood Church*, http://ncvisalia.com/who-we-are/.

7

CENTERED CHARACTER

QUALITIES OF JESUS

Six men wearing red jumpsuits with "prisoner" stenciled on the back file into the multipurpose room where we are gathering for a weekly Bible study in the Fresno County Jail. We shake hands and exchange warm greetings. After reading Mark 1:15, I ask the men what "repent" means. One older man says, "To confess your sin, to turn around, change direction." Jason, a young inmate who is a new Christian, asks, "Why is it that even though I have repented, I keep heading back the other direction and do things I should not do?"

"Good question," I say and silently pray, "What do I say, God?" I could give a theologically correct response, but Jason is not looking for information. He has repented. He has experienced God's transformation of his life, but he wants to know why he still stumbles. I invite the others to respond. They share what they find helpful—spending more time reading their Bible, praying with others, talking with a fellow Christian, resisting the devil, staying away from old friends, and so on.

Wanting to add an indicative element about the nature of God to take the conversation deeper, I make a connection between Adam and Eve and an example of "slipping up" that one of them had shared. I say that God loves us profoundly, and yet Adam and Eve rejected the loving instruction God gave them. They did not trust God and so they reached out for the forbidden fruit. I invite the men to trust that God loves them and because of that love, God calls them to a different path, to repent. I assure them God will forgive them when they slip up.

I start wrapping up so we can begin our prayer time, and then Steve blurts out, "I can't mess up again. If I sell drugs again, I will be in prison for a long time. What do I do?" He talks about how much he is praying and how prayer is helpful, but he has tried it all before—going to church, speaking in tongues, being part of a support group, but nothing has worked. Moved, I pray again for guidance and wonder to myself, "What is behind this? Why did he start selling drugs again?" I start asking him questions, and Steve tells us that he has a college degree, had a good job and a nice house, but when money got tight, he returned to selling drugs. I press further, asking more questions, and he acknowledges that he was driven to sell drugs by his concern about what others thought of him. Selling drugs provided the money he needed to keep up appearances.

I tell the group about a friend of mine who had a good job and bought a new house. When I visited, I was surprised to find the living room totally empty—no furniture. Why?—because he and his wife had used up their money to buy the house. I ask, "What would most people do?" The group says that most people would beg, borrow, or steal to get furniture rather than have an empty living room, because they would fear what people would think. My, friend however, lived within his means and waited until they had money for furniture. Steve admits that this is not what he would do.

We talked about society's lies: that more things equal a better life and that people with more money deserve more respect. I say that when we trust that we are loved by God and trust and obey what Jesus teaches about money, those lies are exposed and they lose their power over us.

The hour is about up, so I encourage Steve to imagine himself back in his house with half the possessions he currently has and then to think of himself resting in God's loving embrace as he imagines what others might say about him. I say a quick, heartfelt prayer for the men, and then the correctional officer comes to take them back to their cells.[1]

---

[1] Adapted from Mark D. Baker, "Going to Jail," *Christian Leader*, December 1, 2010, https://christianleadermag.com/going-to-jail/.

As I reflect back on that Bible study now, I can see how I used some of the methods that I describe in the previous chapter, and yet I know that words are not enough. The study pressed beyond the superficial because of Jason's and Steve's sharing about their feelings of failure. If anyone in the circle had responded with line-drawing judgmentalism, I doubt that Jason and Steve would have opened up so transparently. I am also grateful that I responded to the Spirit's prompting when I hesitated a moment before responding to Steve and prayed for guidance. If I had not stopped and prayed at that moment, I may not have wondered with compassion and curiosity about why Steve was selling drugs.

To practice a centered approach, we need both the words described in the previous chapter and certain character traits, such as compassion, curiosity, creativity, trust, humility, and vulnerability. I think of these traits as akin to the fruit of the Spirit. First, like the fruit of the Spirit, these qualities reflect Jesus, who is at the center. Second, these qualities are similar to the fruit of the Spirit because they are fruit of the *Spirit*—not just of human effort. Someone could try to implement the techniques described in the previous chapter through their own work and effort, but that is not the case with the qualities described in this chapter. Third, like Paul's list of the fruit of the Spirit in Galatians, these qualities are not limited to leaders. As in Galatians, we can think of these qualities as characteristics of both individuals and a centered-church community as a whole.[2] Although the primary point of this chapter is that these qualities are necessary to embody a centered approach, the relationship flows both ways. These qualities facilitate a centered approach, and a centered approach facilitates the development of these qualities.

COMPASSION

Moral outrage reacts against a wrong that has been done. When we are morally outraged, we see an action and do not stop to ask why someone has acted as they have. When we are morally outraged, we also tend to separate

---

[2]For more on the corporate nature of Paul's letter to the Galatians, see my forthcoming *Freedom from Religiosity: Studies in Paul's Letter to the Galatians,* Luminaire Studies (Winnipeg: Kindred Productions, forthcoming), as well as Mark D. Baker, *Religious No More: Building Communities of Grace & Freedom* (Downers Grove, IL: InterVarsity Press, 1999).

acceptable people neatly from unacceptable people. In a bounded church, moral outrage reinforces the dividing line, increases the status of those who are compliant, and shames those who fall short. These responses describe Simon the Pharisee's attitude toward the woman he categorizes as a sinner. Unlike Simon, Jesus sees the woman rather than defining her by her actions. He not only compassionately forgives her, but also compassionately defends her loving actions (Lk 7:36-50). Throughout the Gospels Jesus continually looks with compassion on the people he encounters.

Father Gregory Boyle ministers to gang members in East Los Angeles. Yet even in this context, where moral outrage might seem appropriate, Boyle advocates for compassion. He observes that "the ultimate measure of health in any community might well reside in our ability to stand in awe at what folks carry rather than in judgement at how they carry it."[3] A bounded church practices judgmentalism; a centered church must develop the ability to look with compassion on what people are carrying.

Years ago, I had critical thoughts about the pastor of the church I attended. He was a good orator, but he often appeared to be making up his sermon as he delivered it. He led us in making plans, but not in carrying them out. I could go on, but the point is that I had a list of critical thoughts about him, which I brought to church with me each week. Seeing him through the filter of that list not only made it hard for me to see anything else about him, but it gave me a hypersensitive radar to his negative attributes. This created a critical feedback loop. My growing disdain and frustration became a barrier to my ability to experience the positive things that he and the church had to offer and therefore a barrier to my positive involvement in the church. Doug Frank suggested that during church each week, I imagine the vulnerable, hurting little boy within the pastor (just as Doug had previously led me to imagine the little Mark Baker within me). After going through this exercise for several weeks, I still had critiques about the things the pastor did or did not do, but the starting point for those thoughts was compassion, which made a huge difference. How might it change a church if we wrapped every thought about another person in a blanket of compassion?

---

[3]Gregory Boyle, *Barking to the Choir: The Power of Radical Kinship*, reprint edition (New York: Simon & Schuster, 2018), 51; see also 141.

For many people, the words, "God sees into the innermost parts of your being," provoke fear. If God's eyes were unkindly, the fear would be appropriate. But in chapter four we observed that Jesus' gaze is full of compassion. Church historian Roberta Bondi describes a turning point in her relationship with God and Christianity after she read one of the early desert monastics. She realized "that only God can judge us because it is only God who can look with compassion on the depth and variety of our individual experience and our suffering, and know us as we really are."[4] God looks at us with eyes of compassion.

Note that Bondi does not say that her turning point was realizing that God does not judge us. Similarly, Doug Frank did not suggest that I ignore the pastor's shortcomings. Tolerance feels better than a critical, unkindly eye, but it is less than love. I imagine that a fuzzy approach could look with compassionate understanding about why a person acts in a certain way, but it would stop there. People in a fuzzy church would hesitate to take the next step. They would not seek to use that understanding to work with the person toward change.

Having the God revealed by Jesus, the God described by Bondi, at the center is a key element in creating the character of a centered church. Emphasizing relationship with the center includes the biblical imperative to live in conformity with the center—in other words we seek to imitate Jesus. Being united with Christ calls and enables us to view others with compassion, which will change the character of a church.

A critical posture, on the other hand, feeds a bounded approach. Looking critically at others enables us to feel superior. Even if this is not an intentional effort to grasp superiority, the critical gaze places us over and above others. As I began to look at my pastor through different lenses, thinking compassionately about his hurts and wounds, I found myself at the same level with him. It was not pity; I, too, carry wounds. But all wounds are not the same. Father Boyle sees himself as fortunate rather than superior. He writes, "Every homie I know who has killed somebody—everyone—has carried a load one hundred times heavier than I have had to carry, weighed

---

[4]Roberta C. Bondi, *Memories of God: Theological Reflections on a Life* (Nashville: Abingdon, 1995), 78.

down by torture, violence, abuse, neglect, abandonment, or mental illness."[5] Compassion and humility helped me see my pastor's actions in a new light, which led me to think differently on what might bring change in his life. As compassion grows within us, it will become easier to shift our focus from the boundary line to individuals and their journey toward the center.

CURIOSITY

It is not enough simply to tell those who are morally outraged to "be compassionate." If all we can see is the infraction that has been committed, then moral outrage is an understandable response. Therefore, we must commit to move past the superficial to explore the story behind the action. Thinking of Father Boyle's quote, we will not stand in compassionate awe of the burdens that other people carry if we have no sense of who they are and what they are carrying. Curiosity fosters compassion and is needed in a centered approach for that and much more. For instance, the Bible study in Fresno County Jail would have gone much differently if I had immediately focused on the action of selling drugs rather than inquisitively exploring why Steve was selling drugs. Before exploring various aspects of the curiosity of a centered approach, I want to make clear it is loving curiosity, not the voyeuristic curiosity of snooping.

I have not heard a lot of talk about Jesus' curiosity. Perhaps our curiosity would grow if we gave more time to imagining his. Think of how often he asked questions. A stance of curiosity. Or think of Jesus looking up in the tree at Zacchaeus. Jesus was just passing through Jericho; perhaps he decided to change plans because he was curious—he had a desire to converse, ask questions. What was Zacchaeus seeking when he wanted to see Jesus (Lk 19:1-6)? In the story of the woman at the well in John 4, we have an account of Jesus' conversation with the Samaritan woman, which is full of probing curiosity. I invite you to reread that familiar story and look for examples of loving curiosity.

Curiosity is not just about asking the probing questions of a detective. Loving curiosity cares about the person and assumes that more is going on than we can see on the surface. Imagine the following scene: A young couple,

---

[5]Boyle, *Barking to the Choir*, 132.

who are unmarried teenagers, sit shamefaced in front of their pastor as they confess to having sex. Their pastor responds, "What is the problem?" They look at him, confused, and one of them says, "We are not married." The pastor repeats the question. More confused, they explain that they have had sex a number of times. In a bounded church, that confession would be enough, and so there would be no need to probe deeper. In a centered church, the pastor expands his question to make it clear that he wants to explore their relationship and their individual stories—their root issues, the stories behind their action. The pastor is not fuzzy. He does not ignore the action. Mark Pequegnat, a lay home-church leader, says that we still observe actions and evaluate. "But now [in a centered approach], as soon as I evaluate, I think 'why?' and start asking questions like, 'What is going on in your life? What can I do to help?'"[6]

A fuzzy approach also does not require curiosity; it is you do your thing, and I do mine. In a fuzzy approach, everyone wants to be nice and to avoid shame, but the silence of avoidance or the lack of curiosity can also hurt and shame. A friend of mine went through the pain and upheaval of a divorce, I asked him how his church had handled the situation. He said, "Eighty percent very good." I asked, "What was some of the twenty percent?" He said, "The pastor's wife, whom I interacted with regularly, never asked me about it, never said anything." She displayed no loving curiosity. Her silence increased the shame that my friend felt.

Curiosity also helps in moments of disagreement, or when someone says something that is counter to the beliefs of a church. Rather than simply rejecting, we need to explore. Kurt Willems, a church planter in Seattle, finds himself saying things like, "That's interesting, say more." Or "Help me understand why you think this way. How does Jesus inform this idea?"[7]

Curiosity also includes a sense of discernment and sensitivity to the Holy Spirit. Discernment can lead us to say, "yes," where a more rigid and bounded approach might say, "no, stop that." But the Holy Spirit can also lead to saying "no." Weldon Nisly, who we met in chapter two, recalls two similar situations at his church in Seattle. A man who had attended their church for some time began to roam around during the service more and more each

---

[6]Mark Pequegnat, focus group discussion, The Meeting House, Hamilton, ON, January 20, 2018.
[7]Kurt Willems, interview by author, Seattle, WA, February 21, 2018.

week. One Sunday, he went to the front and began chanting and burning incense. Nisly said, "I did not sense the Spirit. I met with him that week and told him it was disruptive and inappropriate. He stopped doing it." One Sunday, another woman came up to the front of the church and said she wanted to sing a song. Nisly discerned and approved of her singing "Amazing Grace." Afterwards she told him that his was the only church that did not call the police when she began to sing. Nisly reflects, "She was giving us her offering as best she could."

Curiosity in a centered church is broad. Just as we are inquisitive about the story behind any behavior that we deem to be inappropriate, we are also curious about the positive things that God might be calling people toward as we journey with them toward the center. Here curiosity and intentionality go arm and arm. When situations arise, when people come to us, we respond with curiosity, but to encourage movement toward the center, we also take initiative and explore the next steps. A centered church asks, "What is Jesus up to in our midst?" This is a corporate question we ask together, and we also ask individuals—"What is Jesus up to in your life?"

CREATIVITY

As we curiously delve below the surface, we will encounter complex realities. Thus a centered church both opens the space for and needs creativity in order to respond well to those complex realities. In the Sermon on the Mount, Jesus' centered approach opens space for him to creatively move beyond easily defined and measured rules and to press deeper. Both bounded and fuzzy approaches would scurry away from saying something like Jesus' teaching, "You have heard that it was said, 'You shall not commit adultery.' But I tell you that anyone who looks at a woman lustfully has already committed adultery with her in his heart" (Mt 5:27-28). Jesus also displayed creativity in challenging the neatness of bounded categories with the messiness of life. In the process, he exposes the oppressive character of a bounded approach. "If one of you has a child or an ox that falls into a well on the Sabbath day, will you not immediately pull it out?" (Lk 14:5). Similarly, in response to the line-clarifying question, "Who is my neighbor?" (Lk 10:29), Jesus creatively responds with a parable that refuses to play the line-drawing game of determining who is in and who is out, but instead deepens the challenge. In the face of binary options of drawn lines, Jesus creatively introduces a third way, such as, "Give back to Caesar what is Caesar's, and to God what is God's" (Mt 22:15-22; Mk 12:13-17; Lk 20:20-26).

Sherri Nozik, a former nonprofit director in Moldova, recounts one example of centered creativity.[8]

> Drinking is central to Moldovan culture, yet, possibly due to the very high rate of alcoholism, evangelical churches prohibit drinking. My friends own a pizza place in a village. They are evangelical Christians; therefore, they wouldn't sell alcohol in their restaurant. Their patrons would simply bring in their own gallon jugs of beer and get belligerently drunk while eating pizza. A fuzzy approach would require no creativity. Church leaders would not say anything, and my friends would do nothing, allowing for their pizza place to get taken over by a non-family-friendly, non-family-promoting environment, simply because they were afraid of losing patrons. A bounded approach also would require no creativity. Church leaders would likely insist my friends take an even stricter stance against alcohol consumption in their establishment— forbidding patrons from bringing in beer, while also refusing to serve beer. That would decrease or eliminate those patrons from their restaurant—further isolating this Christian family from a relationship with their neighbors.
>
> What happened was a centered approach. Their pastor helped them devise a plan to keep the doors open to their beer-drinking neighbors while curbing the drunkenness, *and* all while increasing their business's profits. They would sell beer at their pizza place, being sure it was the low-alcohol kind; they would be sure everyone was of legal drinking age (which many places don't); and they would limit consumption to three glasses per patron. The patrons came in, had their pizza only with beer that was purchased from the res-taurant, and they didn't get drunk. They (mostly men) ate with their families or went home to their families in a much better state than they had been previously. It actually decreased drunkenness in those patrons and their per-sonal family environments. And with their restaurant being one of the only ones in the village, this actually has a measurable impact on their community. I can state, with some confidence, that decreased drunkenness also decreases abuses within families. The possible positive results of this centered approach are numerous.

---

[8]What follows is from a post to an online class forum, Sherri Nozik, "Following Jesus" (Fresno Pacific Biblical Seminary, October 4, 2017).

SAFETY

While in seminary, Tessa experienced a deepening relationship with Jesus, and she longed to share her new insights about Jesus and the gospel with others in her church, but she remained silent for months. Her experience in a bounded church had paralyzed her, and she did not want to experience the shame of being placed on the wrong side of the line because of her theology, which she worried might be "suspect." She did not trust others to listen with openness. She did not feel safe.[9] While writing this book, I interviewed many pastors and church leaders, seeking to learn key elements in practicing a centered-church model. Repeatedly they mentioned the importance of creating a safe space. If people are going to move toward the center, they will need to seek the help of others to overcome barriers to that movement. Lack of safety, lack of sharing will impede progress.

Safe space is a commonly heard term today. Before exploring how to create a safe space, I want to clarify how I am using the term. An increasingly popular meaning of safe space parallels a fuzzy church. Like fuzzy churches, these societal safe spaces are a reaction to and a refuge from the exclusion and shaming of bounded groups and bounded churches. The safety comes by creating spaces without conflict and confrontation; they forbid anything that would offend or upset someone present. Certainly, the safety of a centered church includes avoiding some of the same hurtful actions that societal safe spaces prohibit. Yet centered-church safe places are not totally absent of conflict or challenging content. The way of Jesus conflicts with and challenges many of the values and norms of society. The fuzzy approach avoids some problems and creates others. When we fail to practice loving confrontation, or when we do not have clear statements about inappropriate actions or inappropriate theology, we create a community environment that is fundamentally not safe because people will not feel safe from others' misbehavior or misguided beliefs.

Fundamentally, the safety of a centered church flows from trust—trust that others have my best interests in mind and will treat me with gentleness and compassion (Gal 6:2). The safety of a centered church is rooted in the

---

[9]Thankfully, when Tessa did take a first tentative step, others responded, "Tell us more." Tessa realized she was living out of fear from a previous church that she had attended.

presence of love and the absence of the self-righteous shaming of a bounded approach. Jesus was the epitome of safety. I encourage you, as you read the Gospels, to take note of the ways that Jesus created a safe space for others. Observe, for instance, the things that he did so that the woman who was caught in adultery—who was feeling very threatened and shamed—felt safe. Think of how Jesus prepared breakfast for Peter and the other disciples to communicate love and acceptance before he began to ask Peter questions about why Peter denied him (Jn 21).

I asked several ministry leaders how they seek to create a sense of safety in their congregations. Often the first thing they said was, "Be vulnerable yourself," because that will display that it is safe to tell the truth, to acknowledge struggles, to seek help from others. In *Culture Code: The Secrets of Highly Successful Groups*, Daniel Coyle writes, "Group cooperation is created by small, frequently repeated moments of vulnerability. Of these, none carries more power than the moment when a leader signals vulnerability."[10] He points to the research of Jeff Polzer, a Harvard professor of organizational behavior, which affirms the reality of a vulnerability loop— one person sends a signal of vulnerability, then another detects it and also displays vulnerability. "A shared exchange of openness, it's the most basic building block of cooperation and trust." Polzer observes that, on the other hand, "If you never have that vulnerable moment . . . then people will try to cover up their weaknesses."[11]

After one of the first focus groups that I met with while researching for this book, I wrote in my notes, "What stands out to me from the session is that little things loom large, tone of voice, word choice, attitude, posture." That general comment is especially true in regard to creating a safe space. Coyle points to an experiment by Will Felps to measure the impact of "bad apples" on groups. Felps hired Nick to be a negative influence in forty different four-person groups tasked with constructing a marketing plan for a start-up. Nick was assigned to be a different type of bad apple in different groups— aggressive jerk, slacker, depressive Eeyore. This one bad apple had a huge impact, reducing the group's performance by 30 to 40 percent—in every case

---

[10]Daniel Coyle, *The Culture Code: The Secrets of Highly Successful Groups* (New York: Bantam, 2018), 158.

[11]Coyle, *Culture Code*, 104.

except one. Though the focus of this study was on the impact of bad apples, it ended up displaying the amazing power of a single good apple. In one group Nick recognized that he was failing, and he tried harder to undermine the group. Nick, the paid actor, ended up infuriated that his negative moves did not work. One person, whom Coyle calls Jonathan, found a way to counter all of Nick's moves. The fascinating part, "from Felp's view, is that at first glance Jonathan doesn't seem to be doing anything at all."[12]

> "A lot of it is really simple stuff that is almost invisible at first," Felps says. "Nick would start being a jerk, and [Jonathan] would lean forward, use body language, laugh and smile, never in a contemptuous way, but in a way that takes the danger out of the room and defuses the situation. It doesn't seem all that different at first. But when you look more closely, it causes some incredible things to happen. . . ." They follow a pattern: Nick behaves like a jerk, and Jonathan reacts instantly with warmth deflecting the negativity and making a potentially unstable situation feel solid and safe. Then Jonathan pivots and asks a simple question that draws others out, and he listens intently and responds.[13]

I have advocated that safety is a quality necessary for embodying a centered approach. This makes it sound like we must work on creating safe space so we can become a centered church. That is true, but it is not that unidirectional. It is also true that a centered approach contributes to the creation of a safe space, whereas a bounded approach undermines it. The implications of this are far-reaching. The safety of a centered church not only enables vulnerable sharing, but it also contributes to the general thriving of the church. Psychologists have found that individuals in groups often spend significant energy in status management. "Their interactions appear smooth, but their underlying behavior is riddled with inefficiency, hesitation, and subtle competition. Instead of focusing on the task they are navigating their uncertainty about one another."[14] Thus Coyle emphasizes safety as a key to success. A bounded church is saturated with status management energy.

---

[12]Coyle, *Culture Code*, 3-5.
[13]Coyle, *Culture Code*, 5. Coyle's book is about how to be a successful group, and his main point in telling this story is that safety and connection are of fundamental importance and having someone like Jonathan is of more value than having someone with great ability to strategize or to take charge.
[14]Coyle, *Culture Code*, xvii.

A centered church not only saves us from the wounds of a bounded approach, but it liberates us from status management. Coyle would tell us that the centered approach will help us do all that we do as a church much better.

Coyle urges us to be thinking constantly about making people feel safe and to seek to practice actions such as Jonathan's to create safe spaces. In a centered church, little things matter because they connect with and contribute to deeper things, such as the sense of being loved. Jonathan's actions would stop working if he did something to lose the group's trust. In a centered approach, we must work to foster trust in the God of the center, trust in the leaders, trust in the community.

What is the fruit of a church becoming a place of trust, a safe space of the Spirit? During a course on Galatians, Malia Mooradian described to the class her experience of it. She observed that often when people are struggling, they turn to an individual they feel safe to confide in. Malia recalled a church she attended where people shared their struggles openly with the whole congregation. She said that the presence of the Holy Spirit was so palpable that to walk into a gathering of that church felt like stepping into a pond of love. She recalled one woman standing up, and with her husband sitting beside her, saying, "I yell at my husband all the time. This is not who I want to be." Another time a woman stood and acknowledged she was living as a prostitute; she told the congregation she wanted to change her life. Malia reports that the in-Christ character of the congregation was so strong that people neither judged nor gossiped. Instead, they gathered around those who shared, prayed for them, and then walked with them in their journeys of transformation. I asked Malia, "Where did the safety come from?" She replied that it started with the pastor and his transparency and that the leadership was so full of love, mercy, and grace that others experienced it, absorbed it, and it became the character of the church.[15]

TRUST

Uptightness was a character trait of mine during my bounded years, as described in chapter one. I was uptight about defining the lines correctly, uptight about staying within the lines, and uptight about what others

---

[15]Malia Mooradian, comments confirmed and expanded on in an interview with the author, April 20, 2021.

thought of me. I was also uptight about those I discipled straying across the lines—again, fearful of what others would think of me.[16] Uptightness impedes the full expression of the characteristics described above. Take a moment and say: *uptight* and *compassionate*; *uptight* and *curious*; *uptight* and *creative*; *uptight* and *vulnerable*. The words clash. In contrast to uptightness, trust in God fosters these characteristics. For instance, the fearful question, What will they think of me? blocks vulnerable sharing. When we are confident and secure in Jesus' love for us, the power of this fear diminishes. True, some people may think, *What a lousy leader!* but our security is in the center rather than in what others think of us. I invite you go through the list of words again, reflect on how a posture of trust in God will open space for and enable each of the characteristics.

Imagine that a person visits a small group and shares the pain of going through a divorce. Hopefully, any Christian group would show this person love and compassion, but as church administrator Katie Double observes, in a bounded setting the leader would feel the pressure to jump in and say, "Just to be clear, the Bible teaches that divorce is not God's best." The bounded approach fears what people will think of us, fears becoming fuzzy, fears people's actions if the line is not emphasized. In contrast, Katie observes, "Ultimately [a centered approach] is about trusting God. Everyone's journey is going to be different. That does not mean hands off, 'God's got this.'"[17] Rather, from a place of trust in God we can actively engage in discipleship free of the uptightness that comes from feeling it all depends on us.

Although the agitators in Galatia likely spoke of the Holy Spirit, the reality is that their bounded approach pulled them toward trusting in rules. They likely critiqued Paul for not providing the Galatians with enough ethical guidance—enough rules. In Paul's letter he did list some behaviors as inappropriate and praise others. But rather than imposing a static list of comprehensive rules, Paul placed his confidence in the Holy Spirit. Using centered directional language, he writes, "Since we live by the Spirit, let us keep in step with the Spirit" (Gal 5:25). Eberhard Arnold observed that without

---

[16]I am indebted to Bill Braun for the connection between uptightness and boundedness, email, June 15, 2020.

[17]Katie Double, focus group discussion, The Meeting House, Oakville, Ontario, January 21, 2018.

emphasis on and openness to the Holy Spirit's role, Christians will tend to replace Jesus Christ with a hardened rule.[18]

HUMILITY

In response to complaints about churches' line-drawing judgmentalism, we might say, "Our church is different. We are not like that." That may be fully accurate. A centered church is different from a bounded one. Yet for someone deeply wounded by a bounded church, those words of reassurance will not be enough—and understandably so. Nor will non-Christians turned off by self-righteous judgmentalism be so easily reassured—and understandably so.[19] Those wounded by bounded approaches must hear more than our defensive words. They must experience our love and the qualities mentioned in this chapter—perhaps especially humility. We cannot ignore the importance of humility, particularly when we interact with those who have been wounded or turned off by bounded Christianity. We can lessen their defensive wariness through the humility of confessing and apologizing.

Picture a college ministry setting up a confession booth in the midst of a university festival that is notorious for its drunken behavior and debauchery. What do those passing by imagine? Now envision the surprise of those who actually step into the booth and discover that the Christian in the booth is not judgmentally accusing people, but apologizing for the ways that the church has hurt others and confessing the ways that he has personally failed to live out what he believed. Donald Miller, who was one of the apologizing Christian students in the booth, writes, "Many people wanted to hug when we were done. All of the people who visited the booth were grateful and gracious." Miller reports changed attitudes among the non-Christians who heard the confessions as well as the confessing Christians.[20] When we apologize and confess to others, we communicate that we do not think we are

---

[18]In Charles Marsh, *Strange Glory: A Life of Dietrich Bonhoeffer* (New York: Knopf, 2014), 411.

[19]This is a growing population. Philip Yancey begins his book *Vanishing Grace* with these alarming statistics: "In 1996, 85 percent of Americans who had no religious commitment still viewed Christianity favorably. Thirteen years later, in 2009, only 16 percent of young 'outsiders' had a favorable impression of Christianity, and just 3 percent had a good impression of evangelicals." Philip Yancey, *Vanishing Grace: What Ever Happened to the Good News?* (Grand Rapids, MI: Zondervan, 2014), 15.

[20]Donald Miller, *Blue Like Jazz: Nonreligious Thoughts on Christian Spirituality* (Nashville: Thomas Nelson, 2003), 117-25.

superior, while we also communicate that there are standards by which we are seeking to live.

Craig Detweiler tells a similar story about being at the Sundance Film Festival with his communications students.[21] One film, a scathing satire of American evangelicals, drew a standing ovation. Jay Floyd, the filmmaker, had grown up in a bounded church in North Carolina. As a gay man, Floyd clearly felt condemned by the church of his youth. Detweiler recounts, "While the filmgoers celebrated this assault on the religious right, I shed a tear, depressed and convicted by the depiction of Christians as judgmental and vindictive." After the showing, Floyd took questions from the audience. Someone asked if any conservative Christians had seen it. His reply, "I'm ready for that fight," prompted more applause. Detweiler felt the Spirit moving him to say something. He stayed seated. Soon the moderator said there was time for two more questions, and Detweiler found himself standing up. He recalls,

> I struggled to compose my words. My voice cracked slightly. I eked out, "Jay, thank you for this film. As a native of North Carolina, a fellow filmmaker, and an evangelical Christian. . . ."
>
> I never use the word evangelical. It is so loaded with negative baggage that I usually attempt to distance myself from such associations. But in this instance, it seemed quite right. I was speaking for my community, responding to a particular stance we'd staked out for ourselves. Jay stepped back, ready for that fight. He tensed up, preparing to launch a counterattack. The crowd sensed that things were about to get ugly. My next words caught them off guard: "Jay, I apologize for anything ever done to you in the name of God."
>
> The entire tenor in the room shifted. Audience members turned around. "Did I hear that correctly?" They craned their necks. "Who said that?" Jay fumbled for words, not knowing how to respond. He was ready to be attacked. He was not prepared for an apology. He offered a modest, "Thank you." The audience was literally disarmed. It had instantly transformed from a lynch mob to a love fest. The Holy Spirit swooped in, surprising us all. The moderator concluded the conversation. Audience members approached me afterward with hugs. A lesbian couple thanked me. Gay men kissed me. One person said, "If that is true, I might consider giving

---

[21]What follows is from Craig Detweiler, *A Purple State of Mind: Finding Middle Ground in a Divided Culture* (Eugene, OR: Harvest House, 2008), 133-34.

Christianity another chance." Tears were shed far and wide. All it took were two little words: "I apologize."

Two little words, yes, but offered with a spirit of humility, they were deeply significant. A centered church will benefit from the type of humility displayed in these two stories and will need humility in other ways as well. It will need the humility of an individual leader turning to a team and saying, "Help me discern, what is the most loving thing to do in this situation?" And it will also need corporate humility. Rather than exuding a sense of "We've got this," a centered church will humbly recognize its need to rely on the Holy Spirit for guidance time after time.

As we seek to live out the centered approach let us put as much emphasis on character development as we do on language (the previous chapter) and strategies and methods (the chapters to come). May we be open to God's Spirit working within us to increase our humility, compassion, trust, curiosity, vulnerability, creativity, and a sense of safety within our churches so that the centered character of our churches may grow and yield much fruit.

Progressing toward the center includes lessening behavior that is counter to the way of Jesus and growing in behavior in line with the way of Jesus. A centered church does not leave people on their own but intervenes to aid in their progress. The next two chapters explore appropriate ways to lovingly intervene.

8

CENTERED INTERVENTION

IMAGINING POSSIBILITIES

As I HAVE MENTIONED EARLIER, when I was in my midtwenties, I lived near Syracuse University. Finding places to park at the university was difficult or expensive, so I often rode my bicycle to ministry events and to visit students. I never wore a helmet—I did not even own one. Then my friend Jim McCauley visited and confronted me directly, "Mark, wear a helmet! You are getting married soon. Be more careful." His exhortation surprised me, and at first I felt shame, but mostly I felt loved. I have used a bike helmet ever since. Jim intervened in an area where he discerned that I needed reorientation. It was not the first time he had intervened in my life.

We had first met in college while working together on campus mopping floors. The very first night I met him, he intervened by inviting me to pray with him and the other members of the wax crew during our break. He later persuaded me to join him in a ministry and encouraged me to take a course on youth ministry. He invited me to a Bible study group where participants regularly challenged and encouraged each other along the path of discipleship. Moments of intervention became mutual as we grew in friendship and love, speaking into all areas of one another's life, from romance to finances—and bike helmets. If Jim and I were college students today instead of in the late 1970s, would we still challenge and exhort each other with the same depth and frequency? Perhaps, but most likely not. Today is an era of moral relativism, where tolerance is seen as the supreme virtue. As the following three snapshots of contemporary Christian college students demonstrate, this fuzziness has seeped into many Christians.

Thomas Bergler, a professor of ministry and mission at a Christian college, stood at the whiteboard and invited his students to list "some traits of spiritual maturity." After the students sat silently, he prodded them again. Finally, they said things like, "Nobody is perfect" or "To make a list like that would be . . . judgmental."[1]

At a different Christian college, John D. Roth's history students read a book about German women who were reflecting on their experience during World War II. One woman, who had worked in a concentration camp, sought to help readers understand how she could have done what she did. Roth asked the class, "What did you think of the choices the woman made who served as a guard in a concentration camp?" None of the students critiqued her. After Roth asked some probing questions, a student replied, "She was in a tough situation. She faced lots of pressures that led her to serve in that capacity." Another added, "She tried to be as kind and reasonable as she could within the constraints of her position." Roth said, "Yes, but was her decision to serve as a guard morally correct?" No one spoke. After several moments of awkward silence, Roth challenged them, "Are there not things that are wrong and society needs to say they are wrong?"[2]

When I asked a recent college graduate about his future plans, he spoke of his hopes to work with a Christian organization and focus on issues related to negative practices of masculinity. He energetically described an alternative masculinity, passionately pointing out faults in common conceptions. But when I said, "So you are working for transformation, to change people," he adamantly said "no." The words *transformation* or *change* were fine when applied to paradigms, but when applied to individuals, they were radioactive. He would not get close to them. Tolerance is so often the supreme virtue, trumping all others. Students do not want to be seen as judgmental, and so they avoid saying anything critical about others.

---

[1] Thomas Bergler, interviewed by Ken Myers on *Mars Hill Audio Journal*, vol. 115, March 18, 2014.
[2] The book was Alison Owings, *Frauen: German Women Recall the Third Reich* (New Brunswick, NJ: Rutgers University Press, 1993). Email from Laura Goerzen to the author, May 29, 2019.

A key driving force today is to avoid making someone else feel bad. True, in a time of such heightened polarization, many are quick to pour out negative words about positions and movements or rant against others on social media, but most hesitate to critique the person sitting next to them. At that level, tolerance is still practiced as the supreme virtue. While there are certainly times and places when tolerance is necessary, is it really the supreme virtue? It is not emphasized in the Bible, which instead speaks of virtues closely related to tolerance, such as humility, graciousness, kindness, nonviolence, and love of enemies. Whereas those who emphasize tolerance assume that the way to forming good relationships is to avoid disagreements or calling someone else's view into question, the Bible emphasizes how we treat other people.

Can you feel the lukewarmness in tolerance? Do we really want our friends to tolerate us? Tolerance is certainly better than judgmental accusations that belittle and shame us, but it falls short of full love. Paul's letter to the Ephesians calls us to speak truthfully to each other (Eph 4:25). Of course, that literally means that we should not lie to each other, but when we remain silent about ways that someone might be hurting themselves or others, we are not speaking truthfully. A fuzzy approach endorses silence. A centered approach practices loving confrontation when necessary.

A few years ago, it pleased me to see one of my colleagues, Chris, commuting by bicycle, but I was concerned that he was not wearing a helmet. Thinking back to the way Jim lovingly confronted me, I later sought Chris out. I praised him for commuting by bike, and I also encouraged him to wear a helmet. A week later, I invited a group of millennial Christians, including Chris, to our home to help me think about how to lead people from a fuzzy approach toward a centered approach. To my surprise, they were not much help because they themselves were fuzzy. In response to my various questions, they expressed discomfort with the notion of communicating to others that they needed to change. Chris, sensing my frustration and confusion, stayed as the others left. He said, "Mark, I did not say much tonight, but I think you are right. Don't let their comments discourage you. The reality is, none of them would have exhorted me to wear a helmet, and I am glad you did."

For people to progress toward the center we must directly address anything that impedes their progress. We must practice intervention not only because the paradigm demands it, but also because Scripture calls us to do so. Jesus tells the disciples, "If your brother or sister sins, go and point out their fault" (Mt 18:15). Paul exhorts the Galatians churches, "If someone is caught in a sin, you who live by the Spirit should restore that person gently" (Gal 6:1). Being quiet and tolerating everything is not an option for a centered church. But as soon as we mention intervention, let alone try to practice it, will the wounded and wary run away, assuming that we are a bounded church? How can we practice what Jesus and Paul call us to do while remaining an invitational and inclusive church community? How can we guide those who are averse to confronting others toward loving intervention?

We cannot jump directly into talking about how to confront others lovingly, which is the topic of the next chapter. If we are going to practice a centered approach today, we must first address the resistance that many people feel to speaking the truth in love. This chapter will explore how we can lower that resistance by leading people to differentiate between two types of confrontation—bounded, exclusive judgmentalism and centered, loving intervention.

SAME WORDS, DIFFERENT MEANINGS

I use the following exercise in classes and Bible studies to help people see how the same words can feel radically different, depending on the images and experiences that we connect with those words.

First, think of a time when someone confronted you in a way that scolded and belittled you. They did not just point out an error but attacked you as a person. Sit with this experience for a moment. What did it feel like?

With that experience in mind, read the following verse and picture it: "For the word of God is alive and active. Sharper than any double-edged sword, it penetrates even to dividing soul and spirit, joints and marrow; it judges the thoughts and attitudes of the heart" (Heb 4:12). How do you imagine the sword? How do you perceive the one who is holding the sword? What did you feel?

Now think of a time when someone confronted you by telling you that you were off-track, hurting yourself and others. They did not scold or attack you as a person but critiqued your action. Though the experience may have been uncomfortable, and you may have felt shame, deep down you felt that the person cared for you. Sit with this experience for a moment. What did it feel like?

With this experience in mind, read the verse again, picture it: "For the word of God is alive and active. Sharper than any double-edged sword, it penetrates even to dividing soul and spirit, joints and marrow; it judges the thoughts and attitudes of the heart" (Heb 4:12). How do you imagine the sword? How do you perceive the one who is holding the sword? What did it feel like?

Repeat this reflective exercise with the following verse: "Our 'God is a consuming fire'" (Heb 12:29). How do these same words produce different images and feelings when you interpret them through the lenses of the two different experiences?

When I do this exercise, people often say that through the lens of the first experience, as they read Hebrews 4:12 they envision being stabbed with a large sword—a thrust that is meant to penetrate in order to hurt and kill. They see the fire as a raging wildfire, destroying everything in its path, as they read the passage from Hebrews 12:29. In contrast, through the lens of the second experience, as they read Hebrews 4:12 they see the sword as a scalpel, carefully penetrating their body to cut out cancer. A surgeon's scalpel hurts, but the intent is to bring healing, and so we are grateful. As they read Hebrews 12:29, they see a fire that is contained and purposeful, one that has been kindled to burn away weeds or impurities.

Generally, I do this as a theological exercise, asking which perspective offers us a correct view of God. I encourage people to use Jesus as a lens for reading these texts as they seek to answer that question. As we observed in chapter three, the way we view God is of vital importance for a centered church. In this chapter, I use the exercise to illustrate that we cannot simply use the words *confrontation*, *correction*, *intervention*, or *discipline* without explaining what we mean. We might be thinking of careful cuts with a scalpel, whereas the person we are talking to is imagining a sword being plunged and twisted in their body.

Intervention in a bounded church often feels like a raging fire or twisting sword as shaming accusations are hurled down from those who are standing above others with self-righteous superiority. We must openly and explicitly reject such interventions. But as we do, let us also offer counter images of loving intervention, such as a purifying fire or a carefully wielded scalpel.

DISINTEGRATIVE SHAMING
VERSUS REINTEGRATIVE SHAMING

To further contrast these types of intervention, I will turn from imagery to sociological description. People do shameful things. To call the people out and shame them for their wrongful actions is one way a society seeks to reduce such inappropriate behavior.

Yet not all shaming is the same. In *Crime, Shame and Reintegration*, John Braithwaite contrasts "disintegrative shaming" with "reintegrative shaming." Disintegrative shaming focuses on making an example of guilty offenders and ensuring that they get what they deserve. Disintegrative shaming ultimately stigmatizes. Reintegrative shaming, on the other hand, acknowledges that the social bond has been damaged and draws attention to the shameful action, but its goal is to heal relationships and reintegrate the offender to the group. Grace Spencer observes that reintegrative shaming "strives to attach shame to the behavior, rather than the person, recognizing that some actions are shameful and inappropriate. This shaming is restorative and momentary—it is different from stigmatization. Stigmatization is . . . shaming the person rather than the behavior and treats the offender as an outcast."[3] A restorative approach focuses on addressing the relational obligations and fractures created by the wrongdoing, so as to promote a healthy community. Braithwaite states, "Shaming that is reintegrative . . . shames while maintaining bonds of respect or love."[4]

What does disintegrative shaming look like? I see it every week when I go to jail to lead a Bible study. One week, Roberto, a middle-aged inmate, filed into the Bible study with several other men. He looked downcast as he sat with slumped shoulders. I asked him what was wrong, and he said he had

---

[3]Grace Spencer, "Naked and Unashamed: Using Restorative Justice to Develop a Biblical Theology of Shame and Equip the Church for the Criminal Reentry Crisis" (master's thesis, Fresno Pacific Biblical Seminary, 2019), 52. Spencer borrows the idea of attaching shame to behavior from Christopher D. Marshall, *Compassionate Justice: An Interdisciplinary Dialogue with Two Gospel Parables on Law, Crime, and Restorative Justice* (Eugene, OR: Cascade Books, 2012), 231.
[4]John Braithwaite, *Crime, Shame and Reintegration* (Cambridge: Cambridge University Press, 1989), 12.

just returned from a court hearing. "The prosecutor read out the list of all my offenses over the years," he said. "I felt so much shame as all the people in the courtroom stared at me—probably thinking, *What a loser, an animal.*" Roberto acknowledged to us that he did a lot of bad stuff as a youth. "I was dumb then," he said, "but that is not who I am now." He had turned his life over to Jesus and had been out of trouble for a few years, but then his mother died, he got stressed, started using drugs again, and slipped up. None of this background was revealed in court. As he sat in court wearing clothes of shame, a red jumpsuit with the word *prisoner* stenciled on the back, he experienced disintegrative shaming. Much of the judicial process and the prison experience stigmatizes those who break social bonds, thereby practicing disintegrative shaming.

Looking at an alternative practice in the criminal justice system will help us understand and imagine the possibility of reintegrative shaming. Victim Offender Reconciliation Program (VORP) recognizes that when a crime takes place, interpersonal relationships between the victim, offender, and community are all injured. VORP practices restorative justice by seeking to heal what was broken.[5] "VORP allows offenders the opportunity to meet with their victims to apologize and make things as right as possible. The process involves first meeting with the offenders and their families to talk about how their actions affected those closest to them. Once they rebuild trust with their families, they meet with their victims to apologize and make things as right as possible."[6] The offenders still experience shame. To acknowledge their offenses to people who love them and to the victim will involve feelings of shame. But the process is not designed in order to shame and exclude the offenders. Rather, it is designed to release offenders from shame by acknowledging the shame and replacing it with dignity and the restoration of relationships. Take a moment and try to imagine yourself as Roberto sitting in that courtroom. Then imagine yourself as Roberto in a VORP mediation session. In what ways do these experiences feel different?

These categories do not only apply to the criminal justice system. Think back to our study of Luke 15 in chapter three. The Pharisees practiced disintegrative shaming. They sought to promote holy living through threatening

---

[5]Howard Zehr, *The Little Book of Restorative Justice* (New York: Good Books, 2014).
[6]Spencer, "Naked and Unashamed," 3.

exclusion.[7] They shamed and stigmatized those who crossed the lines. We feel this sense of shaming exclusion when they mutter, "This man welcomes sinners and eats with them" (Lk 15:2). In a centered church, we will need to avoid disintegrative shaming, but should we embrace reintegrative shaming—the approach if not the term itself? Let us look to Jesus to answer this question.

REINTEGRATION AFTER SHAMING:
JESUS AND THE CHURCH

Jesus spent much more time freeing people from shame than shaming them.[8] How could that be? If people did shameful things, why did Jesus free them from their shame? Was he being fuzzy? No, because much of the shame that people experience is inappropriate. At that time and still today, society has a skewed perspective about what is honorable and shameful. Even when the labeling of something as shameful is in line with God's perspective, the way people treat the person who is doing the shameful thing is often not in line with God's ways. Jesus repeatedly poured dignity into the souls of those who had been shriveled up in shame. He acted to counter the distorted definitions of honor and shame in his day and to counter the stigmatizing, disintegrative shaming of the Pharisees and other religious leaders. Therefore, in relation to shame, as we follow the way of Jesus in a centered church, our first call is to liberate people from inappropriate shame and to help heal their wounds from disintegrative shaming.

When people did things that were truly inappropriate, Jesus did occasionally shame them, but he did so in a reintegrative manner. We will reflect more on these cases, but it is important to note that often Jesus did not shame people even when they acted inappropriately. For example, rather than shame Zacchaeus, he shared a meal with him; rather than shame the woman caught in adultery, he protected her from further shame and did not speak words of condemnation. To people who were already experiencing shame and were aware that their actions were inappropriate, Jesus did not add to their shame. He felt no obligation to shame simply because an act was

---

[7]Mt 9:9-13; Lk 5:27-32; Lk 7:36-50; and Jn 8:2-11 offer other examples of the disintegrative shaming of the Pharisees and the reintegrative shaming of Jesus.

[8]For a fuller treatment of the topic of Jesus and shame, see the chapter on Jesus in Jayson Georges and Mark D. Baker, *Ministering in Honor-Shame Cultures: Biblical Foundations and Practical Essentials* (Downers Grove, IL: IVP Academic, 2016), 91-114.

shameful. Instead, he looked at the heart, the attitude of the person. Jesus responded to people who knew they were on the wrong path with forgiveness and a loving embrace. For their journey of transformation, these people did not need further shaming. Rather than reintegrative shaming, we might call this reintegration after shaming by others. Therefore, in following the way of Jesus, the loving intervention of a centered church will often involve healing restoration rather than shaming. It is easy to slip into shaming others, and so one of the most important things that a centered church can do is to be cautious and ask intentionally, "How might our intervention shame this person? How can we avoid shaming?"

In following Jesus, however, we must do more than try to avoid adding to a person's shame. Jesus also countered shame with loving acceptance by boldly absorbing the shame of others, willingly taking on their shame to protect them from further shame. In Luke 15, Jesus, just like the father in the parable of the lost sons, risks his reputation and suffers shame himself by standing in solidarity with the outcasts and telling three parables. Similarly, in Luke 7, Jesus defends and absorbs the shame of the forgiven woman in the house of Simon the Pharisee (vv. 36-50). She has already been stigmatized as a sinner in her village, and she adds to the scandal by washing Jesus' feet with her tears and letting down her hair.

> Before Jesus speaks up in her defense, all the eyes in the room are glued on the woman with shaming accusation. When Jesus begins to speak, he becomes the object of scandal, and the eyes of accusation shift to him. He takes the woman's shame upon himself. Because of Jesus's surprising defense, the woman leaves feeling more loved, more accepted, and more graced than before. Jesus's actions are a "costly demonstration of unexpected love."[9] Jesus loved the woman so much that he was willing to suffer her shame in order to save her from being shamed. This story is a precursor of the costly demonstration of unexpected love at the cross.[10]

Therefore, in centered churches, rather than pushing people away by shaming them, let us invite people in like Jesus, taking on their shame, absorbing it, making it ours. What might this look like?

---

[9]Kenneth E. Bailey, *Jesus Through Middle Eastern Eyes: Cultural Studies in the Gospels* (Downers Grove, IL: IVP Academic, 2008), 257.
[10]Georges and Baker, *Ministering in Honor-Shame Cultures*, 101.

In Moldova, prostituted women are one of the most shamed groups in society. Many Moldovans look at them with scorn the way that Simon the Pharisee scorns the woman who comes to his house as a "sinner." One woman who experienced sexual exploitation in Moldova got pregnant. Rather than shaming her like Simon, a church-based outreach team invited her into their community. They offered her holistic support and even hosted a baby shower for her. They arranged work for her at the church so she could come off the street, and they continued to walk with her after her baby's birth. They not only sheltered her physically, but they also sheltered her from shame. The reintegrating love offered by this local, Moldovan church was likely viewed by other believers as a shameful promotion of her situation. Like Christ, the church quite literally took on this woman's shame.[11]

The Moldovan woman was cloaked in shame before the pregnancy, but for many Christians, it is the pregnancy itself that clothes the woman in shame. Unfortunately, many bounded churches respond to pregnancies outside of marriage with disintegrative shaming. Even now, decades later, I can still picture two unwed teenagers standing in front of my church, speaking words of confession about the young woman's pregnancy, their bodies weighted down with shame. These youth were bound to their behavior through shameful exclusion. A woman in this situation cannot hide her pregnancy. She will feel shame, but how can churches follow Jesus by working toward reintegration after the shame rather than adding to her shame with practices of disintegrative shaming?

Robert Brenneman shares how he saw a Guatemalan pastor transform a potentially disintegrative situation into a reintegrative one.[12] The church includes middle-class families in Guatemala City as well as lower class families from marginal neighborhoods. Leticia, a young woman on the lower end of the economic and class spectrum, was actively involved in the church. When she became pregnant before getting married, her family was devastated. Brenneman did not know the details of Leticia's personal conversations with the pastor, but he witnessed how the pastor, Ricardo, responded publicly.

---

[11]Story shared by Sherri Nozik, focus group discussion of an early draft of *Centered-Set Church*, October 24, 2019.

[12]What follows is from Georges and Baker, *Ministering in Honor-Shame Cultures*, 234-35. The names used are not actual.

Near the end of a Sunday morning service, he called Leticia to the front of the church, put his arm around her, and told the congregation that she was pregnant and unmarried. He said that he had invited the father to come and be with Leticia that day, but he was not interested. Then Ricardo said, "Well, what are we going to do? How do we respond to this situation?" The response was immediate. Members from the church, including those from a higher social class, started calling out, "We are going to support her! Yes! We are not going to gossip! Yes!" Leticia continued attending the church, and as she started showing signs of pregnancy, there was nothing to gossip about because everyone already knew. When the baby arrived, the church took up a collection and bought a new stroller that was far nicer than one that Leticia or the father could have afforded. The baby got lots of attention and love as he grew up.

Although directly addressing the issue in such a public way may not be appropriate in all cultural contexts, this was a public issue because the pregnancy would become visible to all. Praising the wisdom and skill of the pastor, Brenneman says,

> He allowed the church to continue to say a firm "No" to extra-marital sexuality without permanently shaming the person and in fact giving the congregation the possibility for consistently supporting life. Obviously, it also cut short the possibilities for gossip—which is essentially a powerful form of social control exercised by those who believe that the more formal or institutional forms of control are not working.[13]

While Pastor Ricardo's intentionality was crucial in making this a reintegrative experience, he could not have done it alone. The church already had a centered character. A bounded church would have likely responded to his question differently. It was not in the character of this church to shame in disintegrative ways. It is not, however, just what they did not do, but what they did. They took action to communicate the woman's place in the community, and they made it clear that they were not ashamed to have her in their midst. They absorbed her shame and refused to let shame be the end of the story.

Yet, as mentioned above, Jesus does occasionally shame people, but most often they are people who shamed others in disintegrative ways. What might

---

[13] Robert Brenneman, email to the author, May 28, 2015.

this mean for a centered church? And note, that even in these cases, Jesus practices reintegrative shaming. Again, returning to Luke 15, Jesus exposes the hypocrisy of the Pharisees in his portrayal of the older son in the parable. The Pharisees are not as holy and sinless as they would like to think. While Jesus does shame the Pharisees, he does it through story, and so it is less caustic. More importantly, Jesus' intent is to bring the Pharisees to the table, too. He is not seeking to exclude, but to restore relationships, to include everyone. In the technical sense, he is practicing "reintegrative shaming," but it may be better to not even use the word *shaming* because of how closely this verb is associated with bounded churches and disintegrative practices. Thus *expose* may be a better term. Jesus brings the hypocrisy of the Pharisees into the light.

In order to be centered rather than fuzzy, we may occasionally need to practice reintegrative exposing. The early church did. Consider three examples. First, in 2 Corinthians, Paul counsels the believers against what we could call disintegrative shaming, proposing instead an approach that has a restorative intent. Eugene Peterson captures this intent well:

> Now, regarding the one who started all this—the person in question who caused all this pain—I want you to know that I am not the one injured in this as much as, with a few exceptions, all of you. So I don't want to come down too hard. What the majority of you agreed to as punishment is punishment enough. Now is the time to forgive this man and help him back on his feet. If all you do is pour on the guilt, you could very well drown him in it. My counsel now is to pour on the love. (2 Cor 2:5-8 *The Message*)

Second, in 2 Thessalonians, Paul explicitly uses the language of shaming, but he also clearly warns against a bounded and disintegrative approach: "Take special note of anyone who does not obey our instruction in this letter. Do not associate with them, in order that they may feel ashamed. Yet do not regard them as an enemy, but warn them as you would a fellow believer" (2 Thess 3:14-15).

Third, in Luke's account in Acts, Priscilla and Aquila observe that Apollos speaks boldly about Jesus, but his teachings are not fully in line with the way of the Lord. In their observations, they practice neither tolerant "what-everism" nor public correction in order to elevate their status and shame

Apollos. Instead, "They invited him to their home and explained to him the way of God more adequately" (Acts 18:26). Their response is an example of reintegrative exposure, where their intent is to shine light on a situation that needs to be revealed rather than to exclude or shame.

Scott Carolan reflects on his pastoral work with people who have in some way stepped out of alignment with Jesus, observing that "most often they already feel guilt and shame. They say, 'I am ashamed of my actions.' But at times I have been with people who have done something that has damaged relationships or hurt others and they show no signs of shame. In those situations I seek to expose it in our conversation because the person will not be truly restored and pointed anew toward Jesus unless they acknowledge it."[14]

Social scientists can help us distinguish disintegrative shaming from reintegrative shaming, which clarifies what we must avoid and challenges us toward a reintegrative intent. Yet when we look at Jesus, we see that we are called to do much more than round off the sharp edges of the shaming ways of bounded churches. As the body of Christ today, let us do what Jesus did: liberate people from inappropriate shame and heal them from the wounds of disintegrative shaming. In situations where people have truly done shameful things, we need to discern if they already feel guilt and shame. If so, we are not called to add to it, but rather to work toward reintegration. If not, we are called to practice reintegrative exposure. Let us be radically different from bounded, shaming approaches so that people will no longer fear exposure. As Dan Serdahl observes, "I would have stepped into the light much quicker if I knew a community would respond like Jesus."[15] Let us practice reintegrative exposing like Jesus.

CHURCH DISCIPLINE

The previous section overlaps in several ways with what many would describe as church discipline, but it is broader than that. In this short section, I will make a few comments that are specifically related to church discipline defined as a formalized process of corrective intervention. First, we must leave behind any church discipline that practices disintegrative shaming. We might even leave behind the term *church discipline* itself, but a centered

---

[14]Scott Carolan, focus group discussion of an early draft of *Centered-Set Church*, October 24, 2019.
[15]Dan Serdahl, focus group discussion of an early draft of *Centered-Set Church*, October 24, 2019.

church cannot reject the practice of intervening for correction, which may sometimes include the possibility of excluding a person from the community. Generally, in centered churches, those who are not in relationship with the center will self-exclude. Recall, however, the analogy of a centered pickup soccer game in chapter two. There comes a time when the group must tell the player who keeps grabbing the ball with his hands, "If you are not willing to abide by the rules, you cannot play." The group excludes the person not only because he is showing that he is not centered on soccer, but also because he is disrupting the game for all.

Centered churches must not only practice church discipline, but they are also better able to practice it. As Stuart Murray in *Church After Christendom* argues, fuzzy churches are unable to practice church discipline at all, and bounded churches are so inflexible that they practice it very poorly.

> Centered-set churches are, contrary to what many assume, more suited to this process than others. They have deeply owned core values that shape the community. They are relationally oriented and less likely to apply the process legalistically. They are better able *both* to preserve the integrity of the community *and* to communicate acceptance of those struggling to follow Jesus. They are less concerned about what stage people have reached on their spiritual journey than about the direction in which they are traveling.[16]

The flexibility that Murray describes is possible because a centered church does not prioritize the line itself, but individuals and the community as a whole. Returning to our soccer analogy, a centered soccer group might include someone who disagrees with the established rules as long as she does not disrupt the game. The centered group can allow for some flexibility in one's opinion about the rules. The hope would be that, with time, the player will learn not only to play by the rules, but also to affirm them. We saw this with Weldon Nisly in chapter three. He was quite open to welcoming people who disagreed with the church's Christian pacifist position to participate in the congregation. He did not say, "Unless you believe like us, you can't be here." Rather, he said, "I will walk with you along that journey. If you find that you genuinely cannot accept Jesus as we understand him, I

---

[16]Stuart Murray, *Church After Christendom* (Milton Keynes, UK: Paternoster, 2004), 184. Italics in the original.

will help you find a different church." He did not patrol the boundary, but he did protect the church. He said, "What we can't have is people trying to undermine our position."[17] When someone seeks to undermine a core value of a centered church, the community must take action to protect the identity of the church. At other times, such as in cases of spousal abuse, disciplinary action must be taken to protect the victim.

THE WORDS WE USE

This chapter has used the words *confrontation, correction, intervention,* and *discipline* but I fear that those who are steeped in tolerance as the supreme virtue will hear the word *confrontation* as harsh, and they will only be able to imagine it as a sword rather than a scalpel. Also, we tend to apply *confrontation* to situations of correction, but helping others to live more fully as the person God created them to be will include both correction (to decrease negative habits and practices) and encouragement and affirmation (to increase positive behavior). The word *intervention* can refer to confronting sin in someone's life and also refer to affirming someone or calling them to the next step in their journey toward the center. Thus I will use the term *intervention* throughout the rest of the book.

In the next chapter, we turn to specific examples of how centered churches seek to practice loving intervention.

---

[17]Weldon Nisly, interview by author, February 15, 2018.

9

PRACTICING CENTERED INTERVENTION

DUSTIN, WHOSE STORY APPEARED in chapter one, looks back on his fuzzy-church experience and wishes that those journeying with him had intervened more. He recalls, "I was living in an apartment with four beer pong tables scattered about. No one from church asked me, 'Are you thriving?' or said to me, 'You would be better off in a different living situation.' More direction from others would have saved me from significant grief, pain, and confusion."[1] Out of love for others, there are times when we must intervene. Yet in bounded churches, intervention often causes significant pain. Out of love, then, we must avoid shaming judgmentalism when we do intervene. Is this even possible?

It is. I have recently witnessed loving, centered intervention at the seminary where I teach. Before students graduate, they meet with a discernment group whose members they select: two professors, two fellow students, a pastor or ministry supervisor, a family member, and a couple of friends. Students write a short paper describing their strengths and weaknesses, how they have grown in seminary, and any areas that need attention. They also reflect on their vocation and list questions that they would like to discern with the group. After reading the paper, the group meets and affirms, challenges, discerns, and prays for the student.

---

[1] Dustin Maddox, focus group discussion of an early draft of *Centered-Set Church*, October 24, 2019.

In one discernment group, the participants first poured words of affirmation onto the student and then exhorted her, highlighting some ways that she could grow. About halfway through the ninety-minute session, a participant went much deeper and directly challenged the student about her racial prejudice. It was an intense moment, perhaps the most intense I have experienced in the dozens of discernment meetings in which I have participated. In this student's post-meeting reflection, she wrote, "At first, I felt embarrassed, but the response of the group encouraged me to lean in and face reality. Their response was free of judgment and full of grace."[2] How was that done? How can a group confront someone in such a strong way without judgmentalism? That is one of the things we will now explore through looking at numerous examples of interventions. Before continuing, I invite you to take a moment and pray that the Spirit may use these examples and insights to stimulate your imagination for possibilities in your own setting.

PRIORITIZE PEOPLE RATHER THAN RULES

A centered church does not disregard behavior or belief, but the priority is the person and his or her progress toward the center. A bounded church must pronounce and enforce rules, which can lead to harsh and abrupt interventions. A centered approach does not have the same pressure to focus on the rule and react as if the rule is the priority. This is reflected in the following experience described by Jason Phelps, who is involved in a church plant. One evening, the church had a Labor Day gathering at a member's home. Toward the end of the party, Jason was standing in the backyard with a few people from his church and three other friends—John, Rob, and Chad—from another church. As they were talking, John asked, "Hey, is it cool if I smoke?" Jason said he could, and then John and Rob both lit up and the conversation continued. As Jason recounts,

> A couple hours later we had cleaned up and were hanging out and talking. Then Chad lit up a cigarette. I felt blessed he felt comfortable to smoke with us. Our conversations continued to get deeper as the night grew later.
>
> Chad said, "You know . . . I never smoke around my church. I don't want it to ruin my witness—cause it's taboo. But tonight I was watching you, when

---

[2]Name withheld, discernment follow-up report, Fresno Pacific Biblical Seminary.

your family and kids came out around John and Rob while they were smoking. And nothing! I observed a peace about the situation in you. As if it was just reality, not a concern. Because of that I felt like I could smoke. I felt like I could truly be myself without any masks."

After his comment about the freedom to smoke, we got into a deeper conversation about smoking. We discussed the hypocrisy and inaccuracy of his experience of the church's stance on smoking. The trust he gave to us allowed us to ask other questions about smoking. He confessed he didn't want to smoke cigarettes the rest of his life, which allowed deeper questions about why he does it now, how they help him, or don't help him, connect with Jesus. Our discussion ended talking about the negative effects of needing something (anything) to have a good life other than Jesus. The great thing about the conversation was that he did most of the talking. I didn't need to lecture—just ask questions and listen.[3]

A bounded church promotes change by threatening exclusion. People do not necessarily comply out of understanding and conviction but to avoid shame. Jesus confronted the Pharisees about this very thing—an external behavior modification that does not involve any internal transformation. A centered church does not simply pronounce rules but explains, as we see in the following example from the Honduran church with whom I studied Galatians.

Pressured by a friend to drink beer, a teenage member of the church asked Mario Cantor, the pastor, if it was a sin to drink. Mario responded that he could not really say that drinking was a sin, but he could give a number of reasons why it would be better for this teenager not to drink. Mario talked about his experience as an alcoholic and all the suffering that it had brought to his family. He shared how his alcoholism had started by drinking beer with friends as a teenager. Mario asked the teenager to think about the places where people drink in their neighborhood, at parties or bars, and the fighting and violence that takes place in that environment. He also reflected with the teenager about the reasons people drink and how many drink as a way to escape problems at home or find release from emotional stress. Drinking does not bring a solution to these problems, but it does bring greater

---

[3]Jason Phelps, a post to the online forum of the "Discipleship and Ethics" course, Fresno Pacific Biblical Seminary, September 8, 2015 (used with Jason's permission; he changed the names of the people involved).

economic and emotional pressure. Mario helped the teenager move past the simple question of drinking as a sin, and this teenager does not drink today.

MAKE THINGS RIGHT

When bounded churches prioritize the rules, they focus on the line, which often leads to shaming punishment and alienation if not actual exclusion. As discussed in the previous chapter, a centered church responds to a shameful situation with the goal of restoring the person to relationship with Jesus, the center, and with the community. Borrowing a phrase from the Victim Offender Reconciliation Program (VORP), the goal is to make things right. In the example that follows, a centered approach that seeks to make things right produces results that are radically different from the shaming punishment of a bounded approach.

Grace Spencer served on the staff of a church in an impoverished neighborhood, which met in the cafeteria of a local elementary school.[4] One Sunday she saw many new backpacks that someone had donated to the school. After the church service she walked a group of girls home. While standing on their front lawn talking, she saw their brother, Gustavo, run inside their house with three backpacks—the same backpacks she had seen in the school cafeteria moments earlier. No one said anything, but as he closed the door, he yelled out, "An old lady gave them to me!"

Grace writes, "Moments like these feel pivotal." Before responding, she prayed. Then the following week, she invited Gustavo and several other students to her house. He was the only one who came; he needed help with his homework. He sat down and pulled a few things from his backpack. Grace reports their conversation,

> "Hey, Gustavo. I wanted you to come over to hang out, but I also wanted to talk to you about something. Do you know what I want to talk to you about?"
> He stopped writing and looked up. "You want to talk about the backpacks."
> "Yes. I want to talk about the backpacks. Why did you take them?"
> "Because. Because my cousins didn't have backpacks."
> "Gustavo, I love that you want to take care of your family. You are a problem solver—you see a problem, and you fix it. But, there has to be a way for you

---

[4]Grace Spencer reported this story in an email newsletter (September 14, 2016). The following quotes are from that newsletter. Name has been changed.

to fix problems without getting in trouble. Next time, let me know and we can work something out." He looked down, avoiding eye contact. I said, "You know you have to make this right."

"Can we fill the backpacks up with stuff and give them to homeless people at the park?!"

I tried not to smile. "That is a good idea, but it doesn't quite address who you hurt in this situation. It would be like if you hit your cousin and baked your sister a cake to make it right."

He started chewing on the handle of his backpack. "Grace, I can't. No. I don't want to get in trouble."

"You can. I know you can. And I promise it will be better than you think."

Grace suggested that they go to the principal. Gustavo literally dragged his feet as they walked to the school. He whined and groaned and listed all the punishments he could receive, but he continued to head toward the school with Grace. Unfortunately, the principal was not there, and the vice principal was in a meeting. Disappointed, Grace thought she had missed the opportunity. She doubted Gustavo would agree to try the next day. She recalls,

Gustavo interrupted my disappointment. "Grace, can we go to Target to buy school supplies to put in the backpacks?"

"Yes. Yes, we can! But, how will you pay me back for the school supplies?"

"I will volunteer ten times at Sunday church," he said, lifting his chest to the sky.

"Ten times? I would have settled for five."

"No. Ten times."

After picking out school supplies, Gustavo insisted that we check to see if the vice principal was out of his meeting. He was. He directed us to his office; his facial expression revealed that he was very confused by what was happening.

Gustavo fumbled with his words. "I—I, um. I need to tell you something." He looked at me, and I gave him a nod of confidence. "I stole three backpacks from the cafeteria—the ones that were donated. I wanted to say I'm sorry. We have the backpacks and we filled them with school supplies."

An awkward silence filled the room as the vice principal searched for words.

"Gustavo, tell the vice principal how you will pay me back for the school supplies."

"I am going to volunteer ten times at Sunday church."

"Well," the VP chimed in. "I appreciate that you made the effort to apologize and bring the backpacks back. But, that doesn't make this right. Stealing is wrong; normally we suspend kids who steal. Why did you steal them in the first place?

"Because my cousins didn't have backpacks."

The VP nodded. I silently prayed, "Oh, please don't suspend him. Please. Please. Please."

"Is there anything else I can do to make it right?" Gustavo asked.

"Um. Just keep improving in school. Your teacher said she is very impressed with you this year. Of course, I will have to tell your mom and the principal."

Gustavo agreed to keep up the good work.

After the meeting Grace drove around the neighborhood, looking for people who could praise Gustavo for what he did. As he shared the story, something beautiful happened. His demeanor changed as self-confidence took root in his soul. It wasn't pride—he had set aside the assuming and boisterous persona he normally carries. Grace reflected, "It's like he believed in himself and discovered a sense of self-worth. It was a moment of release— a light in him that was buried deep beneath insecurity and shame rose to the surface. By journeying with people toward reconciliation, I have learned that even the most despairing systems cannot separate us from the love of God."

We see through Grace's final actions that centered, loving intervention goes beyond an infraction-punishment approach—not just by seeking to make right the wrong that was done, but also seeking the restoration and reintegration of the person who did something wrong.

DISCERN DIFFERENT APPROACHES

A situation that came up repeatedly in my conversations with ministry leaders was how to respond to two people who are living together before marriage. A home group leader, "Steve," asked himself this question when a woman from his group started living with her boyfriend, who was also a Christian but attended a different church. The woman knew that what she was doing was out of line, and she hid—pulled back from the group. Steve discerned with other leaders and thought that it would be best for some people from the group whom she trusted to take initiative and address the situation directly. Steve recalls,

I did not say, "I have observed this. It is wrong. We need to talk." Rather, I said, "Hey, I care about you. I am wondering how this is going. I want to see you thrive in this relationship. Can we talk?" When we did talk, I did not start by pronouncing judgment. I said, "I want to understand your perspective."

She said, "I know what I am doing is not ideal."

We did not tell her, "You are out." I think she was waiting for that. If she had not acknowledged struggle, it might have been different. But she did not need that.

Her huddle journeyed with her the whole way.[5] They took initiative—not just the leader. They gave relational support. None of which was about judgement. In time she came back to the group. The couple is engaged and not living together."[6]

I asked Steve if he always uses this same approach. He said "no" and told me that he recently confronted someone else. One eccentric member of the group is a follower of Jesus, but, in Steve's words, is "all over the map, open to every new thing—most recently smoking spirit plants." He kept pushing his new things on others in the group, saying, "Try this" or "Read this," which was bothering several people in the group. Steve had a close relationship with this person and first affirmed him, saying, "I know you are in love with Jesus," and then he challenged him directly, saying, "You are disrupting the flock." Steve agreed to read some of his literature, and then Steve and two others from the group met with him. They said, "This behavior is inconsistent with where we are trying to go." They did not communicate that he was out or tell him that he could not be part of the group anymore. Steve reports, "He responded well. He didn't like it but agreed to back off. He has changed his behavior, and in fact my relationship with him is stronger."

Note the difference in Steve's approach for these two situations. Rather than focusing on the action, Steve focused on the person. This calls for discernment. Scott Carolan, an executive pastor of ministry, says that before any intervention, he has a conversation with other church staff or lay leaders. He asks, "Help me think through this, how do we handle this

---

[5]As described in chapter six, The Meeting House, a large church, has home church groups that meet weekly. Within the home church are smaller groups of three or four, which they call "huddles."

[6]Name withheld, interview by the author, January 22, 2018.

in a centered way?" A key question they ask is, "What is most loving for this person?"[7]

If, like me, you have experienced a bounded church, then when you read a sentence like the previous one you may assume that church leaders have meetings like that to discuss actions and beliefs that land someone on the wrong side of the line. Although these meetings certainly include such issues, we must not limit ourselves to seeing the use of Scott's question to things a bounded church would consider "wrong." A centered approach is not focused on a line but on movement toward the center. Therefore, centered-church leaders will seek input from others on how best to help someone in their discipleship walk on a whole range of things including calling them to positive actions. The interventions will not be limited to a list of "inappropriate behaviors." An experience I had in a Bible study I co-led displays both the benefit of seeking the input of others and the broader range of intervention in a centered approach.

People in the group were sharing ways the biblical text, and our discussion of it, challenged them—how they felt God was calling them to reorient. Positive energy of a centered journey pervaded the conversation, but one person's comment, weighted down with boundedness and language of religiosity, contrasted the rest. It was filled with phrases like "I know I fall short" and "I ought to do better at. . . ." I felt sadness for the person but said nothing. The co-leader of the group intentionally gave a counterexample that he hoped would dilute the person's boundedness.

I thought about it for the rest of the week. Did the person make the connection between what he had said and what my co-leader had said? Perhaps, but I doubted it. How could we bring more freedom from bounded religiosity into this person's life? I called my co-leader. I asked, "What could we have said that would be more direct? What might we do next time?" My co-leader observed that perhaps it would be better to talk about it one-on-one. I observed, "Yes, alone you could say, 'It saddened me when you said. . . .'" It would be harder to say that in a group setting. The person would likely experience any type of correction we offered of their comment in the group through the filter of their boundedness. We could end up leaving

---

[7]Scott Carolan, interview by the author, April 2, 2018.

them feeling called out in a bounded way and increase the weight they feel rather than bringing freedom. We could imagine, however, that in a one-on-one conversation the person might more readily sense our loving concern and not feel judged. Together the two of us came up with a better intervention plan than either one of us would have done alone.

Dan Serdahl walked away from church and lived, in his words, as "a happy pagan" for decades. Then he had an unexpected encounter with Jesus and has been inviting others to turn to Jesus ever since. After being involved in several different church plants, he is now the lead elder of Newlife, a multisite church in western Washington. In the following story Dan recounts how using a centered approach required discernment and enabled him to respond differently to three couples who were in the same situation.

Dan and his wife, Laurie, invited three other couples who did not know each other to read Luke's Gospel together. Dan and Laurie had been married for thirty years, and the other three couples were not married, but were living together, some with children. Dan recalls, "At least one member of each couple was hungry for community, friendship—and learning about Jesus. Others were skeptical—of religion, church, and Jesus—but there they were at the study each week."

Dan acknowledges that he and Laurie initially "felt a nagging impulse to simply tell all three couples to 'get married,' but we resisted that temptation." Instead, they read Luke together week after week for almost a year, learning about Jesus and each other.

Along the way Dan and Laurie began to meet with the couples individually, and stories emerged about their lives growing up, their family DNA, and how the couples had found each other. The stories often included heartbreaking divorce in their family tree. Dan and Laurie listened, empathized, laughed, and cried with the couples—and they all kept reading Luke together.

For one couple, exploring the way of Jesus was completely new; another couple had not yet begun to follow Jesus as Lord; one couple identified themselves as followers of Jesus. Dan says, "We noticed the trajectory of the two couples who were new to faith was increasingly aimed toward Jesus: a genuine curiosity and an appetite for learning about Jesus from Luke's Gospel." The third couple, who had been followers of Jesus for much of their lives, had both been divorced and were averse to the potential pain of another marriage that might end in divorce. Dan recounts, "Laurie and I discerned that they were in danger of slowly moving away from Jesus' bold and risky 'two-becoming-one' call."

In relation to being married, all three couples were the same, but regarding previous experience with the church's teaching on marriage and, especially, their trajectory toward Jesus, the couples were quite different. Therefore, Dan and Laurie responded differently to the couples. The couple who professed faith in Jesus was lovingly, gently, and privately confronted in a straightforward dialogue about the disconnect between their professed faith in following Jesus and their fear of divorce. With the other two couples, Dan and Laurie simply continued to be friends, enjoying each other's company, reading the Gospel of Luke, and praying together.

After some time, two members of this "Luke group" decided to follow Jesus and be baptized. All three couples—on their own, over time—decided to marry. Dan had the honor of officiating all three weddings.[8]

A bounded church would likely use the same blunt instrument with all three couples, an approach that would be easier and quicker. As this story displays, a centered approach can be messy and slow and may require a significant investment from leaders—but look at the fruit!

The following story is about the same type of situation that Dan Serdahl encountered. Yet here as well, rather than imposing a straightforward bounded approach, church leaders discerned how to respond to this particular situation. Dan Whitmarsh has been seeking to pastor in centered ways for over fifteen years, mostly as pastor of a small Evangelical Covenant church. He describes it as "a church of people from a wide variety of theological and political backgrounds who work hard at loving each other and the world in Jesus' name." A man from his congregation moved in with a single woman, who then also began attending the church. Dan acknowledges that he felt he was expected to confront them for their sinful behavior. He heard a voice from his bounded-church past saying, "Sinful behavior must be called out and dealt with in the church." Rather than following that voice, however, Dan consulted with others and they took a different approach. One key voice in the discernment process was an older man, who wisely said,

---

[8]Daniel Serdahl, email to author, February 4, 2020.

"There are probably forty issues in their lives that need attention. We do not have to single out this one. The main thing is to love them and trust the Holy Spirit to convict them at the right time." Then the other leaders invited this older man and his wife to offer to meet with the couple and form an ongoing relationship of discipleship, love, and support. This loving intervention went on for months, and through the guidance and encouragement of the older couple, the younger couple made a number of changes in their lives and eventually got married.[9]

A bounded approach focuses on the boundary line and the presenting issue. The centered paradigm creates space for a broader perspective and allows time for the journey. We are all on a journey, and no one has fully arrived. Therefore, we cannot demand immediate correction or complete alignment with the center after one intervention. Instead, we seek to help people take the next step. And before that, we ask, what is the next step? We ask that with humility acknowledging we need the guidance of the Holy Spirit as we together discern the answer to the question. We also ask questions about the next steps with anticipation, eager to see where God will begin the healing process and how it will continue. These are discipleship questions.

EXPLORE RATHER THAN PRONOUNCE

As the previous stories display, loving, centered intervention does not prioritize the pronouncement of rules but the exploration of stories. Questions are thus foundational to a centered approach. We ask questions to get beyond the surface issue to explore deeper issues. Questions also bring people into the process rather than imposing an intervention on them. When the right questions are asked in the right tone and with the right spirit, an intervention can feel more like a scalpel than a twisting sword. Following are some exploratory questions that ministry leaders have shared with me:

▸ Do you want something else?

▸ What feels heaviest in your life right now?

▸ What are you worried about the most?

▸ What needs are you trying to meet through this?

---

[9]Dan Whitmarsh, interview by author, July 29, 2017.

▶ In what ways is this working and not working?

▶ How do you think this decision or action will affect those closest to you? Spouse, family members, kids, friends, church community?

▶ How can you make this right?

▶ How can we navigate this? How can we work this out together?

Dan Whitmarsh often uses a question borrowed from spiritual direction, "Where is God working?"[10] Dan Serdahl uses a similar question, "Where would you like Jesus to heal you first?"[11] These trajectory questions focus on movement. A centered approach provides space for questions and gives the person responding the space to identify issues that may be different from the ones the question asker might indicate. Many of the Christlike qualities explored in chapter seven are present when we ask questions like these: there must be humility, curiosity, trust in God, and a sense of safety so that the person can respond honestly.

Jon Boyd frequently invites a person to discernment by asking, "Are you actually doing what you want to be doing?"[12] Scott Carolan asks, "Does this bring you closer to Jesus or further away from Jesus?" He uses this question in situations that a bounded church might simply confront as wrong, but he also uses it with things that are not commonly part of a bounded church's line, as when someone is considering buying a new house, or when he is responding to someone's social media or television habits.[13] Pam Yang has used a similar question with youth in her church. In seeking to help them move away from a bounded view of sins, she invites them to ask, How is this impacting my (covenantal) relationship with God? Is this act/thought causing a breach or harm to my relationship with God? Does it pull me closer or push me further from God? She reminds them of God's mercy and forgiveness and tells them that wherever the relationship got stuck, broken, or damaged, is where we can return to seek repair, reconciliation, and/or restoration with God.[14]

Kurt Willems, a church planter in Seattle, asked someone who was considering divorce, "Have you considered what it looks like to make this

---

[10]Dan Whitmarsh, interview by author, July 29, 2017.

[11]Dan Serdahl, focus group discussion of an early draft of *Centered-Set Church*, October 24, 2019.

[12]Jon Boyd, conversation with author, December 12, 2020.

[13]Scott Carolan, interview by the author, April 2, 2018.

[14]Pam Yang, email to author, September 20, 2020.

decision as a follower of Jesus?" The person answered "no," and then they had further conversation.[15]

Asking questions is a great way to begin a loving, centered intervention, and sometimes the best approach is to only ask questions. Dave Obwald, a care pastor at a large church, recalls a time when two leaders were walking with the same person. One leader started demonizing the other, criticizing his approach and praising his own. Dave asked him, "What led you to assume that he is not also lovingly accompanying the person?" As they conversed, Dave continued asking questions, "Do you have a tendency not to assume the best of others? Is your default to think negatively of them?" The man pondered these questions and acknowledged that his tendency was to be negative. Dave asked, "How do you think Jesus would have you respond differently in this moment?"[16]

Beliefs are a part of a church's center, so a centered church must respond when someone's beliefs do not cohere with the center. But it is best to do so in a way that invites further conversation. Consider the following questions to ask when someone's thoughts diverge from the center: How do you see that in Jesus? How do you see that in the Bible? Can you tell me more about that? I would love to converse more about your perspectives.

In a centered church, there is room for people to explore as they journey toward the center. Asking questions or inviting conversation, however, should not be mistaken for passivity. Matt Miles, a home group leader, observes that as he has continued to practice a centered approach, he has become less passive. When some people from his home group decided to leave the church because of a difference in biblical interpretation, Matt did not let them leave without exploring the topic together and having further conversation. In a fuzzy church, he would likely not press the issue or would just say, "It does not matter, we can have different perspectives." In a bounded church, he would see the issue as a line, and anyone who crossed it would be out. But Matt desired further conversation because he loved the people and did not want to see them leave the church, and he also cared deeply about his commitment to the church's

---

[15]Kurt Willems, interview by author, February 21, 2018.
[16]Dave Obwald, focus group discussion of an early draft of Centered-Set Church, October 24, 2019.

center. He longed for them to have the same life-giving experience with that center as he did.[17]

JESUS QUALITIES ENABLE LOVING INTERVENTION

Centered intervention is done from the perspective that ethics is a gift. A centered intervention must be rooted in and wrapped with love and must be seen as part of naming someone (chapter five). Loving interventions require the same essential characteristics of everything we do in a centered church: our humility, compassion, trust, curiosity, vulnerability, creativity, and a sense of safety. In addition, Paul exhorts us to intervene with gentleness (Gal 6:1). From those who practice restorative justice, we note the importance of recognizing that the person involved is more than just the action in question. Rather than trying to shame or stigmatize someone, a loving intervention intentionally seeks to avoid shame or stigmatization. Finally, drawing from both Scripture and the practice of restorative justice, the goal is restoration and reintegration. Jesus models all of these characteristics.

In this chapter, we have already seen the importance of these qualities in practicing effective interventions experienced as centered and loving. In the story of Jason Phelps's encounter with the smokers, reflect on how things could have gone much differently if Jason had not created a safe place or if he had not exhibited humility, trust, and curiosity. The importance of these qualities and other fruit of the Spirit are even more pronounced in *Way of Love*, as Norman Wirzba recounts how a group opted for reintegrative exposure when many would have, by default, practiced disintegrative shaming.[18]

The Lord's Acre is a community garden started by people from several churches in Fairview, North Carolina. It aims to provide fresh, organic produce to local food banks and much more. As people come together to work, eat, or simply enjoy the beauty of the garden, the Lord's Acre has

---

[17]Matt Miles, interview by the author at The Meeting House, Oakville, ON, January 22, 2018. The story became more complex because the people themselves responded in a bounded way. Although Matt and others said, "you do not have to leave over this," they felt they had to leave. For them the church was wrong on this issue, and they could not be part of a church like that.

[18]Norman Wirzba, *Way of Love: Recovering the Heart of Christianity* (New York: HarperOne, 2016), 62. See also Fred Bahnson and Norman Wirzba, *Making Peace with the Land: God's Call to Reconcile with Creation* (Downers Grove, IL: InterVarsity Press, 2012), 92-93. The story that follows is based on Wirzba, *Way of Love*, 62-64.

become a place where, in the words of garden manager Susan Sides, "diverse physiological, social, and spiritual hungers of people can be identified and addressed."

One year at the Lord's Acre, a dozen beautiful sweet melons were getting ripe, and then a few went missing. The staff wondered if an animal might be eating them at night. Then one morning, they were all gone. Garden interns discovered a large, pink cloth bag hanging on the shed with a bottle of beer and one melon. They left the bag and the beer, and the next morning, the bag was gone. Days later, in a grocery store, one worker saw the bag on "Emma's" shoulder. This person knew Emma and her struggles with illness, poverty, and isolation, and she assumed that hunger drove Emma to steal the melons.

Several weeks later, Emma came to the garden to get some of the free produce. "Wanting to understand her better Susan struck up a conversation. After a short while Emma admitted to stealing all the melons and other produce besides." Yes, she had taken some to eat, but she had also given some to others in need. Principally, however, she wanted something to give to her landlord because he was often angry. She saw it as a means of reconciliation—a peace offering.

> Susan was pleased to see a generous disposition in Emma. But it was clear that at some point further conversation about the equitable distribution of the garden's food needed to happen. As that day's conversation continued, it became plain to Susan that Emma was suffering and embarrassed by her own admission of guilt. What had been a calm conversation suddenly turned to rage on Emma's part as she screamed at Susan, trying to cover her shame with a torrent of hurtful and violent words. Susan listened to Emma's verbal abuse for an hour. Susan will tell you it was by the grace of God that she neither retaliated nor retreated. She simply sat with her, absorbing her painful outburst . . . [Emma] left the garden in a fury, vowing that the garden would never see her face again.

Months later Emma called Susan and apologized. Having read a flyer about the garden's purpose to feed the poor and hungry, she realized that her thievery was wrong, a violation of the work and needs of others. She apologized.

Susan asked if it would be okay for garden members to come to her home and build her a garden, one that included a melon patch. Overwhelmed with tears, Emma expressed how wonderful that would be. . . . Emma now comes to The Lord's Acre not to steal but to harvest beans for the local food pantry. . . . When she sees Susan, she often asks, "How did we get here from where we started?" Attending to Emma's story, we realize that she could not have arrived where she is without the love The Lord's Acre attempts to embody.

Emma experienced shame, but the intent of the Lord's Acre staff was integration rather than exclusion. Susan did not have to shame Emma by pronouncing her sin. The shame was already there. The qualities exhibited by Susan and the garden community produced a radically different result than either a bounded or fuzzy approach.

The following story demonstrates how discernment, imagination, and creativity enable a centered church to respond to a situation in a radically different way. Ken, a youth pastor, went to his pastor and confessed that he had been involved in a sexual relationship outside of marriage with a consenting adult woman from a church in another province. Following the guidelines of the denomination, Ken was removed from his pastoral position and suspended originally for two years. During this time, he moved in with his lead pastor's family, who treated him with compassion and helped support him during this time. The denomination offered him counseling, accountability, and support, but Ken experienced these things at a surface level. The focus seemed to be on helping him integrate back into ministry without creating too many waves.

The pastor desired for Ken to return to his role, but the board chose otherwise. Ken began applying for youth pastor positions again but was not hired. It was like he had a scarlet letter. He finally found work managing an Apple Store, met and married a young woman, and began to consider that he may never work in pastoral ministry again. Finally, after six years, a church hired him. Rather than seeing him as damaged goods and morally suspect, the church discerned that his experience had forced him to deal with things that others had not. Two of the six core values of this church were "No Masks" and "Choose Grace." Hiring Ken as a youth pastor was a way to live out the value of "choosing grace," and the church believed that his experience of restoration and growth could help model how to take off masks honestly. The centered approach of this church enabled them to see Ken's experiences as an asset rather than a liability, which would help them grow the kind of culture that they wanted the church to exemplify. Five years later the lead pastor retired, and the congregation called Ken to be the new pastor.[19]

When we see transformation as a journey, we may recognize an intervention as an important step in a process—the beginning of a conversation. More than one intervention will be needed. This can be especially important when we engage someone from a fuzzy orientation who may interpret any confrontation as bounded. We observe this softer approach of starting a conversation in the following excerpt from a letter written by Grace Spencer, calling her friend to turn away from something, but even more strongly calling her to turn toward something better. With humility Spencer reveals her own struggles—her sense of being on a journey and inviting her friend to join her. The letter also displays how a loving intervention can be expressed through various mediums.[20]

Dear_____,

Television, social media, the internet, the incessant checking of the iPhone, etc., have all served as an escape for me. When I would come home from work looking for rest, when I felt alone, when I simply wanted to press pause on whatever was occupying my thoughts, I knew television could meet my needs. I needed it. Little did I know, it was consuming me. It invited me into a different reality, offered me a new sense of self, replaced my feeling of purpose, provided me with a fictional community, and gave my life new meaning. I wanted to escape, but I never thought to ask what type of place I was escaping to. When we watch television, we engage in a world that pervades into our own. We are foolish if we think entertainment stops affecting us when we turn the TV off.

In the last year, and more so in the last couple months, as I continue to walk away from those things, I have found myself. What does that even mean? I don't know that I can explain it, but I feel it. I have planted myself, poured myself into my neighbors, devoted myself to society's outcasts, tried to give 100 percent to every moment, and lost myself in a bigger story. Community is all around me. Before, when I wanted to grow and heal, I solely focused on how to improve myself. Ironically, once I began to lose myself, I found myself

---

[19]Eric Versluis, email to author, November 8, 2017.
[20]Grace Spencer, March 24, 2016.

(I am pretty sure Jesus said this). Unlike any other idol or anything we worship, when we devote ourselves to Jesus, we receive something greater in return.

I encourage you, as you embark on a journey to heal and find yourself, not to allow the virtual world to compete with the real around you. Engage all of your senses in the beauty that surrounds you. Deeply invest in a community, especially with people who make you uncomfortable. Commit yourself to something bigger than you. Reflect on moments when you feel Christ, and pursue those moments with every ounce of your being.

I pray that the love of Christ will overtake you in this season, that you will experience his love in new and exciting ways, and that you will be open to the possibility that finding yourself requires that you first lose yourself.

Love,

Grace

Throughout this chapter we have seen again how love is the foundational element in a centered church. By highlighting the importance of love in a centered approach, I am not implying that sincere love is absent in bounded or fuzzy churches, for I have experienced and observed love in both bounded and fuzzy churches. Yet these paradigms impede people from fully loving others. The fuzzy paradigm leads people to believe that it is inappropriate to intervene. While love may motivate an intervention in a bounded paradigm, the bounded and excluding stance will overwhelm the intent and disintegrative shaming will seep through; a feeling of enforcement will contaminate the intervention. In contrast, in a centered approach the paradigm itself pulls people away from a focus on enforcement and exclusionary shaming, and pulls all to focus on trajectory and growth.

CONFRONTING BOUNDEDNESS

Jesus and Paul both make it clear that we must do more than simply avoid bounded practices, we must also confront and challenge them. Galatians, Paul's most passionate letter, is not reacting to loose moral living, but to bounded-church line drawing. Jesus repeatedly exposed and challenged bounded-group religiosity. Let us follow their example.

In challenging the bounded approach, we must first and foremost attack the power and the paradigm rather than people. I rarely confront someone at a personal level for living out bounded religiosity. Instead, I proclaim an alternative and the possibility of being liberated from bounded ways. Yet line-drawing exclusion is sinful and harmful, and there are times when loving confrontation is necessary, particularly when someone's words and attitudes hurt others. One church leader told me about a person in a small group who was making line-drawing statements. The leader took him aside and said, "That is not how we do things here." He made it clear that the group welcomed him to continue in the group, but his behavior was not welcome.

As much or more than talking about boundedness, I find myself seeking to liberate people from a view of God that contributes to their bounded ways of judgmentalism against others and against themselves. This underscores the fact that no chapter in this book can be applied in isolation from the others. We can have great methods of centered intervention, but if people view God as the big accusing eye in the sky, that concept of God will distort our centered words. They will remain bounded.

Rianna Isaak, who has been involved in various ministry settings, told me about an experience she had when people's concept of God and latent boundedness contaminated a conversation. She began a discussion in a group by asking, "What is your relationship with entertainment?" People engaged well and shared openly. Then she asked, "How does your relationship with Jesus affect your relationship with entertainment?" The feeling in the room changed. One person responded with a sense of resignation as he somewhat bitterly said, "Oh I guess I should. . . ." Rianna did not use bounded language or have an attitude of line-drawing religiosity, but it suddenly appeared.[21] We must work at both the wording of our questions and the foundational elements outlined in chapters three through five.

IT TAKES A COMMUNITY

All the examples in this chapter portray interventions by an individual or a few individuals. Yet centered intervention cannot be done alone. In a number of examples, I identified the role of the group or the loving environment of the church because the community's role is fundamental. If people in the church talk about others from a bounded perspective, their judgmentalism will overwhelm another individual's attempt to intervene in a centered way.

---

[21]Rianna Isaak, conversation with author, confirmed by email, July 17, 2019.

While doing field research for this book, I heard a number of stories about loving interventions that included having to undo the shame and exclusion people felt because of how someone else in the church had confronted them.

Fuzziness in the community also impedes loving intervention. Matt Miles recalls an engaging discussion in a home group where he served as the lay leader. At one point someone said something that clearly differed from the church's beliefs. Matt probed, seeking to understand the person's thinking. Then he asked, "How do you link that back to Scripture?" Immediately the others in the group communicated their discomfort through their looks and body language. They quickly sought to smooth over the disagreement by affirming aspects of what the dissenting person had said—even though Matt knew that they did not fundamentally agree. He sensed that the cultural commitment to tolerance was so strong that the rest of the group wanted to wipe away the uncomfortableness of disagreement.

Matt could not lead a centered group on his own, as the rest of the group undermined his efforts. This underscores the role of instruction and the formation of the whole community. If you are a small group leader, a pastor, or ministry leader, it is not enough for you to read this book and put it into practice. You must also introduce the people in your group, congregation, or organization to the basics of bounded, fuzzy, and centered. Who are others you can invite to read this book? In addition, on the last page of this book there are other resources to use in aiding people to understand a centered approach.

Training people in centered ways will enhance their ability to perceive intervention as a loving scalpel rather than a slashing dagger. For instance, one pastor, who asked to remain anonymous, uses language that many would think of as too direct or harsh, and yet it was received differently because the individual interpreted it within his centered framework.

Chris, who was recently divorced, was active in the church before his divorce and continued to be involved after his divorce. Leaders from the church had worked with this couple to try to save the marriage. To put the story that follows in context, we only need to know that the pastor and several others in the church thought that Chris could have done more to seek healing and reconciliation. They also felt that he was stating things that were not true when he told others in the church about the divorce—things that tended to downplay the seriousness of the issues and the divorce itself.

The pastor, Kevin, and a church leader, Jordan, met with Chris. After some light conversation, the pastor said, "You probably remember us talking about a centered approach," and Chris acknowledged that he did. Kevin continued:

> We believe that what you have done is sin. We are not going to hide that. We believe that your choice for divorce, especially when reconciliation was possible, is against the way of Jesus. But we do not want you to leave our community. You matter to us. We think that it is important that when you tell the story of your divorce, it is told truthfully. You have the opportunity to, in the best sense of the word, repent of this situation—and to take this opportunity to discover yourself, in Jesus, that this decision is not pointing toward the center. It is actually pointing away from the center. We want to help in the process of reorienting your vision of who Jesus is. The evidence in front of us suggests that your orientation has turned, at least in this slice of who you are.

Then Kevin and Jordan discussed some of the inconsistencies they had observed. At various points, they stopped and asked, "Are you hearing what we mean? Are you going to leave this conversation feeling attacked, or thinking we are being legalistic?" Chris repeatedly responded, "No, what you are doing is the right thing considering what I have chosen and done." Because Chris understood the centered approach, he could hear the words *sin* and *repentance* within a centered framework. He responded well to their statements and received them as true.

Kevin told me that even with the direct loving confrontation and all the centered language, the intervention could have played out in a fuzzy way. While it was possible for Chris to make a significant reorientation on his own, they did not think that was likely. They did, however, believe that he wanted to reorient and to become a person of integrity. Kevin and Jordan suggested that Chris prepare a truthful narrative about what had happened in the divorce and then read it to them and three or four other men from the church of Chris's choosing. This group would continue to walk with him, exploring the root issues that had caused him to approach the marriage and divorce as he had and to paint another picture to others. The group would provide the structure he needed to walk in the way he desired.

Kevin acknowledged that part of his motivation for taking this additional step with Chris was how it would impact rest of the community. He said, "There are consequences beyond the person that we do need to think about even in a centered approach. How we treat a person in the community can have impact on others in the community." The arrows heading toward the center are in relationship; they affect each other. They are not autonomous individual arrows.

If the church had allowed Chris to maintain his casual attitude and tell his partially true version of the divorce, it would have confused the church community and may have contributed to others having a more casual view of divorce. The bounded approach is not wrong to be concerned about how people in a community will be impacted when someone crosses a line. The problem is that bounded churches are often more concerned about the line than the person.

As Kevin observed, "These kinds of situations test the integrity of our centeredness. Chris's resources for self-awareness were low. If we had not acted, we would have set him up to progress only so much, and we would have set up the community, at least those closest to him, to have a blurred sense of what our community really represents—what a centered approach is really about."

GUIDE PEOPLE TO THE WELL

As I sat in a Seattle café telling Dan Serdahl about this book project, he passionately began to describe the intentionality of his church's centered approach. When I asked him to share examples of loving intervention, he said, "Most commonly someone from the church will come to me out of a desire to help someone else in the church, saying, 'I am concerned about my friend's . . .' (often it is some sort of addictive behavior). My response is, 'Invite the person to read one of the Gospels with you.'"[22]

I had a pen in hand, ready to take further notes, but that was all he said. At first his answer disappointed me. I wanted more. Then I began to reflect on what he had said. I realized that he had actually told me a great deal about a centered approach. I invite you, before reading some of my reflections

---

[22]Dan offers to work through one of the Gospels with the person who has the concern, equipping him or her to read it with the friend. Dan Serdahl, interview by author, July 20, 2019.

below, to take a few moments to ponder his response. How is it centered? How is it a loving intervention? What can you learn from it?

Dan's suggestion to intervene by inviting the person to read a Gospel together does not dismiss or downplay the presenting issue. It also, however, does not focus on the presenting issue. While the assumption is that the issue will come up in the course of reading the selected Gospel, the approach is relaxed, trusting, curious about how it will all unfold and what else will come up. This method recognizes that there are always deeper underlying issues. Reading a Gospel together facilitates the exploration of deeper issues. The sense of journey is inherent in the intervention itself.

As I reflected with Dan, he observed that shame is often a root issue. That is, the person not only feels shame for what he or she is doing, but deep shame and alienation are also causal factors. Jesus liberates us from shame, and the Gospels overflow with stories that provide opportunities for people to experience that liberation. This Gospel-reading approach is not disintegrative shaming. The Gospel-reading method helps insure a strong and clear restorative intent.

A bounded approach expresses its concern for the whole community by protecting the line that gives security to the community. A centered approach, on the other hand, expresses concern for the community by emphasizing relationships and walking with each other—growing closer to each other as we move closer to Jesus, our center.

Finally, the Gospel-reading method is profoundly centered. Not just because of the characteristics listed above, but because looking at Jesus and talking about Jesus is fundamental to the intervention itself.

I do not close this chapter with the Gospel-reading method because I want to suggest that this is the best approach for all churches in all situations. There is not one right approach. But this method highlights the value of not just taking a bounded method of confrontation and retooling it. Rather, let us be open to approaching loving intervention in radically new and different ways.

CONCLUSION

As I just stated, and this chapter has displayed, there is not one right way to respond to a given situation in a centered way. That is true in the same cultural context, even in the same church but much more so in differing cultural settings. Although this chapter contains examples from different countries and cultures, I did not directly address the significance of culture. The reality is what works well in one culture may not in another. For instance, centered confrontation will look very different in a setting with a high honor-shame orientation. For examples and insights on loving confrontation in a culture that prioritizes saving face, I refer you to the book I coauthored, *Ministering in Honor-Shame Cultures*, especially chapters seven and eleven.

I began this chapter with a student's comment about how she experienced her discernment group's confrontational words as nonjudgmental and full of grace. Her comment left me curious. I wanted to learn more from someone who was on the receiving end of a loving intervention. So I asked her what the group had done to enable her to experience their words of confrontation as a scalpel rather than a dagger. She listed a number of elements, which both affirm and expand what we have seen in this chapter. First, she observed that her previous interaction with the people in the group prepared her to receive their words in love. She said, "It starts with connection, with a relationship, then the exhorting can follow. I don't believe it could work if it started the other way around." But not just any kind of relationship. She noted, "I had already experienced grace from everyone there." That enabled her to hear their words as wrapped in grace, which muted the default response of thinking that everyone in the group was scandalized and was judging her. Second, she had already been vulnerable in the meeting and had acknowledged some areas of struggle, and no one had jumped on her, which created a safe space. Third, the tenor of the meeting was positive, and there was no sense of hostility—even in the challenging comments. People's countenances exuded care rather than contempt—even after the strong, challenging words. As the group processed her prejudice, she felt cared for rather than shamed.

This student's observations sober me, because they reveal that much is required if an intervention is going to be experienced in a loving and centered way. Yet her observations also excite me. Imagine the potential for growth and transformation if developing communities of loving intervention can enable us to engage each other at such depth! I pray that the examples of loving intervention in this chapter will give you models to imitate and ideas to adapt and put into practice.

In the final chapter of this section, we will explore other aspects of discipleship and journeying together. You might think of it as intervention in a broader sense. I have given significant space to corrective loving intervention because so many people have difficulty imagining any confrontation or reorientation outside of a bounded approach. Yet in terms of time, the discipleship interventions in the shorter chapter that follows actually take up more of our day-to-day discipleship. Whereas the present gave examples of interventions that responded to particular situations, most of the interventions in the next chapter are proactive. Chapter ten will offer examples of a type of loving intervention that calls to action and affirms the progress of disciples seeking to follow the way of Jesus. It also will put more emphasis on journeying together.

10

JOURNEYING TOGETHER TOWARD THE CENTER

PROACTIVE AND AFFIRMATIVE INTERVENTION

Anthony, a gang member, had been in and out of prison since his teenage years. When he turned thirty-five, he told me he could only remember one birthday since he was eighteen when he had not been incarcerated. A few months earlier, he had repented and turned to Jesus and had been faithfully attending the weekly Bible study I lead for a high-security pod in the Fresno County Jail. Over those months, I witnessed the Holy Spirit working in his life and producing fruits of transformation.

In my interactions with these men, I am always looking for things that I can affirm, and I often ask questions that invite them to think about God's calling for their lives. Once, when I asked Anthony how things were in the pod, he said it had been tense. Two men were heading toward a violent confrontation. He described how he had talked to them individually and asked why they were upset. He discerned that one of them had said something that had been misinterpreted by the other. Anthony brought the man who had made the comment to talk to someone who had overheard the exchange. Hearing how this third man interpreted the comment helped the man who made it see how easily what he had said could be misinterpreted. Then Anthony invited him to talk with the man he had upset. When Anthony brought the two men together, the man who made the comment apologized and said he did not mean to offend but could see how the other man had heard his words that way. The other man accepted the apology and the tension dissipated. I asked Anthony how many men in the pod would take this sort of initiative, and he said two, maybe three. I asked him what the eighteen-year-old Anthony would think of what the thirty-five-year-old follower of Jesus had done. He just shook his head. I affirmed his wise mediation and urged him to continue to look for opportunities to be a peacemaker there in the pod. Over the months that followed, I asked if he had resolved any conflicts and continued to affirm him and name him as a peacemaker. When he was sent from the jail to prison, I sent him books on conflict resolution and other discipleship themes. I continued to affirm him when I responded to his letters in which he described the risks he had taken to mediate conflicts and lessen tensions.

I intervened in Anthony's life. In contrast with interventions in the previous two chapters, rather than addressing something in his life that was out of line with the way of Jesus, I affirmed Christlike actions. Corrective intervention is essential, but discipleship in a centered church calls even more for affirmation and support. We not only seek to reorient others when they turn from the center but also proactively orient and affirm movement toward the center. The following story invites us to consider whether our questions and comments support character development in line with the center. Do we model for disciples the Christlike values we affirm?

In an article for *The Atlantic*, Adam Grant and Allison Sweet Grant address neither church nor discipleship, yet their thoughts on parenting provide an excellent springboard to reflect on character development and discipleship. They report that over 90 percent of parents in the United States agree that one of their top priorities is that their children are caring. Yet when you ask children about their parents' desires, 81 percent say their parents value achievement and happiness over caring. The Grants write, "Kids learn what's important to adults not by listening to what we say, but by noticing what gets our attention. . . . Kids, with their sensitive antennae, pick up on all this. They see their peers being celebrated primarily for the grades they get and the goals they score, not for the generosity they show."[1] The

---

[1] Adam Grant and Allison Sweet Grant, "Stop Trying to Raise Successful Kinds and Start Raising Kind Ones," *The Atlantic* (December 2019): 36.

Grants observed that many of the questions they asked over the dinner table were indeed about accomplishments: Did your team win? How did the test go?

> To demonstrate that caring is a core value, we realized that we needed to give it comparable attention. We started changing our questions. At our family dinners, we now ask our children what they did to help others. At first, "I forget" was the default reply. But after a while, they started giving more thoughtful answers. "I shared my snack with a friend who didn't have one," for example, or "I helped a classmate understand a question she got wrong on a quiz." They had begun actively looking for opportunities to be helpful, and acting upon them. As parents, we've also tried to share our own experiences with helping—and to make a point of including the moments we've failed.[2]

What questions are we asking others in our Christian communities? What behaviors do we honor? What character values do we reinforce through these questions and affirmations? Of course, some could easily experience the sort of questions the Grants recommend as bounded. They respond, "The point is not to badger kids into kindness, or dangle carrots for caring, but to show that these qualities are noticed and valued."[3] If we hold back out of fear of boundedness, people will absorb societal values through both the questions they encounter throughout their days and the actions they see honored in society. Let us thoughtfully intervene through questions and affirming comments that build disciples' Christlike character and values. Let us wrap those questions in unconditional love and place them in a context so radically centered that people will not interpret them in a bounded way.

THE IMPERATIVE OF DISCIPLESHIP AND PRACTICING THE WAY OF JESUS

At the beginning of this part of the book, I defined discipleship as a formational process of becoming more Christlike. Someone who disciples others walks with them toward Jesus, intentionally sharing life with them, modeling, naming them, guiding them, exhorting them, and learning from the

---

[2]Grant and Grant, "Stop Trying," 36.
[3]Grant and Grant, "Stop Trying," 37.

Bible and the Spirit together. The discipler points disciples to resources for learning, mentors them in practices, values, and character, and gives them opportunities to learn by doing—training them so they can train others.

Discipleship, as described above, was central in the early years of my ministry. I was discipled and in turn discipled others at a Christian camp where I worked, in the Christian Service Brigade program at my church, in the church I attended in Honduras, and as a campus minister with InterVarsity Christian Fellowship. I have remained committed to discipleship and, although with less intensity, have practiced it throughout my life. I did not, however, talk about it much in the ethics course I teach. Certainly, various elements listed above received significant attention, but I did not teach students to lodge them in discipling relationships of shared life and mentoring.

Then, one Saturday morning a few years ago, while working in our vegetable garden I listened to *This Cultural Moment*, a podcast by John Mark Comer and Mark Sayers.[4] They reflected on a serious error of their early church-planting efforts. In the early 2000s they, and many others, looked to new ways of being church. "We turned down the lights, sat in a circle, talked about social justice, and sought to be relevant." In the same time period what Mark Sayers calls "digital capitalism"—that is, the blending of free-market capitalism with the internet—began to dominate life more and more. Digital capitalism combined with a worldview committed to autonomous individualism. The latter told people to not give themselves to any external authority, yet through the former they gave themselves to Apple and Google—autonomous yet increasingly enslaved.

Comer and Sayers planted churches in the context of this caustic mix of digital capitalism and hyperindividualism. Sayers affirms relevance, but it is just not enough. They were sending Christians out to be "relevant," yet these believers were getting sucked into and enslaved by the world they sought to be relevant to. "The iPhone is a greater threat to the gospel than secularism ever has been." Earlier you could assume Christians read their Bible and

---

[4]John Mark Comer and Mark Sayers, "Frankenstein, Sexy Communist Spies, and the Rise of Digital Capitalism," February 19, 2018, in *This Cultural Moment*, podcast, season 1, no. 3, 27:02, https://thisculturalmoment.podbean.com/e/frankenstein-sexy-communist-spies-and -the-rise-of-digital-capitalism/.

prayed regularly, but now spiritual disciplines are disappearing, "if not erased by secularism then by Wi-Fi access." What really caught my attention, however, was their proposed solution—discipleship!

> We must return to formation and discipleship. We can't send people out into the world unformed because the world has so much sway, pull, allure to it. First we must help people be with Jesus and be formed by Jesus. . . . Basic human wisdom is lacking. We must go way back in discipling and teach people how to live in community, how to not be flaky, how to show up, how to deal with conflict.

They were seeking to shape Christians who would read a psalm before touching their phone in the morning and who would share a meal with other Christians a couple times a week. They did not assume that was happening. They were now working at those things through discipleship.

I put down my garden trowel, leaned back, and thought, *Perhaps I need to start talking about discipleship in my class.* If Comer and Sayers are correct, without discipleship people will not be able to live out the ethics I teach in the course. The caustic floodwaters of digital capitalism and hyperindividualism are too strong.

Earlier in this book, I argued that discipleship is imperative in a centered church, by which I meant that movement toward the center requires discipleship. With Comer and Sayers's observations in mind, however, I add that discipleship is especially important in our current times. Discipleship entails both the basic practices of Christian living and the necessity of repetition, working at them—*practicing* them. Comer and Sayers warn us that people cannot do this alone. Members of centered churches need others not just to instruct them, but to walk with them, mentor them, and give them opportunities to learn by doing.

DISCIPLESHIP ACTIVITIES TO FOSTER TRANSFORMATION

In this section, then, I will share some ideas for discipleship activities. Just as valuable as the activities described below, of course, are the many things already commonly practiced in churches. For instance, positive discipleship interventions may include inviting someone to co-lead a small group, teach a Sunday school class, join the worship team, pray together, join an outreach activity, or go on a mission trip. Inviting someone to accompany you in any activity is a possible discipleship moment. I invite you to read again through that list and reflect on the potential of each to name people and help them to move closer to the center. Also, I invite you to reflect on how a centered approach might engage these activities differently than a bounded or fuzzy approach.

As usual, in a weekly men's Bible study I participate in, one person's observation sparked a new insight from another. Someone else's question led us to ponder the text in new ways. One man stated that he felt called by the text to share the good news of Jesus more actively with others. Someone asked him a question about what he had said. His answer led us all to reflect on the ways we talk with others about Jesus and things that inhibit that. Some spoke words of affirmation for ways they had observed other group members taking initiative with Christians and non-Christians. The discussion left us all with a renewed sense of call, and it also led us to experience anew God's radical unconditional love. Hours after the study, I found myself reflecting on how we had practiced several things described in this book. Yet a key difference caught my attention: it had been corporate and mutual. It was not one person calling another to reorientation, nor was one person exhorting the rest of the group. We all contributed to the call to live differently, and we each accepted the exhortation as for us. The first story in this chapter and most of the examples in the previous chapters in this part of the book have presented one person intervening in another's life or one person exhorting an individual or group. That is common in discipleship, but just as common in a centered church is what happened in that Bible study. We journeyed *together* toward the center—learning from each other, challenging each other, and affirming each other.

In the ethics course I teach, I have a number of act-reflect-adjust assignments. Consider ways you can bring that three-step dynamic into discipleship activities in your own setting. Experiences provide opportunities for new insights and growth, and that growth increases greatly if we take time to reflect with others about the experience. The goal, however, is not just to reflect and gain insights, but to listen to how the Spirit calls us to make changes based on the experience and reflection. The following activities are designed for groups to practice as they seek together to live out the way of Christ in their context. All the examples encourage growth—or movement toward the center—but none of them pressure disciples to toe a preconceived line. Rather, they encourage the group to experiment and explore what it means to follow Christ in a centered environment and give them space to share, reflect on, and support one another through significant struggles and hopes.

Money autobiographies. Shane Hipps advocates ways for churches to practice autobiographical storytelling and offers one example of a church's small group experience in sharing money autobiographies.[5] Each week the person sharing prepares their presentation by writing about their best and worst memories related to money as well as their hopes, fears, and sadnesses related to finances. Presenters are invited to make connections to Scripture when possible and to recall messages about money that they received from their families, friends, and culture. Imagine the impact when, as Hipps describes:

> [A] presenter would show up . . . with credit cards in hand and say, "Please hold these for me. I'm in too much debt; I need help." The effect on the group was profound, as it caused them to reconsider the role money played in their discipleship to Christ. They learned about the ways our culture of wealth breeds secrecy and privacy around issues of money. They became aware of the erosive power this kind of secrecy had on their relationships with one another.
>
> These people were never asked to tithe more, reveal their net worth, or hand over their credit cards. And yet the process nurtured a more generous community. The changes in their lives took place when they were given space to tell and hear each other's stories. It developed new openness, trust, and intimacy.[6]

Looking at the mall through a different lens. A discipleship activity can also involve doing something we normally do, but intentionally looking at it from a kingdom of God perspective. In *Desiring the Kingdom*, James K. A. Smith suggests one activity that I have used with small groups.[7] I invite members to spend an hour at a mall individually, observing how it acts as a

---

[5]Faith & Money Network, *Guidelines for Writing Your Money Autobiography*, http://faithand moneynetwork.org/wp-content/uploads/FMN-Money-Autobiography.pdf.
[6]Shane Hipps, *The Hidden Power of Electronic Culture* (Grand Rapids, MI: Zondervan, 2006), 117-18.
[7]James K. A. Smith, *Desiring the Kingdom: Worship, Worldview, and Cultural Formation*, Cultural Liturgies 1 (Grand Rapids, MI: Baker Academic, 2009), 96-101.

religious place of formation and worship. Liturgy and worship practices reflect what matters to us and shape us, giving us a vision for a way of life and calling us to devote our allegiance and obedience to that way of life. I invite people to discern the "liturgies," "sermons," and "worship" practices of the mall. What is the foundational narrative of the mall—that is, its basic truths? What is the mall's view of the human, of "sin"? What is the vision of the good life to which it calls us? What kind of people does it want us to become? How does it communicate its foundational narrative or basic truths? How does it seek to shape us and call us to be the kind of people it wants us to be? When we come together as a group, we reflect on how observing the mall through these questions leads us to new insights about the mall, consumerism, and ourselves. Every time I have done this activity with a group, it has led to awakenings and life change.

Technology fasts. Fasting, from food and other things, serves as a potent intervention. Many people practice a discipline of fasting from technology. For instance, in *The Tech-Wise Family*, Andy Crouch writes that his family fasts from their devices for one hour a day, one day a week, and one week a year.[8] For those who do not have a regular fast, fasting with the purpose of observing and reflecting is an excellent discipleship activity. Students in my ethics course participate in two fasts. The first is a one-day fast from their cell phones. As with any type of fast, we learn new things when we remove something. Participants often make startling confessions, such as, "I kept reaching for my phone even though it wasn't there. I am addicted." Together we process one another's observations, such as the following two:

> I realized how much time and energy I spent caring about what other people were doing on social media, instead of using that energy to focus on today and what I need to get done. I also realized how much social media makes me feel like I need to work harder to catch up to others, yet at the same time is stealing my time to get things done.
>
> In my most consumed moments of social media and technology there are instances where I become aware that I am looking for something. I ask myself in that moment, What am I looking for? What do I need right in this moment that I think social media can fill? Is it friendship? A connection?

---

[8]Andy Crouch, *The Tech-Wise Family: Everyday Steps for Putting Technology in Its Proper Place* (Grand Rapids, MI: Baker Books, 2017).

Personal meaning? Motivation? Am I avoiding something? Am I seeking attention? Recognition?

We then share action steps that we want to take in response to what we have observed and learned. As part of the course, we also do a five-day fast from television and internet-based entertainment. The results are always surprising and significant, even for those who beforehand might say, "This will not be that significant because I do not watch much television." This would also be a great churchwide activity, particularly if there is space to process and reflect together afterwards.

Action-focused experiments in discipleship. Mark Scandrette has sought ways to make discipleship a communal adventure that is rooted in actions. He writes, "Too often our methods of spiritual formation are individualistic, information driven or disconnected from the details of everyday life. . . . Perhaps what we need is a path for discipleship that is more like a karate studio than a lecture hall . . . action focused, communal, experiential."[9] His book, *Practicing the Way of Jesus*, provides numerous examples of just that— action-focused communal experiments in discipleship. The experiments are designed for a particular time period—a day, week, month, or longer. All the activities are inspired by the life and teachings of Jesus and relate to real needs. A group of people commit time and energy to specific practices and times to gather to reflect on the experience and how they can shape ongoing rhythms of life. Scandrette begins the book with a description of one of his more radical experiments.

> A number of years ago I invited a group of friends into an audacious experiment in which each of us would sell or give away half of our possessions and donate the profits to global poverty relief. We were inspired by what Jesus taught about true security and abundance. . . . To our surprise over thirty people signed up to participate. . . . Thousands of dollars were redistributed and we each discovered more heart simplicity and the benefits of less physical clutter. We were surprised at the depth of connection we felt with a diverse group of people we barely knew when the experiment started. Working on an intensive project seemed to produce an accelerated sense of intimacy. . . . For many of us, this and subsequent experiments set a chain of events in

---

[9]Mark Scandrette, *Practicing the Way of Jesus: Life Together in the Kingdom of Love* (Downers Grove, IL: InterVarsity Press, 2011), 14-15.

motion that continues to shape the ongoing direction of our lives. Some of us quit jobs or relocated to impoverished communities. Others have gotten out of debt, reconciled with their families, overcome addictions or discovered significant inner healing. Many of us experienced a greater sense of identity, purpose, security and peace.[10]

Doesn't that have the feel of well water, attracting and pulling both the people who are involved in the experiment and us as we read about it? Consider the following examples selected from the many one-week experiments described in a section of Scandrette's book. As mentioned above they all include times of group processing of the experiment. Which of these activities or practices might you try with a group?

▶ Take a thirty-to-ninety-minute daily solitary walk with God: observe, pray listen.

▶ Practice seeing as God sees: as you look at each person you meet, pause to see him or her as loved by God.

▶ Expect opportunity: each morning, ask God for on opportunity to be an agent of healing.

▶ Eat with the lonely: eat a meal at a local soup kitchen, hospital, or nursing home.

▶ Gratitude: keep a gratitude log, writing down ten things each day for which you are grateful (without repeating anything).

▶ Time/money journal: keep a detailed journal about where you spend your time and money.

▶ Worry journal: each morning, make a list of the worries and fears that go through your head and surrender them to God.

▶ Celebrate abundance: like Jesus feeding the crowds, give a lavish gift or prepare a special feast for friends or family.

▶ Seek reconciliation: is there someone you have wronged, or who has wronged you, a strained relationship? Take intentional steps this week toward reconciliation.[11]

---

[10]Scandrette, *Practicing the Way of Jesus*, 11-13.
[11]Scandrette, *Practicing the Way of Jesus*, 121, 51, 137, 148, 184.

Scandrette's book includes a number of other seven-day experiments and many longer experiments as well. I recommend his book, not just to get more ideas, but because he provides excellent reflection questions to accompany the experiments, offers valuable practical suggestions about the process, and includes his personal stories about the experiments which communicate a sense of adventure and excitement for growth and transformation.

In this section I have presented neither an organized program of discipleship nor a full range of activities. Rather, I have sought to present a variety of activities and practices to stimulate your imagination for ways that will facilitate your journey with others toward the center. For a more thorough program of discipleship practices that John Mark Comer and Bridgetown Church see as imperative today, I encourage you to visit the "Practicing the Way of Jesus" website.[12]

FRUIT OF DISCIPLESHIP

In this third part of the book, which has focused on discipleship, a major theme has been imagining alternatives to bounded approaches. Centered discipleship in community, however, is so much more than just avoiding the negatives of bounded or fuzzy approaches. It produces rich fruit.

When I was just out of college, completing my second year of teaching high school in Honduras, I stood on a balcony overlooking the city of Tegucigalpa with my friend German Medina. He was about my age and worked as a clerk in a hardware store. With other volunteers, we had just finished setting up the chairs in a borrowed space for our weekly church service. As we looked over the city, I asked German about his future hopes, and he immediately responded, "I want to be a pastor and plant a church in another city." At first, his answered surprised me—how audacious! I wondered how a twenty-something hardware store clerk with a high school education imagined he could be a pastor. But then I thought about our church, Amor Viviente (Living Love), and how well it discipled people.

Marvin Lorenzana attended the same church and agrees that Amor Viviente discipled well. He has been a church planter and pastor and is now

---

[12]Practicing the Way, https://practicingtheway.org.

the president of Eastern Mennonite Missions. He recounts his experience of discipleship in Amor Viviente:

> Allan, my fourteen-year old brother, invited me, only ten at that time, to tag along with him to a public school building where he had been going for several months "to learn more about Jesus." In fact, Allan was taking me to "church." About 300 mostly young people had gathered that night in the central patio of a run-down school right in the center of Tegucigalpa, the capital city of Honduras. I heard a missionary from North America preach that night. But . . . who was this man? The man was Edward King, a Mennonite missionary and sociologist who had come to Honduras, along with his wife, Gloria, and their five children, to teach people how to read and write as part of their work with an international faith-based organization focusing on literacy, health and nutritional training, job and skills formation, and community development. I became a believer in Christ that night after hearing Pastor King preach the gospel with such passion that I could only respond with a "yes!" to his invitation to meet Jesus. My discipleship journey with Jesus began on that unforgettable night in 1975 under the starry skies of Tegucigalpa.
>
> From the outset, Edward King's emphasis was on one-to-one discipleship. He believed that anybody—as long as he or she lived under the lordship of Jesus Christ—had potential for kingdom impact in the world. As the good Anabaptist that he was, King fully trusted in the empowering of the Holy Spirit and in a commitment to the "ministry of all believers." The backbone of the movement was the creation of cell groups, made up of seven to fifteen people and led by lay leaders whose main goal was to make not only disciples, but disciple makers![13]

German, like Marvin, was attracted to Jesus through Amor Viviente. After converting and reorienting his life toward Jesus, German was invited to join a cell group. One of the group's leaders visited him, and they spent time together praying and studying Scripture. Soon German accompanied this leader as he evangelized and invited others to the group. German was given small tasks, then larger ones, and eventually became part of a small group that was sent to start a new home gathering. The cell group leader mentored him in leading worship and preaching in the cell group and gave him opportunities to do both. In time he was invited to be the leader of a

---

[13]Marvin Lorenzana, "Not Just Disciples, but Disciple Makers," *Missio Dei* 29 (2019).

new cell group and was included in the discipleship group of the church's lead pastor. Not long after the night that German and I talked, he led worship at the main church service. He had drunk at the well of Jesus, and through the centered discipleship of Amor Viviente, he saw others, like himself, grow and be sent off to other cities to start churches. He had tasted the adventure of serving Jesus at the small scale of a cell group and longed for more. In the context of Amor Viviente's discipleship through doing, his dream of becoming a pastor was not audacious, but was following the discipleship trajectory.[14] Decades later, I stood beside German again, but on that evening, he was introducing me as a guest speaker at the church he pastors in Tela, Honduras.

A bounded-church approach creates a situation where many people are just treading water inside a boundary line, and a fuzzy group contributes to stagnation for different reasons. A centered church requires discipleship, which leads to transformation. Discipleship in a centered church nourishes Christians, such as German, with vision for even deeper engagement in the adventure of journeying with others to become more Christlike.

---

[14]There are, of course, other important layers to this story. In the world I was from, people would weigh the pros and cons of the risky adventure of church planting compared with a job with income security and the potential for advancement. German was from a poor home and had a minimum-wage job with little promise for advancement. He taught me an important lesson about the drag of money and security. German had little of either, and I sensed in him a freedom to leave all, a freedom that I did not see in myself or my peers.

PART FOUR

CENTERED MINISTRY

PEOPLE OFTEN SAY TO ME, "The centered approach attracts me, but there just are situations in which a church needs to use a bounded approach, such as people in recovery." Or they might say, "We are a centered church, but we have bounded groups, such as the leaders, within our centered church." This part of the book counters those assumptions by giving examples of centered approaches in those situations.

Chapter eleven focuses on certain ministries that require clear standards and firmness. Some examples include recovery programs, ministry with those reentering society after imprisonment, homeless ministry, and children's ministry. Whereas in these situations it is the characteristics or needs of the people in the ministry that lead many to assume boundedness is necessary, chapter twelve explores aspects of ministry itself that many see as inherently bounded. Rather than saying boundedness is necessary, it is more that people cannot see any other way than bounded of doing things like membership, evangelism, or having requirements for leaders.

Obviously, a church or organization's ministry consists of much more than these two chapters can cover. Other elements include worship, baptism, pastoral care, conflict resolution, fundraising, and community service, to name a few. Everything that any church or ministry does merits the question, "How can we do this in a more centered way?" By giving centered examples of some of the things that people struggle to conceive of in a centered way, my hope is that these examples will provide guidance for other aspects of ministry as well.

11

FIRM NOT BOUNDED

ADDICTION RECOVERY

When people say to me that some situations, such as recovery ministry, require a bounded approach, I respond by saying "You can be clear and firm without being bounded." While working on this book, I began asking practitioners involved in recovery ministry whether this statement is, in fact, true. Dave Obwald, pastoral care director at a large church, oversees their recovery program. He insists not only that a centered approach works, but that a centered recovery ministry works *better* than a bounded one.

He first sensed the weakness of bounded recovery programs while involved in one. He recalls:

> If I did not look at pornography, I was okay; I was in the circle. Similarly, I felt God loved me if I had not looked at porn for a certain number of days. I observed in myself and others that because of this arbitrary marker of in-ness or out-ness, with the group and God, we minimized deeper feelings. Yes, I did not look at pornography, but fears and anxieties consumed me all day long. I did not talk about that stuff because that was not the goal, not the boundary to the circle. I was trying to learn how to rest my heart on Christ, but we were not talking about that. It was: "Did you do this or did you do that?"[1]

---

[1] This quote and all the material in this section are from Dave Obwald, interview by the author, February 27, 2018.

The bounded approach sent ripples through the whole program. For instance, the line itself determined who was selected to lead the group. They asked, "Who has been sober the longest?" rather than, "Whose life is most aligned with Jesus Christ? Who is most humble and honest and willing to lean into the journey? Who is most willing to acknowledge we are all still in process?"

Dave felt God leading him toward a different approach as he lived out his own recovery, and he desired the same for others in the church where he was pastoring at that time. Some books pointed him in a new direction—a focus on his heart rather than his behavior alone.[2] He combined what he gained from these books with what he knew of the centered-church paradigm and tried an alternative approach. He invited others to acknowledge their brokenness and to move toward the center, who is Christ, together. With 1 John 1:7-9 in mind, he said to the group, "Let's drag things into the light together—into the light of Jesus Christ, our healer and redeemer." He assured others, "As we move toward him together, in this messy process of life, know your pastor is moving toward him just as much as you are."

Dave reports, "As we began to do this in community, in small pockets, there was such a sense of freedom. Our biggest fear is we will be rejected if we actually begin to talk about what is going on in the interior world and the things we do that we are ashamed of. Yet, people felt safe in a way they had not in a bounded setting and shared openly."

Dave is intentional about infusing the whole program with a centered character. It helps greatly that the senior pastor and other leaders do not present the program as being for a certain population that needs to get fixed. They affirm, "We are a church of brokenness." In a bounded church, leaders must pretend that things are okay, whereas leaders who participate in the church's recovery program share honest stories about their journeys and encourage all to participate.

In the church's program they separate by gender, but not by issues. If everyone in the group is dealing with the same issue, the issue becomes the

---

[2] The books he mentioned were Matt Chandler and Michael Snetzer, *Recovering Redemption: A Gospel Saturated Perspective on How to Change* (Nashville: B&H, 2014); Michael John Cusick, *Surfing for God: Discovering the Divine Desire Beneath Sexual Struggle* (Nashville: Thomas Nelson, 2012); Mike Wilkerson, *Redemption: Freed by Jesus from the Idols We Worship and the Wounds We Carry* (Wheaton, IL: Crossway, 2011).

focus, and it more easily becomes a bounded group. Dave says, "We want to focus on the heart. What happens is a person struggling with porn comes into a group. He hears someone else talking about alcohol and what drives him to drink. The porn addict recognizes the same thing drives him to porn. It takes people past the presenting issue."

Though the program is centered, it is not fuzzy, for they have guidelines and take them seriously. They have guidelines regarding group participation—for instance, participants only talk about their own stories, not about others, because people commonly try to fix others rather than focus on themselves. Dave reflects, "Guidelines are important. We train our leaders to the heart of the guideline; the heart of the guideline is trust. We present guidelines as important for building a trustworthy community." Leaders tell participants, "If you do not follow the group guidelines, then you are opting out—communicating you do not want to do this." Although there are times when they do ask people to leave a group, there is not a spirit of policing—three demerits and you are out. The leaders do the hard work of trying to be centered and not fuzzy. It is not easy to interrupt and tell someone, "Thank you, great that you are sharing, but we want you to keep it about yourself. Let Greg speak for himself. Please start again." Yet if leaders do not step in and enforce the guidelines, the depth of sharing in the group will decrease.

Leaders also communicate clear expectations for work outside the group. People begin in an open group format for six to ten weeks and individually do daily homework curriculum to work on their recovery. It includes a daily devotional because, as Dave says, "We believe healing comes through pointing our arrow toward Christ, connecting with him." If participants demonstrate faithfulness by attending a minimum of six times and actively engaging their daily work, then they are invited to join others who have demonstrated the same motivation. To join this nine-month process, each person must commit to engaging the process through daily work, meeting with a mentor, and attending and participating in the group. Dave observes, "We have found that when people do not choose to keep one of these commitments, they then feel disconnected from the movement of the group and will tend to disengage, both affecting themselves and others."

The week before I met with Dave, the leaders had asked a participant to leave a group because he was not doing the personal work, which was affecting him and the others in the group. Leaders had sought to encourage him to do the work, not legalistically, but by pointing out its importance for his healing and transformation. They reminded him that the work is a tool that they all agreed to use. He did not change, and so they asked him, "You said you want to do this. Do you still want to? No shame if you do not. You are not outside of the body of Christ if you do not. You can be in a Bible study with others from the church, but if you want to continue in *this* group, you will need to do the curriculum. Are you willing to do the work you have missed, or do you not want to do this process? We are willing to give you time and work with you to catch up." He responded, "No, I do not want to do this."

Dave acknowledges that this is difficult. Some of the leaders must fight their own fuzzy tendencies, and others must fight their bounded tendencies. The leaders meet and ask themselves, "What is the most loving thing for the individual—both short term and long term? What is the most loving thing for the group? What is the log in my own eye I need to be careful about?" Being firm in a centered way is further complicated by the fact that many people, including the man in this example, have a lot of boundedness from previous church or family experience. You cannot assume that centered language will defuse a bounded approach. For instance, in spite of what the leaders said, the man did feel like he had been excluded—or "kicked out." For this reason, they have follow-up meetings to convey that they are not ending the relationship. Because the leaders communicated that they were thinking of this man, that they loved him, and that they were willing to have him in a group again when he was ready, the man changed how he framed the experience, and he remains involved in the church even though he has opted out of the recovery program.

The recovery program Dave leads also includes commitments, action steps, and "accountability" structures. They are individualized for each participant. Each must ask, "What is repentance? What will it mean for me to turn away from patterns of idolatry? What action steps are needed?" Participants work with leaders and mentors to develop this list. Although it might look like an accountability system, Dave says they do not use that word.

I prefer to call it "structures of care and support," where someone learns to trust and live in the light with God and others. I think accountability, the way it is normally defined, is a bounded word about sharing when you broke a boundary rather than living in a way with one another where we can confess sin and temptation and pray for healing as we point our arrows toward Christ together in authentic community (James 5:16).

Dave said they work against a sense of policing by having the individual, not the mentor, take the initiative and by encouraging sharing not just about particular acts, such as, "I went into a bar yesterday," but also on deeper things, such as, "I am feeling a lot of stress at work and my anxiety level is greater." Dave emphasizes the program's commitment to work against the sense that if people slip up, they are out. "We celebrate when people confess. We train leaders to model confessing. We constantly need to work against how both bounded or fuzzy approaches would lead people to respond—to not feel the need to share or to not share because of fear of shame, the stigma."

Reflecting on the contrast between his early experience and the church's current ministry, Dave explains,

Bounded has to do with separation from rather than connection to. To sum it up, we want to tell people abundant life comes from a connection to Christ, not merely the separation from an addiction or the repair of a relationship. Those are often byproducts along the way but the goal is our entire life centered on Christ. That is what Jesus calls abiding in him; it is where abundant life is.

Their centered approach has further diminished a sense of separation in the church because there is less of an "us" and "them" attitude toward people with addictions. Dave says, "Because all are in need of pointing our arrows toward Christ, it widens the view of neediness and grace beyond just the red-letter bodily sins to all of us being called back to our original design as image bearers truly flourishing in being loved and loving others."

REENTRY AFTER PRISON

Chris Hoke also has shifted to a centered approach, but rather than moving from bounded to centered like Dave Obwald, Chris moved from fuzzy to centered. Chris and I grew up similarly. Unlike me, however, Chris stepped away from exclusionary line drawing much more quickly. Soon after he had newly experienced God's grace in a profound way, he threw away his religious line-drawing marker and became involved in jail ministry. To men who were accustomed to being on the wrong side of lines of exclusion, Chris proclaimed that there was no boundary to God's love. As described in his book *Wanted*, Chris led Bible studies that invited men to see themselves in Gospel stories and to experience forgiveness and Jesus' unexpected, total embrace.[3]

Chris stayed in touch with men when they left jail for prison, writing and visiting them. He knew the immense challenges awaiting the men once they got out, and that they would need more than Bible studies proclaiming God's limitless love. Yet having stepped away from line drawing, Chris hesitated to say anything that might lead the men to think that his love, or God's love, was conditional. Looking back, he now acknowledges he practiced a fuzzy approach. Often when men were about to be released, they would write and ask, "You going to be there for me when I get out?" Chris would respond, "Yeah I will." But what exactly did that mean? What future was the man hoping for? How did it align with the future Chris envisioned? What was required to get there? What would the man have to take on and commit himself to get there? What would Chris do? It all remained fuzzy.

Chris says, "We were allergic to conversation about clear expectations. We were so afraid of being Pharisees."[4] What did this commitment to avoid drawing lines lead to? In Chris's words, ineffective chaos. He recalls:

> We were chasing homies around all the time. Asking nothing of them, cleaning up their messes in hopes of working with them. We were taught that was Christlike, but actually it was a codependent imbalance. We wanted so much for them, but there was no clear agreement or expectations. We would say things like, "We just want to help man. What do you need?" Which was not really honest. We said, "Whatever you need," but actually we had clear ideas of what they needed. We wanted so much more for them. We would spend a lot of time with a guy; we would put a lot of money into paying off fines,

---

[3]Chris Hoke, *Wanted: A Spiritual Pursuit Through Jail, Among Outlaws, and Across Borders* (New York: HarperOne, 2015).
[4]The information and quotes in this section are from Chris Hoke, interview by the author, February 8, 2018.

getting their driver's license, helping them out with stuff, and then just see them not really taking it seriously. They thought they had arrived, we did not.

Chris would get discouraged and then resentful. He began to recognize, "The released prisoners were not taking advantage of us. This was on us. We never told them what we wanted to offer and what we expected of them." Chris did not want to go back to line-drawing judgmentalism that shamed and excluded, but he realized that simply erasing all the lines did not work either. It was not truly loving. Eventually Chris started a new organization, Underground Ministries, and created a new organizational culture.

Chris and his organization continue to love extravagantly—both through gracious embrace and through concrete actions of accompaniment. They provide assistance in getting a driver's license, getting a job, paying off fines and bills, and internal and interpersonal healing. They connect recently released prisoners with a congregation who is committed to walk with them. Rather than showering these services on all those they know and love, however, Chris has come to understand the importance of inviting people to make a turn and commit themselves to the process. He now clearly communicates expectations and enters a covenant with those who receive assistance from the organization.

Underground Ministries believes that resurrection is possible for those who have been buried alive in prison, society's underground tombs. They invite people who are still in prison to start the covenant commitment by completing a personal resurrection and reentry plan. The form uses Lazarus' story as a frame and asks participants to list their goals and dreams and then to name the things that are blocking those dreams of a fuller life—stones that need to be rolled away. They select from a list that includes legal obligations, debts, lack of job, the need for drug and alcohol treatment. The form then states,

> Lazarus still was not free when the stone was rolled away. He was still wrapped up like a mummy. Today we too have wrapped ourselves up in all sorts of "layers" that protected us in the underground life: anger, violence, unhealthy relationships, addictions to kill pain and hold us tight. But now they're getting in the way. Jesus told the community to "unbind" Lazarus. What do you think some of those layers would be that trip you up?

Next, participants write down short-term goals and expected next steps. Finally, by signing their names, they affirm their commitment to put in the work that it will take and invite the accompaniment of Underground Ministries.

In the past Chris shied away from insisting on a commitment such as this, mistaking it for conditional love or a bounded approach. So how is this new approach centered rather than bounded? First, Chris makes it clear that neither God's love nor his love for the incarcerated person is conditional. On an Underground Ministries brochure, it says, "If you have your own path you want to try, cool. We'd love to still stay in touch with you. Our doors and hearts are open to you. No matter what." Second, the directional sense of the program is strong and clear. The participant's commitments are not an end in themselves, nor are they standards to measure up to in order to be accepted by a church or God, but rather they work toward the stated goal of restoration and resurrection life. Third, how Chris describes the "One Parish One Prisoner" program to those who will accompany the formerly incarcerated also contributes to is centered nature.[5] He presents relationship building as the priority and frames the process as a journey of mutual transformation.

I asked Chris what happens when participants fail to keep their commitments, such as when they fail a drug test. "How are you different from your former fuzzy approach? How are you not bounded?" He says that before they had no clarity. "When one of them messed up I might say, 'This is not cool, this is lousy.' They'd say, 'No, I am fine, thanks.' I had no basis to challenge them." Now it is different. There are clear standards, an agreement to which he can point.

This does not mean that everyone who "messes up" gets kicked out of the program. He told me about a recent interaction involving a man who tripped up and got high. But the man was humble and acknowledged he had messed up. He said, "I do not want to go back to prison. I will do whatever you say." Chris explained, "In this case I knew he was serious, he is so on board with other things. So, I asked questions; I explored, 'Why'd you do this?' He knows it is not me being nosey or judging. He had committed himself to this process. He senses I am probing to figure out how we can help him. It is reintegrative." Chris leans back and says, "Before, I was so afraid of being a

---

[5] "One Parish One Prisoner," *Underground Ministries*, https://undergroundministries.org/opop/.

Pharisee that we could not have these strategic, pragmatic conversations about how to care for those we love."

Sometimes, Underground Ministries discerns that a person has broken covenant and is not committed to the goal of restoration and new life and removes them from the program. Even then, especially then, they intentionally undercut the judgmentalism and conditional love of a bounded approach. Referring to such a situation, Chris says, "We told him, this is the path we know, what we offer. This is what you said you wanted and committed to at the start. If you want to try another way, you're free to. We're here if you want to come back and try this again, later. We love you."

Reflecting on the changes that Underground Ministries has made, Chris says that having a stated path to which people commit provides a basis for real conversation so that they can discern next steps together by looking at the disjuncture between their life as it is and the path along which they want to be traveling.

Chris credits Greg Boyle, a Jesuit priest, for helping him imagine an alternative to a fuzzy or bounded approach. Since 1984, Boyle has ministered in a parish in East Los Angeles with the highest concentration of gang activity in the city. In 1988 he started Homeboy Industries, which has become the largest gang intervention, rehab, and reentry program on the planet. It provides jobs, tattoo removal, mental health counseling, case management, and legal services. In addition to his skills in ministering to gang members, Boyle is a great storyteller.[6] His two books overflow with stories and insights he has gained from decades of a life intertwined with gang members. His books do not begin with autobiography, nor with dramatic tales of gang violence or sad stories of addiction and brokenness, nor exhortation about the necessity of providing jobs and counseling—though all these things are found in the books. Rather, the first chapter in both books focuses on God. In the first paragraph of *Barking to the Choir*, he writes, "It is indeed a challenge to abandon the long-held belief that God yearns to blame and punish us, ask us to measure up or express disappointment and

---

[6]Many of his story-filled talks are available online. I recommend "Compassion and Kinship: Fr. Gregory Boyle at TEDxConejo 2012," video, 20:39, June 20, 2012, www.youtube.com /watch?v=ipR0kWtlFkc/. His two books are *Tattoos on the Heart: The Power of Boundless Compassion* (New York: Free Press, 2010) and *Barking to the Choir: The Power of Radical Kinship* (New York: Simon & Schuster, 2017).

disapproval at every turn."[7] Boyle proclaims the opposite and tells moving stories of homies who experience that God is love and that they are beloved by God. Why does he start his books this way? What can we learn from that?

Gang members' relational lives are riddled with abandonment, alienation, and attachment issues. And for most, the God they live with is part of that negative stew of rejection and shame. Boyle has seen the destructive power of a distorted concept of God, and he has seen that homies experiencing the loving embrace of a God looking at them with eyes of compassion and delight is a powerful contribution to healing. Boyle begins his books with chapters on God because one's concept of God is of fundamental importance. His example underlines a key difference between a bounded and centered approach—how we perceive God.

Boyle's approach is centered, but not fuzzy. He combines radical love and acceptance with directional language, a call to something. He says, "'Working on yourself' doesn't move the dial on God's love. After all, that is already fixed at its highest setting. But the work one does seeks to align our lives with God's longing for us—that we be happy, joyful, and liberated from all that prevents us from seeing ourselves as God does."[8] Seeking to "foster an irresistible culture of tenderness" and wanting "harmonizing love to infiltrate the whole place" does not mean that anything goes. Boyle writes, "We often say to the homies: 'We got you' (with a finger pointing) and 'we got you' (with an open-armed abrazo [hug]). I am indeed heartened that gang members can receive, by in large, the occasional critique I send their way and not have them interpret it in any way other than loving, even if it's hard to take."[9]

Homeboy Industries patiently journeys with their workers, but they must sometimes fire people. Yet even that significant disciplinary action is done in an intentionally centered way. "When it seems the best thing for a person, I have, often enough, fired someone. I call the person in and say, 'The day won't ever come when I will withdraw love and support from you. I am simply in your corner till the wheels fall off. Oh, by the way, I have to let you go.' They always agree with me. Nearly always."[10] Homeboy wraps disciplinary action

---

[7] Boyle, *Barking to the Choir,* 13.
[8] Boyle, *Barking to the Choir,* 111.
[9] Boyle, *Barking to the Choir,* 122.
[10] Boyle, *Tattoos on the Heart,* 178.

with love, not just to contrast with bounded religiosity, but, even more so, to the bounded character of gangs. "Gangs are bastions of conditional love— one false move, and you find yourself outside. Slights are remembered, errors in judgment held against you forever."[11]

As in many recovery programs, those who work at Homeboy must do drug testing. Yet, similar to Dave Obwald's description of his church's recovery program, the focus is not on the line or the drugs themselves, but deeper issues. Boyle observes, "Embarking on 'the good journey' requires confronting the inevitable emotional obstacles in that path. It's always a painful process, and we don't want them to numb themselves by self-medication. Once they let go of the hatred for their gang rivals—every homie's starting point—they are left to deal with their own pain."[12]

Certainly, how people in recovery think about the lines, such as drug testing, is a key factor in how they will experience the program—as centered or bounded. Yet the attitudes of the leaders and others who walk with those in recovery is even more important in preventing a program from having a bounded nature. This brings us back to matters of character in chapter seven. Father Boyle underscores the absolute necessity of compassion. "Judgement never gets past the behavior. . . . Judgment keeps us in the competitive game and is always self-aggrandizing."[13] As we already observed, he calls us to turn from judgmentalism to compassionate accompaniment, saying, "the ultimate measure of health in any community might well reside in our ability to stand in awe at what folks have to carry rather than judgement at how they carry it."[14]

Moving past the surface behavior, looking with eyes of compassion, Boyle sees abandonment, deep wounds, and pain. And he sees shame. At the root of addiction, violence, and gang membership is shame.[15] Boyle captures the reality of pervasive shame with great images, such as: "There is a palpable sense of disgrace strapped like an oxygen tank onto the back of every homie

---

[11]Boyle, *Tattoos on the Heart,* 94.
[12]Boyle, *Barking to the Choir,* 84.
[13]Boyle, *Barking to the Choir,* 52, 54.
[14]Boyle, *Barking to the Choir,* 51.
[15]For more on shame as a fundamental issue contributing to gang membership and violence, see Robert E. Brenneman, *Homies and Hermanos: God and Gangs in Central America* (New York: Oxford University Press, 2012) and James Gilligan, *Violence: Reflections on a National Epidemic* (New York: Vintage, 1997).

I know. . . . They strut around in protective shells of posturing." Whereas the shaming tendencies of a bounded approach add to the disgrace, Boyle seeks to counter "the wreck of a lifetime of internalized shame" by communicating the reality that "God finds them (us) wholly acceptable. . . . One of the signature marks of our God is the lifting of shame."[16] Boyle seeks to follow Jesus in showering the shamed with love and dignity through radical inclusion and kinship. "Precisely to those paralyzed in this toxic shame, Jesus says, 'I will eat with you. . . .' He goes where love has not yet arrived. . . . Eating with outcasts rendered them acceptable."[17]

HOMELESS MINISTRY

Ministries that provide services to homeless people have certain dynamics that are not present in other examples in this book—foremost that many of the people participating are neither part of the church nor aligned with the church's center. Because their actions can have significant consequences for other homeless people served by the program, rules or boundaries are important. Therefore, many people might think it is necessary to impose a bounded approach in this aspect of a church's ministry.

As we observed in chapter two, after hearing a lecture by Paul Hiebert on bounded and centered churches, Weldon Nisly left seminary with a passionate commitment to the centered approach. He is now retired, but in his last pastorate with Seattle Mennonite Church, he sought to apply the centered approach both within the church and in the church's community ministry. He recalls that the church's homeless ministry "initially emerged from being faithful to what God was setting before us by listening to our friends without homes living on the neighborhood streets. It became a way of embracing people who felt unwelcome most places and welcoming them to be present in the church, including in worship in ways they chose to be present."[18] As church members got to know homeless people through fellowship meals, the church's involvement grew from providing bag lunches for day laborers in the church foyer to buying a nearby house that has "daily drop-in hours during which time people can access laundry facilities,

---

[16]Boyle, *Tattoos on the Heart*, 43, 52, 44; *Barking to the Choir*, 135.
[17]Boyle, *Tattoos on the Heart*, 70.
[18]Weldon Nisly, email to author, May 27, 2020.

showers and hygiene, community kitchen, internet and phone, resource referral, food closet, nursing care, personal storage, blankets and clothes, and a safe, secure place to just 'be.'"[19]

Weldon affirms that in the services and spaces they provide, rules are important. He acknowledges that they have, at times, had to get restraining orders. Yet, like Dave Obwald and Chris Hoke, he recognizes the benefits of doing homeless ministry in a more centered way. "We do have rules, for instance: no drugs, no alcohol, no sex, no violence." But the rules have grown out of a process with the homeless people. Weldon recalls, "We asked them, 'What do you need to come here and be safe?' When new people come, we do not simply state the rules. We go over them and tell their purpose and origin." The focus is on self-monitoring and community monitoring. The church both encourages participants to take the lead and trusts them to do so. Weldon observes, "People in the program itself help monitor and talk to each other and get others to comply. They are very good at helping each other. Still, problems arise that you have to work with, but the framework is totally different." It has produced a setting where the rules are taken seriously, but it does not feel to the homeless community as if they are doing something that has been imposed on them. Instead, they sense that it is good for the community.[20]

CHILDREN'S MINISTRY

Some have commented to me that a bounded approach is important in children's programs because children of certain ages need clear statements about what is right and wrong. However, that confuses clarity with boundedness. While bounded lines are clear, not all expressions of clarity are bounded. The clear lines of a bounded church are draped with conditional love, a centered church can communicate with clarity and simplicity, but clothe the statements, and especially the enforcement of them, in unconditional love.

Connie Nicholson, a children's ministry pastor at North Fresno Church, trains Sunday school teachers to be invitational rather than condemning when articulating rules or behavioral expectations. For instance, she

---

[19]"Community Ministry," *Seattle Mennonite Church*, https://seattlemennonite.org/community
-ministry/.
[20]Weldon Nisly, interview by the author, February 15, 2018.

regularly reminds children about the expectations for their sharing time, but rather than saying, "Don't talk when others are sharing," she says, "When someone is sharing, we will listen with active ears." Yet Nicholson says she also seeks to limit the amount of rules they do have. For instance, rather than having a list of rules during playtime, she encourages teachers to see it as an opportunity for teaching that goes deeper than rules. She says, "We do not have the rule, 'Don't push someone off the jungle gym,' but when I see a child do that, I gently draw the child aside and ask, 'What just happened?' to make sure the child is aware of what he or she did. Then I ask, 'How do you think that made the person feel? Was pushing loving?'"[21] Nicholson seeks to encourage children to think about how their behavior might be affecting someone else and what it means to love others and love God—rather than just imposing rules on them. Her priority is for children to feel that church is safe and that God is good.

As we observed in chapter two, the paradigms have power. A bounded approach not only communicates with clarity, it also pulls us to focus on the line. Focusing on the line has consequences. Jennifer McWilliams, the children's pastor at The Meeting House, observes, "So much children's curriculum is focused on getting children to behave. With much of it, you could just pull out the Bible verses and what is written would work fine in Boys and Girls clubs."[22] McWilliams explains that it's "not that we do not deal with behavior, but we don't start there. We start with Jesus. What Jesus lives and teaches has implications for behavior, actions." Just as the bounded approach pulls children to focus on the line, the centered approach pulls children to focus on the center—Jesus. This focus changes the character of the whole.

While children of certain ages do need simplicity and clarity, a bounded approach draws clear lines for all ages—even when the children could handle more complexity. The Meeting House encourages teachers of some age groups to work toward creating safe spaces for children to ask questions. They train the teachers to accept children being in different places—rather than focusing on having one "right" answer. Natalie Frisk, author of *Raising Disciples: How to Make Faith Matter for Our Kids* and the writer of The

---

[21]Connie Nicholson, interview by the author, October 7, 2019.
[22]Jennifer McWilliams, focus group discussion, The Meeting House, Oakville, Ontario, January 22, 2018.

Meeting House's children's curriculum,[23] observes that youth, and especially their parents—often want a simple focus on what they are allowed and not allowed to do. She tells youth, "If you are looking at the line and what you are allowed to do, then you are not actually looking at Jesus." She can see the light bulbs going on in their heads, and they say, "Oh, I see what you mean." This approach begins a conversation, "You're saying we should look at Jesus and consider all things relationally with him."[24] This focuses on reorientation rather than a particular set of rules.

We do need to be aware of the stages of development. Children of different ages process and understand information and ideas differently. Yet, I believe a bigger factor leading some to use bounded approaches with children is fear of them misbehaving. A bounded approach feels stricter; it is more threatening, and it carries a bigger stick. Many grasp at anything they think might work to keep kids safe and out of trouble. This raises two important questions. Does such an approach actually work better? Do the positives of behavior enforcement outweigh the negatives? Fear is a short-term motivator, and as we have seen in the above examples, a centered approach gets past the superficial and leads to deeper transformation.

Furthermore, we also need to consider what toxins we are pouring into our children that may affect them for years—even for life. If they grow up with a bounded-church experience, they will carry toxic shame and the toxicity of conditional love—including a God of conditional love. Aundrea Ascencio shared with me that she recently experienced God as gracious and loving, but she is still working to cleanse herself from the toxins of a distorted concept of God—a result of the boundedness she experienced as a child and youth. She recalls, "I had always been taught that God will punish and judge me every time I stepped out of the limits set by the church. Even if it were a small transgression, the church's portrayal of God was unforgiving and conveyed to me that I needed to be spotless." Eventually she grew weary of church and felt distant from God.[25] Was whatever behavior

---

[23]The Meeting House makes their own curriculum and shares it freely: https://onestorycurriculum
.com/; http://kidsandyouth.themeetinghouse.com/.

[24]Natalie Frisk, focus group discussion, The Meeting House, Oakville, Ontario, January 22, 2018.

[25]Aundrea Ascencio, written assignment ("Discipleship and Ethics" course, Fresno Pacific Biblical Seminary, Fresno, CA, April 8, 2021). As Aundrea reflects on her past, she displays the centered character of compassion described in chapter 7: "After discovering this counter message to what

compliance gained through the bounded threats worth it? My Old Testament professor in seminary, Francis Andersen, insisted that the most important thing we can do as parents is to make the love of God credible to our children. Thus we must reflect on how a bounded approach might discredit the love of God for our children.

CONCLUSION

We began this chapter with the question, "Do some populations, such as those in recovery, need a bounded approach?" The practitioners in this chapter would answer the question by saying, "No, those in recovery do not need a bounded approach. In fact, they would be better served by a centered approach." The practitioners would affirm that clarity, standards, and firmness are important in recovery situations. The distinction is not that a bounded approach is clear and firm, while a centered approach is not. Rather, the contrast is between the sense of conditional love in one and unconditional love in the other, between shaming judgmentalism in one and compassionate curiosity in the other, between a fixation on the standards in one and seeing standards as tools in the journey of recovery and transformation in the other.

I grew up with, I had feelings of empathy rather than resentment for the church I was raised in. I understand their logic behind it more, in that we as human beings are uncomfortable in our own inadequacy and desire to feel worthy of God's love and salvation."

12

IMAGINING CENTERED ALTERNATIVES

WE NOW TURN FROM SITUATIONS where some have assumed the needs of the people demand a bounded approach to elements of ministry where some see boundedness inherent in the aspect of ministry itself. In this chapter we will explore centered ways of practicing church membership, setting higher standards for leaders, and doing evangelism.

MEMBERSHIP

Megan Ramer, the pastor at Seattle Mennonite Church who followed Weldon Nisly, acknowledged in a sermon that "a traditional membership model wasn't working for many people here. It felt too bounded, too boundaried—keeping track of who was in and who was out."[1] Her comments reflect a common sentiment, as I frequently hear comments about the tension between membership and a centered-church paradigm. Membership requirements are fundamental for all bounded groups—not just bounded churches. Even in bounded groups that may not exude judgmental superiority, membership communicates some degree of exclusivity and, even if subtle, some sense of distinction. Often membership communicates something about rights and entitlements for the members.

---

[1]Megan Ramer, sermon manuscript, Seattle Mennonite Church, May 15, 2016.

Bounded-church membership can contribute to anemic discipleship by communicating that if you meet certain requirements, you are "in," even if you are just a spectator or your attendance is sporadic. As we observed in the case of the Honduran woman who was a member in good standing, but whose marriage was deeply troubled, bounded-church membership tends to focus on certain requirements and remain indifferent to other ways that members' lives might not align with the way of Jesus.

Many practitioners have told me, with a certain degree of pride, that their church does not "do" membership. While abandoning membership solves some of the problems caused by bounded-church membership, it does not solve the anemic discipleship problem. Opting for fuzziness loses the positive aspects of church membership.

A moment after Megan Ramer made the above statement, she continued, referring back to the time when Weldon Nisly had been the pastor at the church, "Wise congregational leaders here at Seattle Mennonite Church didn't want to altogether do away with offering an opportunity for newer-comers and longer-timers alike to name a commitment to this church, this particular manifestation of Christ's body in the world." But what might a centered approach to church membership look like? In the examples that follow, I will share how Seattle Mennonite and other churches responded to this question. Before turning to these specific examples, I will list some key qualities that need to be considered when discerning a centered approach to church membership.

Key qualities in centered membership. First, it is important to begin by asking the question, "Why?" What are the purposes for church membership? Seeing discipleship and transformation as a fundamental purpose for membership will help insure an approach with a centered character. In relation to shaping a membership practice, Scott Carolan suggests asking, "How can we shape the membership process so that it might help someone point toward Jesus?" He sees membership as a tool to help shepherd the congregation rather than to police who is in and who is out.[2]

Second, centered membership will highlight relational aspects over institutional ones through a sense of commitment to the body and others in the

---

[2]Scott Carolan, interview by the author, February 27, 2018.

body. Third, a centered approach to membership will include a sense of invitation—not just to be part of an organization, but to join in a mission. Finally, a centered approach will describe membership by using language of orientation to, alignment with, and commitment to the center rather than language of requirements and boundaries.

Static membership (once you're "in," you're "done") contributes to anemic discipleship, whereas centered membership conveys a sense of movement toward the center. This does not mean that the centered approach will avoid all lines. When we move toward something, we intentionally take steps that shift us from one position to another. A centered church must provide its members with clear opportunities to turn toward the center. In many churches, baptism provides this clarifying turn, and a commitment to membership can provide this as well. Ongoing opportunities to commit to membership invite members to evaluate their position and realign with the center.

In bounded membership, a church's statement of faith serves as a fence. For membership to function in a centered way, beliefs must function as a well rather than a fence. Because a centered church focuses on one's journey, there is space to affirm that someone is heading toward but is not necessarily in total agreement with all the beliefs of the center. At the same time, there is a center, and beliefs are an important part of the center. As we observed in chapter three with Weldon Nisly and his church's peace position, it is one thing to be exploring and another to stand against what is at the center of a community. Pulling down the fences enables an approach to membership that focuses on the thriving of the individual and the congregation. This is reflected in the way that Aaron Carlson explained the statements of belief in a congregation he pastored:

> These are teaching positions of this fellowship. You don't have to be in complete agreement with them in order to be a member here. We recognize that we are all in process. But if these teaching statements are going to cause major friction for you, and are going to be constantly grating against you, if they are going to cause you to be constantly pushing back—then maybe this isn't a great fit.[3]

---

[3] Aaron Carlson, email to author, October 2, 2017.

One way that some churches seek to diminish friction is to ask members to affirm key elements rather than a complete statement of faith. While such an approach can serve to heighten the sense of importance of those "key" elements, it can also feel like the church is just building a lower fence. Even with minimalist faith statements, it is still necessary to do the work of reframing from a bounded to centered perspective.

A church's center consists of more than beliefs, and in a centered church, membership should include more than affirmation of beliefs. Raymond Bystrom, a professor of pastoral ministries, advocates including values as part of membership commitment, especially "Jesus' values since we are Jesus pilgrims, traveling in his direction individually and corporately." A bounded approach does not lend itself to including values in membership requirements. Someone's living out values cannot be measured and used as an in-or-out criteria in the same way as beliefs or some other membership requirements. As Bystrom observes, "We are all at a different point in our journey toward understanding and embodying our Lord's values."[4] A centered church recognizes that, and its directional focus enables it to include values like generosity, integrity, mercy, justice, hospitality, and other Christlike values such as those described in chapter seven.

The word *member* itself tends to be laden with bounded-group associations, and so it is essential to reframe it. Thankfully, the Bible strips away negative associations with the word *member* by relating it to the metaphor of a body, which is made up of many parts (see Rom 12:4-5; 1 Cor 12:27; Eph 5:30). Saying that we are "members" of the body of Christ centers on an organic connection to Jesus and other members of the body. As members of a church body, we are joined together as living, active, functioning parts of a whole.

Centered membership can take on many forms. I share here three distinctly different approaches. As you read these examples, first look for things that might help the people in the church experience membership in a centered way, such as the characteristics described above. Then read through the examples a second time and let them stimulate your imagination about how to enhance your church's membership practice.

---

[4]Raymond O. Bystrom, email to author, February 6, 2021.

Seattle Mennonite Church. Seattle Mennonite Church annually invites those participating in the congregation to renew their covenant. The covenant is sent out ahead of time with an invitation for people to discern their commitment. Both the statement itself and the way it is explained contribute to the centered character of the covenant process. Before the covenanting, Megan Ramer's sermon clearly invites people to choose the covenant (or not) and extends a wide welcome to those who do not to remain in the community.

> And for those who may not yet be ready, you are welcome here in this place and among this people. Fully and without hesitation or limitation. We don't and won't track who's in and who's out. That doesn't even compute in our understanding of what it means to be church. We will keep gathering around our center, who is Christ, and we pray that all in this place, on any given day, will be invited and drawn into that center together.

She invites thoughtful reflection on the covenant by asking, "Where do you particularly resonate. . . ? Do you sense a 'Yes' welling up within you?" She also invites people to consider what shifts they notice in themselves and adds that "this is a living, moving covenant." Then those who want to covenant are invited to read the following statement together:

> As an Anabaptist community of God's people, we at Seattle Mennonite Church receive with joy and humility the mystery of God's grace, truth and love. In response to God's initiation, we make this covenant with God and with each other, to join in worship, praise, and service.
>
> We affirm our faith in God, the source of life and love, the Creator of the world. We commit ourselves to follow Jesus Christ, who reconciles and reveals God to us through the Holy Spirit. We welcome God's Spirit to transform, empower, and guide us, as together we discern and follow the Gospel of Jesus Christ. We pledge to care for each other, including our children, nurturing the gifts of each person, and living towards just, nonviolent, and transformative relationships in community.
>
> We renounce evil, both personal and corporate, and join God's plan for healing the earth, and bringing just peace to its people. We accept God's call to share the good news of transforming love, and welcome others to faith in God and belonging into Jesus Christ's beloved community.

We encourage and pray for each other as we live out this covenant which gives us hope for the time when God brings all of creation into wholeness and an end to all suffering.[5]

Ramer's comment, "We don't and won't track who's in and who's out," could be interpreted as fuzzy and individualistic. I asked her what she meant by that. She explained that they do not keep a list of members. That does not mean they wrap membership under a blanket of privacy. For instance, after conversations with newcomers about covenanting, she invites them to share with the congregation about their decision to covenant.

The less rigid and less formal nature of the covenant membership does not imply a lack of seriousness. Even after switching to this approach, pastors and church leaders at Seattle Mennonite Church have at times met with people who have hurt others, or something happens that constitutes a breach of the congregational covenant. And, occasionally, when efforts of walking with the person did not lead to reorientation and repairing the harm done, the leaders stated clearly to the person that they had breached their covenant commitment. Those statements included an invitation to repent and a reiteration of the church's desire for the person to be in covenant relationship once again.[6]

Mile High Vineyard. Mile High Vineyard is a family of neighborhood Vineyard churches in Denver, Colorado. Rather than *member* they use the term *covenant partner*. They want to move from a sense of someone with rights and privileges to someone who has a sense of ownership and commitment. Mile High Vineyard does not press people to commit quickly to covenant partnership. They encourage people to first participate in discipleship training programs. When people are ready to consider commitment, they participate in a two-hour meeting over lunch that includes three teaching sessions with a small group discussion after each one. The teaching is based on a document that the leadership team worked on together called "Covenant Community." Each participant receives a copy of the document. What follows is based on that written work.

---

[5]Megan Ramer, sermon manuscript, Seattle Mennonite Church, May 15, 2016.

[6]Megan Ramer, emails to author, September 21 and 29, 2020. Ramer clarified that she generally assumes people in the church are covenanted, addresses them as such, being open to being corrected. If a person is more on the fringe, she would ask rather than assume.

The first teaching addresses the question, "Why make a commitment to a local community?" It is seven pages rich with cultural observations and biblical insights. As I summarize the main points, I invite you to reflect on ways they differentiate their centered way from both bounded and fuzzy approaches. The teaching begins by acknowledging that the United States is becoming a commitment-phobic culture, hesitant to commit to personal relationships or social organizations. The first section, "Commitment Confronts Contract," states that for many people membership in a church is similar to gym membership: it is an exchange of goods and services. This contractual approach is then contrasted to biblical covenant and its relational character. The following section, "Covenant Confronts Consumerism," includes the statement,

> In a culture where we don't make commitments, we don't need to forgive—we just move on. We don't need to really serve from our hearts out of love, out of compassion, out of care. We can fulfill an obligation if that's what we're required to do to be a part of the group, but the Scriptures want more than just simple obedience or frustrated compliance. The Scriptures call us to love and care and bless and sacrifice for one another. And that has to happen in the context of a covenant agreement where we're choosing to commit to one another relationally because we know that we love and follow Jesus.[7]

The next section, "Covenant Confronts Individualism," uses the analogy of church as a swim team. Swimmers on a team receive words of challenge, instruction, correction, and encouragement from coaches, and they exchange words of encouragement and correction with others on the team. In contrast, for many, church is more like individuals swimming in a pool on their own. They would be quite surprised, perhaps resentful, if someone shouted out instructions on how to improve their stroke.

> Most people see the church as something where they're just sort of coming and hanging out. They kind of get that it is a benefit to them, but their responsibility to others, their understanding or expectation that everybody is there to help them grow or change or challenge them is really limited. And even if they want challenge, it will come only on their own terms—not on the terms of what a coach might think or the team might need.[8]

---

[7]"Covenant Community," Mile High Vineyard, December 12, 2018, 5.
[8]"Covenant Community," 5-6.

In contrast,

> When Jesus called people, he called them disciples. . . . And disciples in the
> Scriptures never exist alone. They were part of a team. When the Scriptures
> talk about what it means to know God, the Scriptures always tell us that we're
> suddenly included within a body. We're connected to others. Very plainly
> the Apostle Paul writes in 1 Corinthians 12:27, "Now you are the body of
> Christ, and each one of you is a part of it." Or we're connected in a family;
> we're living life with others. . . . So you see, to enter into life with God,
> through Jesus Christ, immediately throws you into connection and com-
> mitment with others.[9]

The following section, "Covenant Confronts Anti-Authority," adds that
just as authority is given to coaches to exhort us and call us to something, so
too in a covenant community pastors and other leaders have that role. From
that perspective,

> it completely makes sense when a pastor says, "Hey, I want to talk to you about
> your marriage." "Hey, I'm concerned about how you're thinking about your
> money." "I've noticed that maybe you don't have a heart for the poor or for
> your brothers and sisters—you seem isolated to me." "Hey, can I talk you
> through how you form a prayer life, how you grow in your understanding of
> the Scriptures or a greater connection to God or to mission or to calling." See,
> if you've understood yourself as being a part of a family, on a team, or part of
> a body, that all seems natural. That all seems clear. This isn't just about you
> and getting your needs met.[10]

After these sections of contrast—that is, describing what covenant is *not*—
the final section makes the positive statement, "Living in Covenant with
Others is for God's Glory and Your Good." It plants a sense of vision and
calling. It states they covenant together with others to show the world there
is a God and that through Jesus, people who are very different join together
and display that grace is real, forgiveness is real, and hope is real. Then,
moving to the last part of the section title, they explain,

> And frankly this serves you too—not just the watching world. The truth is, you
> can't make it on your own. You can't just live out of your own resources. To be

---

[9]"Covenant Community," 7.
[10]"Covenant Community," 7.

submitted to others, to serve others, to be trained and challenged to put yourself in life with others means strengthening for your marriage, for your own life with God, for the way you think of yourself in a business or as a parent. You're no longer living within your own resources; your life now includes the gifts that God gives across the body that are used to serve one another and care for one another. This goes way beyond just saying, "Yeah, I'll agree to do this and agreed not to do that." It's saying "I choose to live as a part of a family that has a local expression, because that's the way that God designed for me to live out and to fulfill the best life that God would call me to."[11]

After this first teaching session, the group discussion questions include

▶ What have you been really committed to before? School? A gym? Friendship?

▶ How did that help you and what was it like being part of something larger than yourself?

▶ What is your greatest desire and your greatest fear regarding personally committing yourself to a local church?[12]

The second teaching session, titled "What Am I Being Asked to Do?" begins by explaining that although covenants differ from contracts, they still have structure and stated expectations. The teaching then explores in-depth commitments listed in the covenant statement below. The third session describes Mile High Vineyard's shared theology, values, heart, and structure. After the final small group discussion, the participants are invited to sign the following commitment statement if they desire:

Committing to Covenant Community

Giving my Word

As a covenant partner in my church, I recognize that . . .

▶ I represent Jesus Christ, his kingdom and my church to the people I encounter, both inside and outside the church.

▶ I am a model—others will follow the example of what I think, say, and do.

---

[11]"Covenant Community," 8.
[12]"Covenant Community," 10.

Therefore, as a covenant partner in my church, I commit to grow into the following:

▶ To maintain and grow in my relationship with Jesus, through the practice of consistent Bible reading, worship and prayer (2 Pet 3:18).

▶ To attend weekend services regularly (Heb 10:25).

▶ To live in consistent, intentional relationship with followers of Jesus in this church community (Jn 15:9-17).

▶ To demonstrate moral purity as defined in the Bible, which includes refraining from all premarital and/or extramarital sexual activity, not cohabiting with a significant other before marriage, refraining from inappropriate speech (both spoken or in writing) and avoiding addictions (drugs, alcohol, pornography, gambling, etc) (Gal 5:16-21; 1 Cor 6:18-20; Eph 5:3-7; Jas 3:5-12).

▶ To honor all marriage covenants, especially my own, and when necessary, to resolve any marital problems with the care and counsel of the church's pastoral staff (Mt 19:4-6; Eph 5:31-33).

▶ To seek to display Christian character in my relationships with others by being kind and courteous; expressing loyalty, honor and appreciation; refraining from gossip; willingly offering and receiving forgiveness; and recognizing and encouraging other's gifts and abilities (Eph 4:1-3, 20-32; Gal 5:22-23).

▶ To work through proper pastoral relationships when I desire to speak about matters of concern in the church regarding what I see or experience personally.

▶ To be faithful with my finances by giving at least 10 percent (a "tithe") of my income to the Lord through the church or to formulate a plan to work toward this goal (Lev 27:30; Mal 3:6-12; Prov 3:9-10; Lk 6:38; Mt 5:17-20).

▶ To cultivate a lifestyle of neighboring and service, prepared to share Jesus and provide help to any whom I might encounter who are in need (1 Pet 3:15; 1 Jn 3:17-18).

▶ To use my spiritual gifts to serve and build up my church community and my city (1 Cor 12).

▶ To resolve any dispute I may have with the church or one of its members according to Matthew 18. If that fails, I will pursue mediation to resolve disputes and not pursue lawsuits in court against the church, its employees or partners (1 Cor 6:1-8).[13]

Although they include theological beliefs as part of the instruction of what it means to be a covenant partner, they do not include a list of beliefs that people must commit to. I asked Corey Garris, pastor of one the churches and chief of staff of the family network of churches, about this. He explained that theological beliefs are an assumed part of the covenant commitment. They do not, however, present them as a checklist that people must affirm, but rather the teaching in the last section is framed as "this is who we are, what we believe in. We want you to know who you are committing to partner with."[14]

Throughout their materials on covenanting and the actual commitment statements, it stands out that they work as hard against fuzziness as they do against boundedness. Their list of commitments is certainly not fuzzy! Yet they include the word *grow* in the commitment statement. It communicates a sense of a work in progress, a journey. A bounded group could not use that word. You either are fulfilling the requirements, or you are not. So, in one sense, the word *grow* lessens the strictness of the list. At the same time, it also raises expectations beyond a bounded church's static meeting-the-criteria membership. As Garris points out, it communicates that you cannot remain the same. They expect everyone to continually work at growing.

Keller Park Church. Keller Park Church is a close-knit, intergenerational church in a diverse neighborhood in South Bend, Indiana, which is affiliated with the Missionary Church. David Cramer, a bivocational pastor, is leading the church through a process of reframing their membership in a centered way. The following statement came out of that process. Cramer imagines they will use this statement both when people become members and in an annual reaffirmation of membership.

At Keller Park Church (KPC), we take a centered-church approach to membership. This means that we regularly proclaim Jesus and the kingdom that Jesus calls his followers to embrace as the center of everything we do. . . .

---

[13]"Covenant Community," 29.
[14]Corey Garris, phone conversation with author, February 17, 2021.

Being a member doesn't mean that you've signed off on a list of doctrines and practices, nor does it mean that you won't ever have days when you are pulled away from the center rather than toward it. What it does mean is that you freely commit to being part of a community that defines itself by who and what is at its center and that you freely commit to opening your life to being drawn closer to the center as part of that community. . . .

If KPC defines membership as freely committing to a community defined by its center and freely committing to being drawn closer to the center, then how does KPC define the center toward which we are drawn? The short answer is (1) Jesus and (2) the life to which Jesus calls his followers—often called the kingdom of heaven or kingdom of God. . . . [The longer answer that follows] begins to resemble lists of articles of faith and practice, though, again, these articles are understood not as exclusionary boundaries (believe them or you're out!) but rather as the beating heart of what makes the church who and what it is.

Then follows their first statement of faith:

At Keller Park Church, we believe that Jesus is . . .

1. the risen Lord.
2. the Word of God.
3. the Son of God.
4. the suffering messiah.
5. the new human.
6. the savior of the world.
7. the liberator of the oppressed.
8. the authoritative teacher and healer.
9. the initiator of the kingdom.
10. the sender of the Spirit.
11. the head of the church.
12. the victor over Sin and Death.

Their second statement of faith is

At Keller Park Church, we believe that the kingdom of God is the realm where . . .

1. the love of God reigns.
2. the peace of God reigns.
3. the goodness of God reigns.

4. the holiness of God reigns.

5. the righteousness and justice of God reign.

6. the generosity of God reigns.

7. the faithfulness of God reigns.

8. the kindness of God reigns.

9. the gentleness and patience of God reign.

10. the truth of God reigns.

11. the freedom of God reigns.

12. the joy of God reigns.

These statements are followed by ten questions for potential members of KPC to consider:

1. Where do I currently stand in relation to Jesus?

2. Where do I currently stand in relation to the kingdom of God?

3. What might it mean for me to be drawn closer to Jesus?

4. What might it mean for me to be drawn closer to the kingdom of God?

5. How might KPC be a context for being drawn closer to Jesus and the kingdom of God?

6. How might I help others at KPC, the Keller Park Neighborhood, and beyond move closer to Jesus and the kingdom of God?

7. Do I freely commit to a fellowship of others who are being drawn ever closer to Jesus and the kingdom of God in the context of the Keller Park community?

8. Have I enacted my commitment to Jesus and the kingdom of God through baptism (at KPC or another Christian church)?

9. Do I regularly memorialize my commitment to Jesus and the kingdom of God through the practice of Communion at KPC?

10. Am I willing to offer and receive mutual counsel, discernment, admonition, and accountability at KPC regarding our shared commitments to Jesus and the kingdom of God?[15]

I hope this section, and these examples particularly, have stimulated ideas on how you might move to a more centered approach to membership. I also

---

[15]David C. Cramer, "Membership at Keller Park Church," unpublished draft, March 2020, quoted with the author's permission, https://www.ambs.edu/publishing/hope-and-resilience/resources.

imagine that for some the section may have stirred some longings, but also a sense of resignation. You might be thinking, *It would take a lot of work to redesign the process, and rewrite the commitments, and even more work to go through the steps of getting it approved by the congregation and instituting the changes.* Or perhaps in your denominational setting you cannot make changes at all.

Eric Miller is teaching pastor at Journey, a multisite Mennonite church in south-central Kansas. He and the rest of the pastoral team are passionately committed to centered ministry, and Journey has intentionally taken steps to become more centered. Yet Eric acknowledges, "We still have a rather bounded system of membership with a significant number of people on the roll who have moved away or are 'inactive' for a variety of reasons. The leadership team desires to change to a centered approach to membership formally, but in the midst of so much transition, we've never had the energy to make the shift." That does not, however, mean they have done nothing. Even now when they talk about membership, they seek to use centered language and call it a covenant relationship. And they have looked for ways to bring in centered dynamics even before the full overhaul. Eric observes,

> Several times over the past ten years, when we've introduced a renewed vision for the congregation, we've asked those who are ready to join together, to come forward and sign a large poster with the vision printed on it as a way of covenanting together as we move in this new direction. The poster was then displayed in a central corridor of each campus, and as others joined the congregation they could add their names.[16]

This practice, however, has never been linked to membership. They hope to continue moving toward the goal of being a more Jesus-centered church; pivoting their practice of church membership toward a centered approach in the future.

LEADERSHIP

People often view church leaders as an elite, bounded group that must meet higher standards than the rest of the congregation. Some churches use

---

[16]Eric Miller, email to author, February 15, 2021.

language that makes this hierarchy explicit. For example, some of the churches I visited in Honduras shamed leaders who failed to meet expectations and told them that they had lost their privileges and could no longer lead worship, sing in the worship band, hold a leadership position, and so forth. While these leaders can still be part of the church, they can no longer be part of the privileged inner circle.[17] In these churches, leaders are a bounded group within a larger bounded group.

I have heard many people who embrace a centered approach to church say, "But there are aspects of a church that will remain bounded—such as leadership. There must be higher standards for leaders." The latter is certainly true, but is the former? In part this depends on how we define bounded. The narrowest definition of a bounded set is a group of people who have the same select characteristics. In that sense leaders who meet certain standards and take on specific roles would be viewed as a bounded group. But if we think of the definition of bounded used in this book that includes the characteristic of judgmentalism and a sense of superiority of the insiders, then we would say the leaders are not necessarily a bounded group.[18] Regardless of which definition you prefer, the key question is: How might a church approach having higher standards for leaders in a way that avoids the negatives of bounded approaches described in this book?

I asked this question of Bruxy Cavey and Darrell Winger, senior pastors at The Meeting House, a multisite church in Ontario, Canada.[19] The Meeting House is a large church, and their mid-week home church groups, which are led by lay leaders, are central to their ministry. The church has stated requirements for these leaders, which include theological alignment, but also include things like "able to guide a small group discussion with focus and clarity" and attending training events. Cavey observed, "Biblically there are qualifications for leadership. Therefore, we appropriately hold leaders to a higher degree of alignment and agreement." Expanding on that, Winger added, "A centered set does not mean there aren't places of clarity. We ask, 'Are you aligned with the direction of this movement? Can you steward the

---

[17]See Mark D. Baker, *Religious No More: Building Communities of Grace & Freedom* (Downers Grove, IL: InterVarsity Press, 1999), 23-24, 28, 51.

[18]See explanation of this definition on pages 24-25 of this book.

[19]What follows is from Bruxy Cavey and Darrell Winger, focus group discussion, The Meeting House, Oakville, Ontario, January 22, 2018, and email exchange, September 26-27, 2019.

ethos in the full sense of what it means to follow Jesus as an ever growing, ever committed disciple? We want you with integrity and authenticity to be able to help cultivate this ethos that we feel is so critical.'" Cavey stated,

> Often people who disagree with a position our church holds will complain to me, "Why can't I be a leader?" I respond, "Leadership means that, among other things, you feel called to officially and publicly affirm, support, and represent the views of that organization. To be a leader here you would need to represent our view instead of your own, with your heart not just your head. If you cannot do this with authenticity, that would put you in an unacceptable position. I don't think either of us want you to be a hypocrite." They usually respond, "I do not want to be a hypocrite." They get it.

Winger added, "We tell people, 'If you can steward the position, we will journey with you. If not, it is not that you are a bad person.'"

As we have observed elsewhere in the book, here as well there is not one right way to approach leadership standards in a centered church. Some are more formal, some less; some list explicit criteria for leaders, others do not. Yet centered churches will share the qualities discussed above. In order to avoid having a bounded group of elite leaders within a church, it is also important for leaders to seek to live out the qualities described in chapter seven. This includes a commitment to avoid using positional authority or adherence to certain standards as a way to elevate themselves or shame others.

A centered approach to church leaders is evident not only in relation to standards, but also how the church responds when leaders act in ways incongruent with expectations. I asked Cavey and Winger how they respond when they discern a change in alignment within those who are already leaders. Winger responded,

> We, of course, first meet, discuss and work for realignment. We try to do it relationally, patiently. The issue is not how many times a person has fallen, but orientation. We seek to wrestle with a person's heart orientation. Are they teachable? We do at times get to the place where we have to say, "This is not helpful for you and is hurting the group." We do not say, "You are a bad person," but we do ask them to step away from leadership. Some continue with us in the church; others move on.

The centered approach Winger describes not only avoids the negative fruits of a bounded approach, but it holds the promise of positive fruit. It also entails more work, as evidenced in an example that Christa Wiens shared with me from her experience leading a youth group.[20] One of the volunteer leaders repeatedly did things that undermined the ministry, such as gossiping, speaking harshly to students, oversharing, and undercutting the youth pastor's authority. After conversation with a copastor, Christa met with the volunteer and shared her observations and concerns. Rather than tell the volunteer she could no longer serve as a leader, however, Christa sought to work with her. They had multiple conversations, working together to identify root causes and develop a plan to build her leadership skills. A seasoned volunteer offered mentoring. Eventually this mentor, Christa, and pastoral staff determined that even these supports were not enough; the problems continued. They discerned together how they might end the volunteer's role with the group in a way that would not hurt her or the community. They met to tell her she would no longer be able to serve in the youth group, they named her gifts, reminded her of the growth they had seen, and shared ideas for other ways she might be able to connect in the church that would better utilize her skills. They made clear that if she demonstrated growth in the areas that they had discussed, there may be an opportunity for her to try it again. They did not report to the youth or other volunteers why she was leaving. They did not shame her, nor create fertile ground for gossip. In the volunteer's last meeting Christa invited the group to share words of gratitude to her and blessed her transition.

EVANGELISM

Many people also assume that evangelism is bounded, and so as they move away from a bounded approach, they simply stop evangelizing. Yet conversion, or turning toward the center, is a fundamental element of a centered church. How can centered evangelism be distinguished from a bounded approach?

Centered evangelism is about alignment with the center. In the words of Peter and Paul, it is about repenting and turning to God

---

[20]Christa Wiens, phone conversation with author, October 2, 2020, and email confirmation, October 5, 2020.

(Acts 3:19; 26:20).[21] Rather than conveying that someone needs to get on the right side of a line like us, the centered approach invites others to join us and walk with us as we follow Jesus together. However, we can still talk about line crossing in the process of turning to Jesus; it is a decisive step when we recognize our need for God's liberating grace, when we choose to trust Jesus and follow him.

While centered evangelism lacks the judgmentalism of a bounded church, calling someone to turn toward the center does communicate that some paths are better than others. Centered evangelism is not "whateverism." So how can centered evangelism call for repentance without being imposing or judgmental?

Fundamentally, centered evangelism is not imposing because the church is focusing on Jesus rather than the fence. As a church sinks more deeply into the character of Jesus, its evangelism will change, for Jesus is not only the content of the evangelism, but also shapes the means of evangelism.

The journey character of a centered church facilitates understanding evangelism as a process. While conversion as a one-time encounter with a gospel witness might still occur in places in the world where many people hold a general belief in God or the supernatural, conversion in secular contexts is rarely a response to a single, isolated evangelistic action. Don Everts and Doug Schaupp listened to the stories of recent converts to learn how to improve their evangelistic efforts, which they discuss in *I Once Was Lost: What Postmodern Skeptics Taught Us About Their Path to Jesus*.[22] The thesis of their book is that "one-trick" evangelism does not work well because it treats all people as if they are in the same place. The authors outline a common path that many people follow when they turn to faith in Jesus today: first, they move from distrusting Christians to trusting a Christian; second, they move from being complacent to curious; third, they move from being closed to open to change; fourth, they move from meandering to seeking; finally, they decide to cross the threshold of the kingdom of God.

---

[21]In a video on bounded, fuzzy, and centered conversion, Eric Miller explores these and other biblical texts that point to the centrality of repenting and turning in the Bible. Eric Miller, "Leading a Jesus-Centered Church, Vol. 2," video, 22:23, April 24, 2019, https://www.youtube.com/watch?v=qkmn1qO6sVo.

[22]Don Everts and Doug Schaupp, *I Once Was Lost: What Postmodern Skeptics Taught Us About Their Path to Jesus* (Downers Grove, IL: InterVarsity Press, 2008).

Thus, in centered evangelism, discernment is fundamental. If someone is only at threshold 2 on the path described above, the evangelist should not invite the call of threshold 5. When we are discerning, we will not impose our will on others, because we will seek to meet people where they are. Although it is the ultimate aim, calling for the step of conversion is not something we should seek to do in every conversation we have with someone who is not centered on Jesus. Everts and Schaupp's approach is centered in the way that it identifies evangelism as a journey and recognizes the importance of inviting people to turn toward God at the appropriate time. This is significant, because some who emphasize conversion as a process may never actually invite people to repent and turn toward Jesus.

The words *conversion* and *repentance* may make some readers uncomfortable, and they would certainly turn off many non-Christians or fuzzy-church Christians. Though a centered church will need to embrace and practice conversion and repentance, it does not necessarily need to use these words. Robert Hill preaches in the chapel at Boston University, a context where many in his audience are in the fuzzy category. Note, however, how he preaches in a centered way and makes a strong, clear call to turn to God without ever using the words *conversion* or *repentance*. The following is excerpted from a sermon on Mark 1:14-20.

> To lay hold of faith, you may just have to turn. You may have to leave the nets, or leave the nest. To lay hold of the future you have to let go of the past. To lay hold of life we may need to summon the courage to leave. To leave the inherited for the invisible. To leave the general for the particular. To leave existential drift for personal decision. To leave the individual for the communal. To leave renting for ownership. To leave auditing for registration. (Some of us have been auditing the course on Christianity long enough. It's time to register, buy the books, pay tuition, take the course for credit, and get a grade!) To leave engagement for marriage. . . . That takes the courage to turn.
>
> Faith, as human response, is a decision, a choice, that inevitably includes some risk. As D. Bonhoeffer wrote on this passage, "When Christ calls a man he bids him come and die."[23]

---

[23]Robert Hill, "The Courage to Turn," sermon delivered in Marsh Chapel, Boston University, January 25, 2015, https://blogs.bu.edu/sermons/2015/01/25/the-courage-to-turn/.

There is much more to say about centered evangelism; it merits a book itself. But here I will make just one more point. While much of this section focuses on how a centered approach avoids the negative problems of bounded evangelism, the following testimonials reveal the dynamic potential of centered evangelism.

First, Michael King describes how centered worked in ways bounded and fuzzy did not.

> I owe my being a Christian to the centered understanding of conversion. The bounded approach didn't work. The formulas never meant anything to me. I tried making my commitment through them, but nothing life transforming happened. Then I tried the unbounded [fuzzy] approach. I tried having no particular boundaries and no particular center. That left me cold, sad, lonely, unfulfilled. I gazed at a sky whose stars couldn't guide me because I didn't believe there was any home toward which they could point me.
>
> Finally I tried making a simple commitment to point my life toward Jesus as a way of pointing through him to God. I would accept whatever meaning that offered me as I walked step by step. . . . I've been taking those steps now for many years, and lo, my faith . . . has become to me more precious than gold.[24]

Mark Pequegnat, a lay leader who is involved in a centered church after years in bounded churches, describes how he now has many more talks with coworkers about faith. He sees the change flowing from his centered approach. He says,

> I recently had the thrill of coming beside a coworker going through a divorce. The conversation started when he asked how I got through mine. Five months later, he is a Christ follower. (He prayed with me on the Thursday before Good Friday). He recently told me that if I had shared the same message he had heard before, he would not have given me the time of day! He only listened because of the relational, irreligious, shame-liberating, Jesus-centered focus of my words![25]

CONCLUSION

In order to challenge us not to settle for becoming partially centered churches or ministries, chapters eleven and twelve have focused on some

---

[24]Michael A. King, *Trackless Wastes & Stars to Steer By* (Scottdale, PA: Herald Press, 1990), 123-24.
[25]Mark Pequegnat, email to author, May 23, 2019.

ministry areas in which people find it difficult to imagine centered alternatives. We need not accept the logic that some things just "have to be" bounded. I urge you to apply what you have observed in these chapters to other areas in your church or ministry. May the examples feed your imagination and excite you with the promise of living out of a centered approach in your context.

13

THE RICHNESS
OF THE CENTERED WAY

I BEGAN THIS BOOK with stories of those who have suffered from the toxic shame that flows from bounded churches or stagnated in the blandness of fuzzy churches. I have advocated for a centered approach as a corrective. May we seek to become more centered not just to avoid negatives, but because of the richness that flows from the centered approach. I conclude with three examples of this richness.

THE UNCONDITIONAL LOVE OF A COMPASSIONATE GOD
Earlier in the book, I stated that the categories of bounded, fuzzy, and centered, along with the accompanying diagrams and explanations, are not the gospel, but are tools. That is true, but perhaps I overstated it. I was recently reading end-of-the-semester reflection papers from my ethics course, one student commented on the class session where I explained bounded, fuzzy, and centered approaches. In that class, my focus is on explaining the concepts. I draw diagrams on the whiteboard, clarify paradigms, and give many examples. There are times when I intentionally proclaim the gospel of Jesus Christ in the course, but I would not point to that class session as one of those. However, reflecting on that day one student wrote, "When I heard the difference between bounded and moving toward the center, for the first time in a long time, I was able to feel God's grace, love and compassion. His

presence felt overwhelming. In the moment I did not realize I was in the middle of a classroom filled with people. In that moment I felt closer to Jesus than I had in a long time."[1] Clearly God was at work; God used an explanation that distinguished between bounded and centered in a way that profoundly moved her.

While these diagrams are tools, they are gospel tools, so let us draw them widely—on whiteboards, napkins, and presentation slides. I encourage you to draw the diagrams and share explanations with someone in the next few days. (And keep doing it! Use the videos described on the last page of the book.) Let us pray that through explanations of these paradigms, people will not only see a different way of doing church, but they will also experience liberation from the conditional love of a bounded God and, like this student, experience in new ways the richness of the unconditional and compassionate love of Jesus Christ.

AUTHENTIC RELATIONSHIPS

Commenting on the centered recovery ministry described in chapter eleven, Scott Carolan said:

> The more time I spend with leaders of the groups, the more I want to be around them. Because of a centered mentality there is a willingness to walk toward Jesus in the light, be open about it. They are the most attractive people around because they are who they are authentically—good, bad, and the ugly. They are who I want to hang out with, as opposed to people who are trying to figure out where the line is and who is in and who is out. These people are just continuing to walk toward Jesus. That has real-life implications. They are making changes in their lives. They are not fuzzy—not anything goes. They feel free to me.[2]

Let us seek to increase the centeredness of our congregations so that all may grow in freedom in Christ and have richer experiences of authentic relationships. And may this freedom and authenticity attract others to our centered communities and draw them to Christ.

---

[1] From a student paper, used with her permission, May 11, 2020.
[2] Scott Carolan, interview by the author, April 2, 2018.

JOURNEYING TOGETHER: REPENTANCE, FORGIVENESS, REORIENTATION, LOVE

I recently sat in a living room with fifteen people who had been invited to gather by David. The circle included a few members of David's family and several of his friends. Some of us knew each other well, and others just met that evening. We all shared two things in common: we loved David, and we had been hurt by David.

After David thanked the hosts and thanked us all for coming, he explained the reason he had asked us to gather. He acknowledged that he had strayed this past year and turned away from Jesus. He told us of the shame he felt for things he had done. He apologized for the ways he had broken trust, caused people in the room to suffer, hurt some people deeply, and caused others to take on his responsibilities. He told us that he had turned back to Jesus and made a commitment to keep close to him. He spoke humbly and realistically, acknowledging that he had a long road of healing and restoration ahead of him. Then he thanked all of us in the room for the way we had confronted him and sought to point him back to a path of *shalom* over the previous year. He expressed gratitude for the way we had confronted but not abandoned him, even when he continued to stray further and sought to isolate himself. He thanked individuals for the specific ways they had repeatedly expressed love through words and actions.

David then explained that he had asked Rick to lead the rest of the evening's conversation. Rick stood up and invited each of us to express our forgiveness to David by picking a slip of paper from one of three piles: "broken trust," "carrying David's responsibilities," or "scaring and/or concerning David's friends and family." One by one, we each picked the slip of paper that most aligned with how we had been hurt or suffered because of David's actions and then put the slip in a box marked "forgiveness." Rick removed the box from the room and told David, "These things have been forgiven, put away. You do not need to take them out of the box. They are gone."

Then Rick passed out blank slips of paper and invited us to write words of blessing to David. We each read our words of blessing out loud to David, showering him with statements of affirmation, love, respect, promise, and hope. These statements affirmed David's identity as a man who is loved by

God and loved by us and explicitly communicated the bonds of our relationship, making it clear that we were not rejecting David. As we put our blessings in another box, David's shame seemed to drain from the room. Rick gave this box to David and said, "These slips go with you; keep them; reread them." Then we all prayed for David as our brother and friend. As others prayed out loud, I silently thanked God for the opportunity to participate in this expression of the body of Christ. After prayer, people exchanged hugs, thanked Rick for his leadership, and spoke a final word of encouragement to David.

I stood waiting for an opportunity to give David a hug and realized that we had just experienced the very dynamic I had been writing about in this book. We had lived out a centered approach that evening. Our time together was a rich gift to David and to all of us. Then Lynn, my wife, turned to me and said, "I want more of this in my life." May it be so—for her, for all of us.

ACKNOWLEDGMENTS

I BEGAN WORK ON THIS BOOK near the end of 2017, but its origins stretch back decades. As I narrated in chapter five, in the fall of 1983, Doug Frank's lecture on religion and faith, relying heavily on Jacques Ellul, captivated me. I left the lecture shaken but convinced and asking, "How about the church? How do we have a nonreligious church?" I sought to answer the question in a paper, pouring more into it than I had any previous paper. Yet clearly I was not done. In different ways, the question was one of the strands of my MA thesis, my PhD dissertation, and my first book, *Religious No More*. I did not know it in 1999, the year that book was published, but I was still not done. Thank you, Doug, for that lecture and the rich conversation over the years. I am "turning in" this book as my final draft of that paper.

As I already recounted in the introduction to part one, a second critical moment that led to this book occurred twenty years ago when Larry Dunn suggested I read Paul Hiebert's work on bounded, fuzzy, and centered sets. If Hiebert had not had the insight to borrow set theory from math and apply it to churches, this book would not exist. Hiebert is the original spring, the source of any talk of bounded, fuzzy, and centered churches today. I dedicate the book to him with deep gratitude and a desire to acknowledge my indebtedness to him and honor his work.

Fresno Pacific Biblical Seminary, formerly Mennonite Brethren Biblical Seminary, has contributed to this book in numerous ways. First, by providing seminary training to Paul Hiebert decades before I began teaching there. Second, the contribution of my students to this book is multilayered and immense. Their challenging questions pressed me to refine and clarify my explanations of bounded, fuzzy, and centered sets. That process continues; a student's comment and question just one week prior to submitting the manuscript led to one of my final revisions. Students' pertinent questions on application motivated me to produce a book to answer them. Things I learned from former students' efforts at doing centered ministry provided many of the examples and insights in the book. With deep gratitude, I dedicate this book to my students at Fresno Pacific Biblical Seminary/MBBS. It has been a privilege to teach you, learn with you, and learn from you.

In early September 2017, Terry Brensinger, then dean of the seminary, invited me into his office. He had just finished the book on ministry in honor-shame contexts that I coauthored with Jayson Georges. Terry, not knowing that I had in mind to write a book on centered church someday, said, "The chapter on community is excellent. We desperately need what you are writing regarding centered church. I urge you to write a book on that." I sat amazed, speechless for a moment. Then I explained that I actually hoped to do just that but had a few other writing projects, including a book, to complete first. He exhorted me to put them aside and get to work on this book. I left his office with a sense that I and the project had been blessed. Terry, thank you for the blessing that I have carried with me through this project. (And you, the readers, can thank Terry for this book being available now and not a few years in the future.)

Valerie Rempel, as dean of Fresno Pacific Biblical Seminary, continued to offer the support and encouragement that Terry initiated. I am grateful to Fresno Pacific University and the seminary for a research grant that facilitated field research with focus groups beyond the immediate Fresno area and for a one-semester sabbatical leave in 2018 to do that research and begin writing the book.

I am deeply indebted to the more than forty people I interviewed, individually and in groups, seeking to learn how they were living out a centered approach. I could have written much of the first few chapters without further input, but they would not have been as rich. However, I could not have written the rest of the book without the insights and examples I gained from the interviews and focus groups. Some of you are named in the book; many are not. I am grateful to all of you. Thank you for your contribution.

I interviewed pastors and lay leaders from over fifteen churches or ministries. Scott Carolan not only provided rich material in two interviews, but also connected me with others who provided excellent content. A conversation with Bruxy Cavey and Matt Miles over Mexican food in Fresno planted seeds that helped me imagine how to use others' stories and insights in the book. And they suggested Meeting House pastors and lay leaders as a great source for input. A few months later I was in Ontario doing what they had suggested. I am grateful to Darrell Winger and Keturah Duncan for graciously and enthusiastically taking on the extra work of organizing five focus groups and individual interviews at different Meeting House sites. I needed the focus groups to learn things I did not know; I also needed to learn how to do focus groups and research interviews. Thanks to my friend and sociologist, Bob Brenneman, for the crash course. Your tips served me well.

It is common in acknowledgments to encounter what you see in the following paragraphs, lists of names. As authors we list these names to acknowledge that although our name is on the cover, the book was more of a team project than that implies. We benefit from the insights, questions, critiques, corrections, and edits of others. We thank them in this way, but simply including their name in a list falls short of the recognition their contributions merit. I feel that especially with this book. Many of the people mentioned gave feedback on the manuscript as others have done with my previous books, but they did so with passion for and commitment to the project that I have not experienced before. And many of them did more than just give suggestions to improve the text: they helped me fill holes in the book by connecting me with people to interview and pointing me to other resources. I am deeply grateful.

Just as I needed the help of so many others for the ideas in the book, so too in the writing and revising process, I benefited from the help of many. I am grateful to the following who read and gave feedback on a complete draft of the book: Darrin Cantrell, Matt Miles, Mike Taetzsch, and Kurt Willems.

I offer thanks as well to those who gave input on parts of the manuscript: Nick Chandler, David Cramer, Christie Dahlin, Jayson Georges, Chris Hoke, Ryan Kenny, Teresa Leonard, Connie Nicholson, Ivan Paz, Jamie Pitts, Brian Ross, and John D. Roth. And thanks to Nate Fast, a social psychologist, for providing me with helpful resources.

A group of ministry practitioners, in addition to reading the entire first draft and making written comments, spent a day in October 2019 discussing, chapter by chapter, how to improve the manuscript. I hoped that a group processing and working together would produce better results than individuals on their own. That was definitely the case that day. Numerous times we ended up with something different from what any one of us had brought to the table. I benefited from critiques and suggestions. Also, however, I benefited from spending the day with people so passionate about the topic's importance. Writing is a solitary task; I left that day recharged and feeling that I was not alone. Thank you to April Alkema, Lynn Baker, Jonna Bohigian, Scott Carolan, Dustin Maddox, Sherri Nozik, Dave Obwald, and Dan Serdahl. This book is much better because of our work together that day. Thank you also to those who donated to cover the day's costs: Laura and Rob Maxey, Ruth and Randy Ataide, and Libbey and Nathan Davis Hunt.

I sought a freelance editor's services with the hope that she would see things I did not in the second draft and guide me to produce a much better manuscript than I would on my own. Karen Hollenbeck Wuest exceeded my expectations. The book you hold in your hands is much better because of what she suggested I cut and what she challenged me to add. Karen, I am grateful for your skill, expertise, and commitment to excellence. Thank you for treating me and the manuscript with such care and respect.

I am again grateful for the privilege and honor of working with the team at InterVarsity Press. Special thanks to my editor, Jon Boyd. Your enthusiasm for the project has buoyed me, and your wise counsel is deeply appreciated.

So many have prayed for this work, expressed interest, and supported and encouraged me in the effort. I am grateful to all. A special thanks to my parents, Bruce and Marcella Baker, for your loving support.

Finally, I thank my wife, Lynn, and daughters, Julia and Christie. How many times over the years, during a meal with guests, have you seen me grab a piece of paper, draw a circle and start talking about bounded, fuzzy, and centered? Thanks for your patience. Thanks, too, for leaning in and engaging my questions as I learned from each of you and your experiences of bounded, fuzzy, and centered churches. Thank you for your love, for believing in the importance of the project, and for the various ways you have supported me as I worked on it.

GENERAL INDEX

SCRIPTURE INDEX

CENTERED-SET CHURCH
VIDEO SERIES & DISCUSSION GUIDE

I hope this book has excited you with the potential of a centered approach to ministry. Of course, none of us can do this single-handedly. We need others in our church or group to join us. Before they can do that, they must understand the concepts. That is why I have worked with others to create *Introducing Centered-Set Church.* This video series presents the basics of bounded, fuzzy, and centered sets similar to the content of the first three chapters of this book. The videos engage viewers through stories, diagrams, and examples. Discussion questions lead participants to imagine possibilities of how God might use this approach in their lives and community.

This resource is designed to inform, excite, and inspire others to turn from bounded or fuzzy approaches and together center on Jesus.

More information about the
Introducing Centered-Set Church
Video Series and Discussion Guide is at
centeredsetchurch.com